The Education of British South Asians

The Education of British South Asians

Ethnicity, Capital and Class Structure

Tahir Abbas

Director
Centre for the Study of Ethnicity and Culture
University of Birmingham, UK

First published 2004 by
PALGRAVE MACMILLAN
Houndmills, Basingstoke, Hampshire RG21 6XS and
175 Fifth Avenue, New York, N.Y. 10010
Companies and representatives throughout the world

PALGRAVE MACMILLAN is the global academic imprint of the Palgrave
Macmillan division of St. Martin's Press, LLC and of Palgrave Macmillan Ltd.
Macmillan® is a registered trademark in the United States, United Kingdom
and other countries. Palgrave is a registered trademark in the European
Union and other countries.

ISBN 1–4039–1691–8

This book is printed on paper suitable for recycling and made from fully
managed and sustained forest sources.

A catalogue record for this book is available from the British Library.

Library of Congress Cataloging-in-Publication Data
Abbas, Tahir, 1970–
    The education of British South Asians : ethinicity, captial, and class
    structure / by Tahir Abbas.
        p.   cm.
    Includes bibliographical references and index.
    ISBN 1–4039–1691–8 (cloth)
    1. South Asians—Education—England—Brimingham—Case studies.
    2. Educational anthropology—England—Birmingham—Case studies.
    I. Title.

LC3485.G7A33 2004
371.829′91′4—dc22

                                                        2004046492

10   9   8   7   6   5   4   3   2   1
13   12   11   10   09   08   07   06   05   04

Printed and bound in Great Britain by
Antony Rowe Ltd, Chippenham and Eastbourne

For Kamilah and Nabeel

Contents

List of Tables

List of Abbreviations

BCC	Birmingham City Council
CRE	Commission for Racial Equality
DES	Department of Education and Science
DfEE	Department for Education and Employment
DfES	Department for Education and Skills
ERA	Education Reform Act 1988
GCSE	General Certificate in Secondary Education
GNVQ	General National Vocational Qualification
ILEA	Inner London Education Authority
LEA	Local Education Authority
LFS	Labour Force Survey
OECD	Organisation for Economic Cooperation and Development
OfSTED	Office for Standards in Education
PSI	Policy Studies Institute
UCAS	Universities Central Admissions System
UCE	University of Central England
YCS	Youth Cohort Survey

Acknowledgements

Education is the only way in which people from all backgrounds can develop themselves in the hope of social and economic betterment. Ordinarily, investment in human capital leads to accreditation, a social and cultural awareness and monetary reward in the labour market. Prevented from obtaining a 'good education' means that many people will not be able to contribute effectively to the economy or reach their potential as fully integrated British citizens. For many, education is the route out of poverty and disadvantage. For others, given the range of circumstances and opportunities available to them, it is an extension of what is merely expected of the individual or group in question.

Why is it, therefore, that many ethnic minorities seemingly under-achieve in education while others perform exceptionally well? How do the factors of ethnicity, capital (economic, cultural and social) and social class impact on the education of ethnic minorities compared with majorities? What roles do different types of schools play – both selective and comprehensive? What are the roles of teachers and parents? These questions are answered through qualitative research on British South Asians (Bangladeshis, Indians and Pakistanis) in education in the multicultural city of Birmingham, UK (a city of one million people, approximately a third of which is non-white ethnic minority). This study is about how Britain's three largest and most significant South Asian groups first survive and then thrive in a seemingly alien society. It is about the educational efforts of some groups and the successes and failures of others. As an academic enquiry it pushes the boundaries of what is known about South Asians in education but it might also help people of all ethnicities and social classes better understand the processes at work and find within them the routes to success.

Whilst working on this research, I had the joy of spending time with a number of people who were able to provide me with intellectual stimulus, an income to fund my research and access to other spheres and domains in which the lives of British South Asians in Birmingham are affected. I engaged and worked with a number of researchers from Warwick and other universities, who, like me, were embroiled in the often-fraught task of carrying out primary sociological research in the field of ethnic relations. I thank Sheila Rampersad, Edgar Hassan, Rajinder Kumar

Dudrah, Nusrat Shaheen and Sameera Tahira Ahmed for the good times I had and all that I learnt about life. I thank Javed Khan, Mohammed Younis, Shabbir Akhtar, Shafaq Hussain and Abdul Ghaffar for the time I had working with the Kashmiri and Pakistani Professionals Association. I express my appreciation to Dilpazir Raja Khan for helping me in many different ways, from vociferously debating and engaging head-on with the important research and practitioner issues of the day in this field to obtaining access and interviewing hard-to-reach groups for my study. In relation to the research we carried out on ethnic enterprise, namely the ethnic independent restaurant sector in Birmingham, I express my sincere gratefulness to Monder Ram and Upkar Pardesi. We worked to develop racial equality councils across the West Midlands region and I convey my appreciation to Waqar Azmi for the opportunity, and to Frank Reeves who is not only a very knowledgeable man but an artist and poet too. Employed by the civil service at the Home Office Research Development and Statistics Directorate and the Department for Constitutional Affairs Research Unit, London, I thank a number of colleagues for their encouragement and advice. They include Trevor Hall, Paul Wiles, Carole Willis, Judy Youell, Sultana Choudary, Bhonny Mhalanga, Andrew Zurawan, Mavis Maclean, Roger Hood and, not least, Judith Sidaway. Special mentions go out to Caitriona and Chris. There are a number of specific people in the field of sociology of education, 'race' and ethnic studies who helped me in my scholarly efforts and I warmly thank them all. They include John Rex, Sally Tomlinson, Tariq Modood, Jorgen Nielson, John Eade, David Gillborn, Zig Layton-Henry, Máirtín Mac an Ghaill, Mark Johnson, Alison Shaw and Jochen Blaschke (of the Berlin Institute for Comparative Social Research).

Researching the educational achievements of South Asians was a stimulating challenge and I relished the opportunity to explore a subject matter that is both important but frequently misunderstood by the South Asian community and the rest of society. It was an undertaking that was sometimes precarious but I had the satisfaction of working with somebody in the industry experienced in the business of social research. I express my deepest gratitude to Muhammad Anwar for his supervision and guidance. There are too many people to name at the Centre for Research in Ethnic Relations, University of Warwick, but want to thank all the people I met and worked with, past and present. It was a blast! I also, very much, want to thank the many secondary school pupils, further education college students, parents and teachers who gave up their valuable time to support this research through the interviews, responding to the surveys and, in general, having to put up with my incessant demands.

I thank my current employers and colleagues at the University of Birmingham, Department of Sociology for the support they have exhibited towards my work and me. My students are a constant source of inspiration, always keeping me on my toes and I am grateful to them. I thank the editors of the *British Journal of Sociology of Education, Oxford Review of Education, Cambridge Journal of Education*, and *Race Ethnicity and Education* for permitting me to reproduce in this book some of my work published in these journals.

Finally, to Briar Towers and the staff at Palgrave, many thanks. Any errors or omissions remain my own.

T. A.
Birmingham, England
10 January 2004

1
Introduction: Immigration, Settlement, 'Race' and Education

In post-war Britain, the education of ethnic minorities, including South Asians,[1] has attracted considerable academic and policymaker interest in relation to *outcomes* but despite the volumes of evidence it remains difficult to draw firm conclusions on *processes*. This study is about how British South Asians achieve in education. It attempts to explain variation in performance in terms of ethnicity and capital – which is a function of the individual's or group's ability to generate, maintain and cultivate the 'resources' that help to mobilise social and economic advancement, which include information, knowledge and networks, and social class. It does this by systematically exploring the important stages of education, from leaving primary school to entering secondary school (11–18), the processes of achievement and entering higher education (18+). The development of the central questions in this study are based on the review of relevant theoretical and empirical literature in the field of 'race',[2] ethnicity and education; in particular, current research on the educational achievements of South Asians.[3] Methodologically, this study endeavoured to determine processes in both selective (fee-paying independent and grammar) and secondary 'modern' comprehensive schools, including voluntary-aided and foundation schools thus exploring the entire range of education in Britain. Qualitative research tools and techniques, in-depth interviews with pupils, parents and teachers and surveys of further education college students (16–19) and teachers provided the empirical data. To explore the experiences of South Asians within this wider conceptual and methodological framework, the city of Birmingham, UK, was chosen for this study because of its rich post-war immigration history, present-day economic, cultural and social diversity and the remaining number of selective schools within it, permitting valuable comparisons to be made between different South Asians in different schools and further education colleges. Indeed, for many decades the city has been the preferred location for sociological research on the experiences of ethnic minorities (Rex and Moore, 1967; Rex and Tomlinson, 1979; Ward, 1983; Back and Solomos, 1992). In addition, since 1982, Birmingham Local Education Authority (LEA) has been committed to a 'strong multicultural, antiracist, and equal opportunity perspective' (Coles, 1997).

There are three significant parts to this introductory chapter. First, there is an historical overview of the economic and social processes of the immigration and settlement of South Asians in Britain and in Birmingham. Second, it identifies the essential religious and cultural characteristics of South Asian communities to determine the nature of racialisation and ethnicisation, revealing specific residential and occupational patterns. Third, crucial developments in education research and policymaker thinking are expounded, exploring the politico-ideological positions of assimilationists, integrationists, multiculturalists and antiracists and how they have jostled to gain hegemony at various stages in recent educational history.

Post-war immigration and settlement

The end of the Second World War left Britain short of domestic labour to meet growing indigenous demand. Workforce scarcity was also common to a number of other Western European economies at the time, including France and Germany. However, British policy differed from that of other European nation-states because it failed to capitalise upon initiatives to exploit immigrant labour for the specific purposes of domestic economic expansion. Realising that newly recognised British citizens from the Caribbean and South Asia would make Britain their home, the restriction of net immigration effectively hindered economic growth. The Labour government of the time, in essence, reduced the inflow of immigrant labour to meet domestic political concerns; regarded by Miles (1989) as a 'paradox'. Labour demonstrated a profound preference for 'aliens' rather than British citizens. Their attitudes and behaviours towards visible ethnic minority immigrant labour remained hidden from the public at large, however (Joshi and Carter, 1984).

The economic recession of the late 1950s eliminated the need for labour – both domestic and immigrant. By then, nevertheless, local communities and national institutions had already developed outward hostilities towards ethnic minorities. It was increasingly becoming the case that ethnic minorities were concentrated in the inner areas of older industrial towns and cities, living close to working-class white indigenous inhabitants. The somewhat limited acceptance on the part of the white indigenous working classes was based on the belief that ethnic minority workers would return to their sending regions once their employment had terminated. Rarely was it imagined or, for that matter, wished that ethnic minorities would remain, forming communities, establishing over time. In many senses, in Britain, as was the case for a number of other advanced Western European economies, immigrant labour, originating invariably from once-colonised lands, filled the gap at the lower echelons of society. Ethnic minority immigrants were, in effect, placed at the bottom of the labour market, disdained by the host society and systematically ethnicised and racialised in the sphere of capitalist accumulation. These workers were recruited into those industrial sectors most in decline and, as such, their positions in society were located below the white working class. The latter was able to attain social mobility, progressing from *lumpenproletariat* to *proletariat* and from *petty bourgeoisie* to *bourgeoisie* (Castles and Kosack, 1973).

At the beginning of the 1960s, the number of immigrants entering Britain from South Asia was at its height. Towards the end of the 1960s, however, immigration from South Asia had all but ended. Both the peak in 1961–1962 and the decline in 1968 were the result of the Commonwealth Immigrants Act (1962) and the Commonwealth Immigration Act (1968). The 1962 Act changed the pattern of South Asian immigration – rather than 'pioneer' men, it was their wives, children and fiancées that arrived with many South Asians from India and Pakistan seemingly rushing in an attempt 'to beat the ban' created by the Act (Deakin, 1970). Subsequent amendments to the original 1962 Act in 1968 led to tighter restrictions on immigration from New Commonwealth countries. On each occasion the move was affected by the politicisation of ethnic minorities in Britain. As a consequence of the change to legislation the South Asian settlement became more permanent and family-orientated.

In the city of Birmingham, immigrants settled in the 'zones of transition' which were being increasingly vacated by mobile Britons experiencing 'white flight'. Subsequently, these areas became impoverished with new employment created elsewhere and in other economic sectors. At present, the ethnic minorities are concentrated in various inner-city areas in Birmingham, forming 'the middle ring' – encircling the central business district of the city.[4] The 1971 Census showed second-generation ethnic minorities, in particular South Asians, preferred to remain within the same geographical locations as their parents. Two decades later the 1991 Census showed that second- and third-generation South Asians chose to do the same (Phillips, 1998). This trend is argued by Robinson (1996) to be a function of the younger generations wishing to continue the religious and cultural traditions of the generation before them as well as because of the negative experiences found in the labour market. Analysis of first-generation economic migrants and their labour market experiences found all ethnic minorities experienced an 'ethnic penalty', including East African Asians, who were generally better qualified compared with other ethnic minorities. Nevertheless, it was African-Caribbeans, Pakistanis and the Irish who suffered the greatest. Indians, Pakistanis and African-Caribbeans all underwent very substantial ethnic penalties, even after controlling for their age and education (Cheng and Heath, 1993). Further-more, a 'racial division of labour' ensured African-Caribbean and South Asian workers were kept apart, prevented from organising together as part of a wider collective struggle. It deskilled workers, kept wages down and segregated ethnic minorities in the dirty, low paid jobs that white workers did not want (Sivanandan, 1982). Further analysis of Census data shows that the 'ethnic penalty' or 'ethnic disadvantage' experienced by first generations has largely translated to second generations. Heath and McMahon (1997) acknowledge that they expected some elimination of the ethnic penalty, since the second generations are UK-born and have received their education in Britain, but both direct discrimination and cultural differences must play a part, they argue, as the range and size suggest complex explanations.

It is apparent that the current position of ethnic minorities in the labour market is a feature of the different periods of post-war immigration and settlement. As such, the extent to which different ethnic minorities experience racism and discrimination in the labour market is a function of this historical specificity. Pakistani and Bangladeshi households are characterised by high male unemployment and low economic activity of women, with low pay and large families as the norm (Modood *et al.*, 1997). Recent national Labour Force Survey (LFS) estimates made at the end of 2002 continue to indicate the variability of economic activity between ethnic minorities. 'Black-Caribbean' women (72 per cent) had almost as high an economic activity rate as white women (74 per cent). Bangladeshis had the lowest economic activity rates among men (69 per cent) and women (22 per cent). Pakistani women had economic activity rates of 28 per cent (White, 2002). Reduced rates of participation for Bangladeshi and Pakistani women reflect their limited education levels before immigration and the negative consequences of that for subsequent generations (Brah and Shaw, 1992). However, among women with children in paid employment, ethnic minority women are more likely than white women to be in full-time employment, irrespective of their occupational group (Holdsworth and Dale, 1997). Current analysis of labour market participation suggests that many young South Asian women demonstrate high aspirations *and* levels of participation, particularly in relation to the educational and occupational levels of their parents. National statistics show a marked increase in the numbers of young Pakistani and Bangladeshi women in full-time undergraduate courses in recent years (Dale *et al.*, 2002). But, it is very apparent that religion is an important dimension in ethnic inequality in the labour market. An analysis of the fourth Policy Studies Institute (PSI) Survey confirms that there is a complex picture of employment within the Muslim/non-Muslim dichotomy. It is Bangladeshi and Pakistani Muslims who suffer a more detrimental experience in the labour market compared with Indian Muslim counterparts (Brown, 2000).

Over the last four decades, in most advanced industrial societies economic and social divisions between rich and poor have continued to widen. During this time, certain South Asian groups, throughout Britain as a whole, have achieved upward economic and social mobility, live in more affluent areas, work in professional occupations or have become relatively successful in enterprise. Many do not. At the beginning of the twenty-first century, even after continued economic restructuring and the internationalisation of capital and labour, there are still many ethnic minorities who are restrained at the bottom end of the labour market and located in concentrated inner-city areas. It is there that they continue to remain.

Religious, social and cultural characteristics

It is important to understand how the 'capital' and 'resources' ethnic minorities were equipped with at the time of initial immigration has subsequently mobilised into ethnic communities, exhibiting different economic, social and cultural characteristics. It is useful to evaluate the nature of South Asian groups in Birmingham through an analysis of community characteristics and to discuss the importance of taking into account religious as well as cultural differences. A brief introduction to the Bangladeshi, Indian and Pakistani community in Britain and in Birmingham is provided below. They are explored on the basis of their relative size in the population.

Pakistanis are the largest single ethnic minority group in Birmingham (104,000 – a figure of one in ten of the city's one million people based on the 2001 Census). Pakistanis in Birmingham almost exclusively originate from the Mirpur district of *Azad* (Free) Kashmir (which is annexed to Pakistan).[5] A number of British Pakistanis also originate from the Punjab region of Pakistan but have largely settled in the de-industrialised inner cities to the North or South East of England. Before migration, many of the Pakistanis in Birmingham lived and worked in rural areas. Families were usually extended, with up to three generations living in one household. The men worked on small land holdings or in specialist craft-type work, while women maintained domestic order and looked after livestock (Dayha, 1974). Families lived in close proximity to each other and were knowledgeable of each other's affairs. Shaw's (2000) socio-anthropological study of a Pakistani community in Oxford shows how strong the village-kin network is in the sending regions among rural-origin immigrants from Northern Punjab and how it has remained relatively intact as part of their adaptation to Britain.

Pakistanis first arrived as merchant seaman after the Second World War (which also includes groups recognised today as Bangladeshis), settling at the English seaports. Only men were first prevalent as migrants who thought of their stay as temporary. Younger men from the sending regions replaced older Pakistanis. Early Pakistani immigration was dependent upon this form of chain-migration and, in particular, the remittances of capital back to the sending regions (Khan, 1979). It was how the Pakistani migration process differed from Punjabi-Sikh and African-Caribbean immigration. These 'pioneer' Pakistanis worked hard to ensure their existence as did other South Asians. Many had to fully adapt to the host society to persevere and, for some, it resulted in forsaking distinct cultural and religious traditions and values for more 'westernised' ones (Dayha, 1988).

The Indians in Birmingham (56,000, based on the 2001 Census), comprising Sikhs (29,000) in the main with fewer Hindus (19,000) are more affluent than their Bangladeshi (20,000) and Pakistani peers and are not generally restricted to the same inner-city areas. These Indians tend to be occupationally more mobile and are more likely to be engaged in entrepreneurial activity. Indians in Birmingham have originated from the Punjab and the Gujarat areas of India or via East Africa – and from a combination of urban and rural settings. The East Africans arrived via Kenya, Tanzania and Uganda bringing with them the acumen for business (Mattausch, 1998). As a result of this distinction at the point of entry, Indians have become successful in many economic and occupational spheres. The Indian economic success is also related to struggles experienced in the labour market, leading to self-employment as a way in which to realise further upward mobility, utilising their human (intellectual, social, cultural and economic) capital which they might regard as having been misrecognised by society. Unlike their white peers, certain Indian small business owners are a well-established section of the *petty bourgeoisie* (Desai, 1963; Ram and Jones, 1998).

Bangladeshis in Birmingham are a group almost exclusively originating from the *Sylhet* region of North West Bangladesh. The largest British concentration is found in the deprived neighbourhoods of the East End of London (Eade, 1989). The second largest Bangladeshi community in Britain is found in parts of inner-city Birmingham. As with Pakistanis, Bangladeshis live in close-knit communities in strong local community structures. Increasingly, they too are establishing an entrepreneurial presence as well becoming more organised at the community level. They nevertheless remain an impoverished group with large families as the norm and with men working in the catering industries or otherwise unemployed. In relation to religion, there is a strong desire for the Islamisation of second and third generations. Present-day second-generation South Asian Muslims (which include all Bangladeshis and Pakistanis and approximately 15 per cent of all Indians) are increasingly questioning their ethnic identities from their religious identities. The nature of Islam among groups is questioned and re-examined in the light of generational development. Young Bangladeshis experience a similar reality to young Pakistanis as the re-evaluation of their individual identity has necessarily involved return to a more literal Islam.

In contemporary Islam, there are three sects, *Shia, Sunni* and *Wahabi*. In addition, the *Barelvis*, the *Tablighis* and the *Ahmadiyas* are all variants of *Sunni* Islam (Robinson, 1988). In Birmingham, the far majority of all Muslims are *Sunni* and the high numbers of Mosques are part of a commitment to remain in Britain and teach younger Muslims the values and ways of Islam. In certain Birmingham localities, there are specialist goods and services outlets such as *Halal* butchers, travel agents, clothing stores, fruit and vegetable markets, restaurants, jewellers and bookshops – and here, all owned and managed by Muslims. Such ethnic enclave entrepreneurial activity reinforces a sense of community as local businesses gear their activities towards the needs of the local people, and in the case of South Asians, whether they are Muslim, Sikh or Hindu. It helps further the creation of community groups holding close various manifestations of religious and cultural value.

In general, immigrants have arrived and settled in Britain for nearly a thousand years (CRE, 1996). In late nineteenth century, Indians from upper-class backgrounds came for the specific purposes of education and enterprise. It could be argued that current South Asian population possesses similar educational and entrepreneurial ambitions but it is drawn, however, from the more impoverished areas in the sending regions of *Azad Kashmir* in North West Pakistan, the *Sylhet* region of North West Bangladesh and the *Punjab* region of India. Invariably, the principal aim of South Asians at the beginning of the 1960s was to create as much wealth as possible before returning to their countries or regions of origin, supported by a 'myth of return' (Anwar, 1979). This did not happen – whether by chance (opportunity) or by design (legislation). East African Asians arrived, essentially because of the 'Africanisation' of former colonised lands by the British in the late 1960s and early 1970s. Their economic characteristics were middle class and professional in the sending societies and they sought to achieve those very ends in Britain. In 1973, Ugandan Asians were forced out of their country and those accepted by Britain were encouraged to settle away from already densely populated South Asian population pockets known as 'red areas'. Bangladeshis arrived when severe economic hardship and the desire for family reunification forced many to seek refuge in Britain during the late 1970s and early 1980s.

The experience of South Asians in Britain and in Birmingham is one of diversity – in terms of economic, cultural and religious relations with the white majority. Life for British South Asians is a complex mesh of identity, culture and religion as well as the maintenance of strong transnational links to the sending regions (Ballard, 1994).

Political ideology and educationist rhetoric

For ethnic minorities arriving in significant numbers to Britain, education was not a primary concern. It came after housing and employment. In the beginning, the number of ethnic minority pupils entering schools was negligible and remained relatively inconsequential for central government and LEAs. As children joined parents during various stages of immigration and settlement, difficulties soon began to emerge for pupils and the schools they attended. Early problems included pupils starting intermittently throughout the academic year.

At first, ethnic minority pupils did not absorb easily the culture of the school or mainstream society. South Asians originating from poorer rural areas were thrust into a vast urban metropolis with a peculiar system of schooling and, consequently, it was disconcerting for some. In addition, pupils were perceived in stereotypical terms by both teachers and white pupils. Early policy responses insufficiently dealt with the more sensitive issues at hand, particularly in terms of language support. Initially, one of the ways in which central government attempted to address 'the problems' in schools was through actively recruiting teachers to take up posts in areas of severe socio-economic decline. For policy-makers, this move was related to the notion that teachers of lower ability worked in such areas. The policy of vigorously conscripting teachers backfired however as central government found it difficult to attract the more able teachers it wanted. High numbers of similarly qualified 'poorer' teachers made the applications and took up the posts. A further problem was that by labelling certain schools as requiring 'special needs' led teachers in the schools to believe the root of educational inequality rested explicitly within the pupils and their communities – and not elsewhere (Glennerster, 1972; Reeves and Chevannes, 1988). In effect, a policy of assimilation was applied to incorporate immigrants groups through adaptation.

As ethnic minorities first began to appear in schools in increasingly visible numbers it was considered that 'difficulties' with pupils could be eliminated by integration into the culture and structure of the school. The apparently high numbers of South Asians at all ages were problems for which the education system was not prepared (Rose *et al.*, 1969). The dilemma was thought to reflect greatest on teachers and, as such, their interests were believed to be the most important (Grosvenor, 1997). Ethnic minorities were expected to abandon their modes of social and cultural behaviour and become absorbed into the school and ultimately into society. Policy attempts were made to incorporate ethnic minor-ities into a relatively homogenous British state – the notion that English society was a unitary whole, politically and culturally indivisible, was central in this period. It resulted in the recognition of ethnic minorities in terms of how well they had internalised middle-class norms and values. Eventual change in emphasis came about when cultural superiority was replaced by cultural tolerance. The latter was more flexible as it began to accept the variability of the ethnic minority experience. It recognised the existence of racism in society and how it potentially permeated all aspects of education.

In the late 1970s and early 1980s, two movements took place in the field of education – multicultural education and antiracist education. Each was based on a different conceptualisation of racism in society leading to ideologically divergent programmes of educational reform (Rattansi, 1992). The broadly liberal position is associated with multiculturalism and Left-radicalism synonymous with antiracism. More liberal than integration and assimilation but drawn from similar underpinnings, multiculturalism assumed a centre-ground position. Power relations between ethnic minorities and whites and how they affected education, however, remain unchallenged. Schools in society were encouraged to introduce multicultural programmes to reduce educational inequality by providing both the pupils and their teachers with positive histories and images of ethnicity. The Department of Education and Science (DES, 1977) green paper entitled, *Education in Schools*, affirmed the multicultural education impetus. Schools and the teachers working within them were instructed to learn to appreciate and respect other faiths and cultures so as to overcome ethnocentric overtones in the curriculum. Multicultural education was an attempt to breakdown stereotypes by calling for 'greater tolerance'. It involved the school in creating an appropriate environment where respect would to be given, for example, to dietary preferences, dress, custom, religions and cultural heritage, and sensibilities (Figueroa, 1995).

In effect, multicultural education extended the philosophy of cultural pluralism. Certainly, it was able to reduce racism but it was *not* able to eliminate it (Parekh, 1989). Furthermore, some LEAs were reluctant to promote multicultural education to hesitant schools. It permitted certain teachers at the everyday teacher–pupil-interaction level to go about undetected. It helped teachers to maintain a 'colour-blind' approach and legitimise the *status quo* (Troyna, 1985). As such, many radical commentators regarded multicultural education as 'essentialist' and 'reductionist'. Multiculturalists, it is argued, viewed racism as merely a product of the few as it was a personality-orientated frame of reference and not structural and, as such, the perspective perpetuated the socio-pathologisation of ethnic minorities (*cultural reproduction*). The problem of educational underachievement was felt to emanate from individuals and not from the workings of institutions and structures in society implying that ethnic minorities possessed deficiencies requiring 'compensation'. As a result, the multicultural education programme was seen to be an instrument of social control. By reducing structural issues to cultural, questions of individual empowerment to combat racism were largely ignored.

Multicultural education 'catered for difference', 'watered down' the curriculum and 'cooled out' ethnic minorities in education (Troyna and Williams, 1986; Lynch *et al.*, 1992). Exasperated sentiments felt by radical teachers and ethnic minority intellectuals, permitted antiracist education to come into existence, especially as the concept of 'institutional racism'[6] became central to race equality legislation at the time. Antiracist education-ists argued that potentially all schools are an integral part of the generation of institutional racism in society. Antiracist education ideology endeavoured to extend attention not just to the socio-pathologisation of ethnic minorities but also to institutional racism. In relation to policy, it wished to de-racialise the curriculum and apply antiracism as part of the syllabus. On the other hand, antiracist education was criticised for assuming that *all* white groups are party to the educational underachievements of *all* ethnic minorities. Moreover, the aphorism, 'racism=prejudice and power' was thought to be over-simplistic and overly generalised. Furthermore, the movement was considered politically motivated and concerned only with racism. It focused on radical struggle in education as part of a wider programme to eliminate racism in society (Sarup, 1991). Even for ethnic minorities, the antiracist education movement lost credibility, especially when the *other* saw it as opposition to racism *per se* (Gilroy, 1990). Furthermore, new forms of cultural racisms, differentiating the experiences of African-Caribbeans and South Asians began to require altogether different sets of responses from ethnic minorities and majorities (Modood, 1998).

The late 1980s and the whole of the 1990s revealed a new agenda in relation to national educational policy but as the layers of rhetoric are peeled away it is clear little has changed since the early 1980s. The education system, since the Education Reform Act 1988 (ERA), has been concerned with issues of league tables and performance outputs. The move to the educational *New Right* throughout the late 1980s and the 1990s was also found in North America. The origins of both were based on the desire by central governments to be removed from the workings of the education system leaving more to market forces (David, 1991). The education system today bears scant resemblance to the Education Act of 1944. Competition between schools and the centralising of core curriculum subjects has become the norm. It has led to a system riddled with inequalities, with tendencies for disparities to deepen and widen between groups. The national curriculum has closely redefined what it is to be a British citizen – and it possesses a narrow interpretation of our cultural heritage. Unsurprisingly, some sociologists have called for a move away from the New Right hegemony in educational discourse (Mac an Ghaill, 1999). As the number of school 'exclusions', particularly for African-Caribbeans, continues to remain high, it is clear discrimination persists in educational settings.[6] Issues in the education of ethnic minorities have been systematically removed from the current policy agenda. At the same time schools have been required to deal with other burgeoning pressures. Racism continues to extend its influence on the lives and opportunities of ethnic minority students.

The Macpherson Report (1999) on the Stephen Lawrence murder inquiry revealed the extent of institutional racism[7] endemic in an organisation such as the London Metropolitan Police Service. The inquiry was a major landmark in British race relations history as it laid open the acute extent of structural racism in a particularly large establishment. Media interest generated by the inquiry report was wide-reaching but teacher union reaction was initially defensive (Richardson, 1999). Furthermore, at the beginning of the twenty-first century, the issues experienced by ethnic minorities in society are broadening, cutting across a number of equality of opportunity issues – namely, disability and gender. In recent periods, racism in social settings has required a more inclusive range of solutions. At the same time, racism in educational settings has revealed itself in more culturally defined terms.

As New Labour passes the midway mark of its second term in power it is important to explore the extent to which it has shaped an understanding of 'race inequality' and the policy and practice needed to increase 'race equality'. Back *et al.* (2002) argue that although there have been genuine shifts in New Labour's approach to multiculturalism, citizenship and social justice, it is very much the case that during the second term it is the policy of assimilation that has been rejuvenated. Blair's Britain is defining a new ethnicity – *Englishness* as opposed to *Britishness* in an era of globalisation and devolution. Eager to embrace the capitalist project, Blair is also at pains to offer answers to the anxieties and tensions faced by Britain's poor, within which are contained a significant proportion of its ethnic minorities (Kundnani, 2000). The young men of Oldham, Bradford and Burnley who conflicted with the police in such a dramatic way during the summer of 2001 did not suffer the problems of being 'under-assimilated'. Indeed, their predicament is of a society divided by racism and discrimination.

Research objectives and book structure

It can be seen that there are a number of important historical periods to take into consideration when exploring the question of how South Asians achieve in education. Certainly, there is an episode of immigration history that has been fundamentally important to look at – as issues in relation to integration and adaptation are based on the time of immigration, the capital (resources) people possessed on arrival, where they located residentially and into which occupational sectors they entered. Furthermore, the experiences of South Asians and African-Caribbeans in the labour market have been contextualised so as to provide a useful perspective on the positions of ethnic minorities in society. The religious and social characteristics of the three South Asian groups under study help to show important variations and how they are operationalised at the everyday level. Politico-ideological explanations for the experiences of ethnic minorities and South Asians in the education system have moved from groups being considered over-aspirant, not adapting appropriately, lacking confidence or a kind of self-esteem, to being subordinated by the institutionally racist structures of education and back again. Here, the sociology of education research moves from a focus on structure as the main determinant to the role of individuals and groups as agents in their own success. The present position is one that can be described as antiracist-multiculturalism and the explanations of how different ethnic minorities perform in education have taken such a standpoint.

This study, therefore, aims to come to terms with the differences in educational performance between Bangladeshis, Indians and Pakistanis in the city of Birmingham as a specific location, with its particular post-war immigration and settlement history and its varying selective and comprehensive schools. Chapter 2 provides a discussion of the important theoretical positions in relation to the sociology of educating ethnic minorities. There is an exploration of the capital that different groups possess; apart from the *economic*, which has been a focus of the current discussion, there are also issues of the *cultural* and *social* to consider. There is also a reflection of the experiences of South Asians and other ethnic minorities in variously different Western European and American settings. The aim here is to provide a wider theoretical framework in which to situate this study. Chapter 3 reviews some of the more salient research carried out on the achievements of South Asians and ethnic minorities in education. First, looking at 1970s studies on South Asians in education, moving to an analysis of the Rampton Report (1981) and Swann Report (1985) – both commissioned by central government. The huge interest in school effectiveness that raged throughout the 1980s, the roles and functions of teachers (including the sensitivities of potentially labelling teachers as racist) and how South Asians enter and experience further and higher education are contemplated in detail.

Chapter 4 is the first of the empirical chapters. It discusses processes in the early education of South Asians. It explores the initial experiences of South Asians in education, evaluating the nature of difference between groups. Selective school entry is an aspiration for many South Asians – findings from the study and analyses show how it is successful for some and not for others. Chapter 5 expands upon how subject choices are made. The ways in which South Asians select General Certificate in

Secondary Education (GCSE) and 'A' Level subjects are explored in detail. The perceptions of pupils, students, parents and teachers are used to discuss the different routes that South Asians take and why. Chapter 6 draws attention to *prima facie* performance differences to illustrate and describe relative achievements. It assesses the results obtained by respondents and how they shaped eventual higher education entry. Chapter 7 is an assessment of the role of home and the school in educational achievement processes, and establishes the significance of each for different South Asians. A perennial dichotomy exists between how far educational success is a function of the social and cultural capital that exists within the South Asian domestic sphere or of how effective schools are. Critical issues explored in relation to South Asians are those of teacher ethnicity and the role of religion and culture within the home. Chapter 8 focuses exclusively on teacher's perceptions of South Asian parents, gender, religion, educational aspirations, language-use and educational policy. Teachers provide their views on teacher ethnicity and how educational policy affects pupils and students. The final chapter attempts to place together the various strands from the findings. A taxonomic framework is developed and suggestions for further research are provided.

The methodology is found in the appendices. It explains the rationale for conducting the study and the way in which it was carried out. It also reflects upon the data gathering process and expands upon the specific outcomes from interviews and surveys. The appendices also contain information on specific educational outcomes data in the city of Birmingham, UK.

2
Theoretical Debates: Formations of Capital

Sociology of education in the 1950s and 1960s was characterised by a focus on educational opportunity. Social class was established as the major theoretical and policy worry of the time, largely because of its perceived impact on educational outcome. There was a concern about the impact education was having on meritocracy and social mobility. It included an exploration of the apparent association between social class and education, for example, coded through language. The close policy-function of the research permitted changes to general administration systems to stimulate educational outcomes. Mac an Ghaill (1996) refers to this as the 'old sociology of education'. This approach reached a peak in the 1970s, when a 'new sociology of education' emphasised the micro-analytical dimensions of teaching and learning processes. Rather than presenting education itself as the route to eliminate structural inequalities the very structures of education were considered vehicles in their reproduction. Neo-Marxist critiques focused on wider questions of power, hierarchy and cultural reproduction. It has led to further dialogue between the disciplines of sociology and education (Shain and Ozga, 2001).[1]

Theoretical debates in relation to the education of ethnic minorities and South Asians in capitalist societies need to be assessed. The idea of 'capital', *economic, cultural* or *social*, is an important consideration because it expresses class relations in the classic Marxian sense, but more developed. In the post-war era, Bourdieu and his concept of cultural and social capital and more recent re-inventions of social capital help to theoretically examine the experiences of immigrant groups or ethnic minorities and how they relate to the structure and functioning of the education system. It is crucial then to set the scene further by discussing ethnic educational inequalities from a wider European and North American perspective.

Bourdieu: field, cultural capital and habitus

In *The Forms of Capital*, Bourdieu (1986) expands the notion of capital beyond its economic determinism, to include the 'immaterial' and 'non-economic', specifically in the form of cultural and social capital. Different types of capital can be acquired, exchanged and transformed into other forms. As the structure and distribution of capital represents the inherent structure of the social world an understanding of the multiple forms of capital help to elucidate the structure and functioning of education. Cultural capital theory has its origins in the education systems (the field) of advanced Western societies, with their inbuilt systems of stratification leading to differential levels of scholastic development, credentialisation and subsequent entry and development in the labour market. The theory of cultural capital represents the collection of different economic and cultural forces, such as family background, status, social class, income, wealth and varying interests in and obligations towards education itself.

Bourdieu distinguishes three forms of cultural capital. First, the 'embodied state' is directly linked to sand incorporated within the individual and represents what they know and do. Embodied capital can be increased by investing time in self-improvement, through learning, for example. As the individual embodies capital, it becomes a type of *habitus* (the embodiment of cultural capital). Second, the 'objectified state' of cultural capital is represented by cultural goods and material objects such as '*books, paintings, instruments* or *machines*'. They are appropriated both materially by economic capital and symbolically by embodied capital. Finally, cultural capital, in its 'institutionalised state', provides academic credentials and qualifications which generate a 'certificate of cultural competence which confers on its holder a conventional, constant, legally guaranteed value with respect to power' (ibid.). Academic qualifications can then be used to create additional cultural and economic capital.

Bourdieu argues that everyone has a 'cultural history' accumulated through primary ('family resources') and secondary ('educational choices') socialisation processes. In general terms, these include anything that gives an individual an advantage or disadvantage in certain situations. For example, gender and ethnicity, under certain circumstances, can be either advantageous or disadvantageous to opportunities in life. Moreover,

Bourdieu developed the idea of *situational constraints*, to demonstrate how the working classes (and ethnic minorities) are systematically blamed for their relative failure within the education system: *cultural reproduction* (socio-pathologisation). Cultural reproduction, in this context, is the way in which schools in association with other social institutions help to perpetuate social and economic inequalities across the generations. For Bourdieu, the relationship between the education system (considered as part of the politico-ideological *superstructure* in capitalist society) and the economic infrastructure (*base*) is a dependent one. In capitalist society, where the economic infrastructure is highly stratified, this *inequality* is reflected in the education system. According to this theory, schools are forced to produce students differentiated in ways that fit them into the economic system. Here, some students (the few) will leave school to go onto higher education and professional employment, while others (the majority) will leave school to go into lower paid employment and lower status jobs (*elimination*). The class that dominates the economic system (the bourgeoisie) dominates the other classes culturally and ideologically. Schools are seen as agencies of cultural and ideological transmission and the dominant economic class (based on the ownership of the means of production) dictates through the transmission of its cultural values via the school. Upper- and middle-class children, for example, may expect to enter highly-paid, high-status employment and, therefore, are more-likely to see the value of educational qualifications as a means of upward social mobility (even if they might find education monotonous and boring). Working-class children, on the other hand, with a family history of low-paid manual labour may not see education in the same way and, consequently, react to structural subordination, which impacts on them negatively, further marginalising their positions in economy and society. Likewise, teachers may expect and demand more or less from students with different levels of perceived cultural capital (Bourdieu and Passeron, 1998). There is a great deal of sociological evidence that supports the idea that teachers classify their students in terms of stereotypical concepts of 'ability' – which, in turn, determines the extent to which teachers believe their pupils are capable of succeeding educationally *and* the different levels of knowledge that can be taught to such pupils (cf. Gillborn and Youdell, 2002; see Chapter 3 on teachers).[2]

Research has used the concept of *habitus* although there are reservations about some of its potential. Reay (2000) has noted the significance of family background as a 'primary site of social reproduction'. The concept of 'emotional labour' is used to describe what is seen as the crucial role played by mothers in the educational life chances of their children. It is argued that middle-class mothers, for example, are 'better-placed' (that is, they have greater reserves of cultural capital) than their working-class peers to provide the support required by children throughout their school career. This 'emotional investment' works on a number of levels, from being better-placed to provide their children with 'compensatory education' (help with school work, for example), having more time to spend on their children's education (middle-class women, for example, are less-likely to spend large parts of their working day in paid employment, although not all) and have the status (and confidence) to confront teachers when they feel their children are not being pushed hard or taught well enough. According to Reay (1995), there are a number of potential uses for the concept of *habitus* in understanding educational processes even though there are strong criticisms of it too. Most of the critiques have focused on the ambiguity of the concept. For Jenkins (1992), the concept contains both seductions and pitfalls, 'the processual and ontological mysteries of the *habitus*' remain unsolved [although the concepts are 'enormously good for thinking with'] (ibid., p. 11). But for Bourdieu (1990), the concept of *habitus* demonstrates not only the ways in which the body is in the social world but how the social world is in the body, 'the habitus as the feel for the game is the social game embodied and turned into a second nature'. Thus, *habitus* is continually modified by the individuals' encounter with the wider world. Schooling, in particular, provides a general disposition, 'a cultured habitus'. While the social position is constructed it also carries within it the genesis to permit it to transcend the social conditions in which it was produced. *Habitus* can be seen as a continuum with either extremes lowering or raising aspirations.

Cultural capital is a very general theory, in the sense that it attempts to construct explanations for outcomes such as differential educational achievement in a way that combines a wide range of differing influences. In this respect, almost any cultural feature of people's lives can, under the right circumstances, be applied to an explanation of achievement or underachievement. This, in some respects, is both a strength and a weakness of the theory. A strength in the way the theory recognises that a multi-causal approach is required to understand the complexity of achievement and a weakness in that it is difficult to pinpoint the relative influence of particular cultural influences. In addition, Bourdieu argues that there is no objective way of differentiating between different class cultures (upper-, middle- and working-class cultures, for example). That is, the high value placed on the dominant cultural values characteristic of an upper or ruling class is simply a reflection of their powerful positions within capitalist society. A dominant class is able, in effect, to impose its definition of reality upon all other classes. Thus, each economic class develops an associated 'class culture', which involves different ways of seeing and doing things in the social world. These things are specific to and develop out of the experience in the social world of social classes. Children are not merely socialised into the 'values of society as a whole'. Rather, they are socialised into the culture that corresponds to their class and, in Bourdieu's terms, this set of cultural experiences, values and beliefs represents a form of cultural capital. Bourdieu's basic argument is that the role of education is mainly one of social reproduction that serves the ideological purpose of enabling a dominant social class to reproduce its power, wealth and privilege.

Although notions of 'race' and ethnicity are not explicitly found in Bourdieu's concept of *habitus*, they can still be understood as part of it – as racial oppression informs the understanding of racialised *habitus*. Prejudice and racial and ethnic stereotyping ingrained in the *habitus* of people in dominant groups can impact the life chances of other groups seen to be different in any number of ways, 'the collective social history of different groups in society informs their understandings of the social world and the dispositions and predispositions embedded in collective habitus' (Reay, 1995, p. 122). As a method for analysing the dominance of dominant groups in society and the subsequent domination of subordinated groups, *habitus* is important. It can be straightforwardly extended to racial and ethnic groups. Furthermore, the concept of *habitus* permits an analysis of social inequality which is not simply dependent on fixed notions of economic and social location (Reay, 1998).

Social capital: ethnicity and education

Bourdieu (1986, p. 248) defines social capital as, 'the aggregate of the actual or potential resources which are linked to possession of a durable network of more or less institutionalised relationships of mutual acquaintance and recognition'. An individual's social capital is determined by the size or their relationship network, the sum of its cumulated resources (both cultural and economic) and how successfully (and quickly) the individual can set them in motion. Social capital theory potentially permits the exploration of class and ethnic factors in the education of a particular group. Using the notions of *bonding, bridging* and *linking*, how the different South Asians mobilise group norms and values into class and social action in the sphere of education can be considered in social capital terms.

A great deal has been said about social capital in recent periods. It has been re-invented as a political project by various advanced Western economies. It is considered to be the 'glue' that holds democratic society together. Theory and empirical research suggest that social capital may be thought of as a measure of the cohesiveness of a society (Print and Coleman, 2003). In general, social capital is generally regarded to be an attribute of communities, whereas human capital is considered to be a characteristic of individuals, comprising a stock of skills, qualifications and knowledge. Putnam (2000) refers to social capital in terms of social networks and the associated norms of reciprocity and trust – with social capital possessing both private and public spheres of influence benefiting the individual, community or nation. The World Bank and the Organisation for Economic Cooperation and Development (OECD) have defined social capital as, 'networks together with shared norms, values and understandings that facilitate co-operation within or among groups' (Cote and Healy, 2001, p. 41). In spite of this, the idea of social capital is not a late twentieth-century fascination. Hanifen (1916, p. 130) talked of the 'importance of community involvement for successful schools'. There is a reference to 'those tangible substances that count for most in the daily lives of people', which helps to generate 'goodwill, fellowship, sympathy and social intercourse among the individuals and family who make up a social unit'. Furthermore, 'the community as a whole will benefit by the co-operation of all its parts' (for Bourdieu, social capital is part of cultural and economic capital). Such social relations facilitate co-operation for mutual gain. Social capital is generated when individuals share and exchange knowledge, norms, values and behaviour that are reinforced by trust and obligations.

The idea of social capital has re-emerged in recent years, popularised by American political scientists. There has been a great deal of thinking and elaborating about the concept itself, issues of measurement and potential public policy relevance, but there is, however, little by way of empirical research, especially of a qualitative nature and particularly in relation to ethnic minorities or in education. This is largely because of conceptual contradictions. Indeed, education is regarded as both an outcome and a cause of social capital. There is disagreement on the way in which social capital is seen to *flow* – with Coleman (1988) arguing that it is an outcome and Putnam (2000) a cause of educational achievements. Distinctions emerge in how the concept is thought to be reified – based on whether communities are disaggregated at the level of the individual *or* the individual aggregated at the level of communities. Coleman argues that education provides resources and knowledge facilitating individual social action. Putnam's argument states societal impact is produced through the collection of associated social behaviours. The apparent relationship between social capital and education, whether perceived or realised helps, nevertheless, to explain some of the current government interest in citizenship education.

Bonding (or 'exclusive') social capital refers to relations amongst relatively homogenous groups such as family members and close friends and is based on strong ties. Portes and Sensenbrenner (1993) state that 'reciprocity, bonded solidarity and enforceable trust (social obligations)' are key features in these ties. Individuals and communities with shared ethnicity, values and culture bond together for mutual benefit. Ethnicity serves as a 'source of adaptive change', using social capital for initial guidance and support. Ethnicity can serve as a powerful tool in the creation of human and social capital but if politicised it is argued that ethnicity can eliminate social capital (Bates *et al.*, 1998). High levels of internal trust may generate distrust of non-kin members and institutions, preventing potentially productive relationships. The work on Southern Italy by Putnam (1993) showed that dense family networks may limit economic growth by imposing barriers to integration with external networks. As such, an adverse effect of strong bonding social capital is that it may exclude others. It constitutes what could be termed as the 'downside' of social capital. Certain South Asians are very well bonded, as social ties among family, kin and communities are strong. The downside of such bondedness can lead to segregation, which often results in community alienation from mainstream society. It generates localised struggles and interventions that are not recognised by the local or national majority (Kundnani, 2001).

Another issue is of inter-generational differences – which become acute precisely because of the particular household and social structures in which, in particular, young South Asians are a part of. Inter-generational differences remain and they exist within family structures that would ordinarily suggest high levels of shared-ethnicity bonding. But, British-born South Asians possess a whole host of attitudes and behaviours analogous to their parents. For example, questions are raised about parental interpretation and practice of religion with many British-born South Asian Muslims attempting to return to a stricter form – often in an attempt to empower themselves against parents [who may insist that 'cousin marriages'[3] are a Qur'anic edict, for example] and against wider society which may seek to contain Muslims in marginalised positions as specific workings of global capitalism and international geo-politics.

Adolescents in many Western cultures come to an age when they begin to conflict with their parents – a socio-biological predicament facing young people and their parents in all societies. Youth rebellion is an almost universal phenomenon; a journey of self-discovery in the transition from childhood to adulthood. It is not unsurprising therefore that some young British-born South Asians oppose many of their parents' values. A generation gap begins to take shape when youngsters begin to question their identity, beliefs and reasons for existence. They are caught between the culture of their parents and that of their everyday lives outside of their homes. For some, the lives of young South Asians are filled with inter-generational conflict as a result of language, issues of social integration and the problems of educational aspirations versus the reality of opportunities. Some youngsters want to feel more a part of Britain, declining much of their existing cultural norms and values, influenced by media, music, technology and society at large. Others seek an identity in religion and politics.

Bridging (or 'inclusive') social capital refers to relations with distant friends, associates or colleagues. These ties tend to be weaker and diverse but important for 'getting ahead' (Granovetter, 1973). For South Asians, the ability to interact with other South Asians is impacted by ethnicity and social class. The effect is to strengthen the bond with one's immediate ethnic and cultural group. There is much that brings South Asians together but an important bridging opportunity with the majority is lost (a) as a function of the group's inability to trust, work and reciprocate with others largely because of alienation and (b) because of racial and religious discrimination. In terms of educational achievements, it is apparent that bridging social capital provides the opportunity to share with and learn from other people dissimilar to oneself in order to gain advantage. Finally, 'linking' social capital refers to relations between individuals and groups in different social strata to a hierarchy, where groups have various levels of access to power, social status and wealth (Cote and Healy, 2001). Woolcock (2001) extends this definition to include the capacity of individuals to lever resources, ideas and information from institutions beyond the community. It is apparent, nevertheless, that linking social capital is a limited feature in the experience of poorer South Asians. There exist a handful of South Asian role models who are academics, entrepreneurs, parliamentarians, civil servants or sport stars in Britain today, although numbers continue to rise.

Relatively homogeneous ethno-religious communities may be characterised by strong trust and cooperative norms within the community but low levels of trust and cooperation with the rest of society. Although strong bonding ties provide some South Asians with a sense of identity and common purpose without 'bridging' ties that transcend various social divides (e.g., religion, ethnicity and social class) bonding ties can become a basis for the pursuit of narrow interests and can actively exclude outsiders (Portes and Landolt, 1996). While ethnic networks may serve as a source of 'adaptive change' when immigrants first arrive, it is bridging capital that enables greater social and economic participation in the host society. That is, bridging social capital is important for minority groups to expand their networks beyond their own ethnic community and to acculturate into society so as to generate further social and economic opportunities. To accumulate bridging capital requires the willingness of ethnic minorities to connect with society at large but more importantly, *the willingness of the receiving society to accept* *other ethnic groups*. As a result, ethnic minorities may well be excluded from the mainstream society because of 'race', ethnicity or religion.

The concept of social capital does, however, receive a certain degree of condemnation. Critics argue that social capital is the latest *buzzword*; it lacks empirical specificity and it neglects considerations of power. It arouses suspicion because of the huge range of social relations it attempts to hypothesise about. It is argued that the recent surge in interest has generally been imported from North America ignoring the socio-cultural context of its conceptualisation. What the explanation of social capital does, in effect, is play to the hands of the functionalists who argue that the lack of ethnic minority social capital is a 'function' of their inability to internalise and actualise the norms and values of dominant society so as to take part in a meritocracy as fully integrated citizens. If groups assimilate and play a more engaging role in society, utilising more fully ethnic resources that exist through ethno-religious inter- and intra-ethnic bondedness, they would potentially stand an equal chance of upward mobility. What this ignores, however, is the historical and economic context of slavery, the British in India, colonialism, post-colonialism and decolonisation and the extent to which many South Asian groups are currently some of the most socially and economically marginalised groups in society.

With the central components of *bonding*, *bridging* and *linking* social capital theory does, on the other hand, provide *some* insight into the educational underachievement processes of South Asians. Bonding is made stronger by cultural and ethno-religious forces as well as the impact on them of economic and social exclusion. South Asians who underachieve in education are more likely to be 'locked' into specific ethno-religious social and cultural relations within their spatial context. Those that perform well possess social relations with other people of similar cultural capital but of a different ethnicity to their own. The idea of bridging helps to show the extent to which some South Asians are able to develop stronger relations with people of a different ethnicity. These groups are civically engaged, participate politically and become involved in interest groups in the orthodox ethnocentric sense. But for British South Asian Muslims (Bangladeshis and Pakistanis in the main), for example, relations with non-Muslim ethnic majorities are restricted because of segregation [as a function of both housing and employment] and alienation, as well as certain instances of rising Islamophobia and hostility towards Muslims in the post-September 11 climate, at the micro and macro levels. Linking involves precisely the notion of developing improved relations with those who hold power in government, media, civil society and academe. They require bearing an influence and leveraging resources. For some South Asians who are often disadvantaged ethnic minorities these opportunities are limited because of the marginalised social, political and economic positions they are in. The opposite is true for South Asians from higher social class backgrounds. The ability to link positively is hampered or encouraged by existing class positions. Meanwhile, the polarities between the bourgeoisie and the proletariat continue to widen exacerbating the positions of some South Asians. Bonding, bridging and linking are inextricably linked for British South Asians.

International comparisons: Western Europe and North America

In the lives of immigrant groups and ethnic minorities in many Western and European economies and societies education remains a precarious juncture. It is important to explore issues impacting ethnic minority groups in education in other European economies and in North America. It is the case, however, that South Asians tend not form a significant part of the populations of ethnic minority groups in other European countries or North America and this subsequently impacts on the way in which they are treated in education systems and sociology of education research. Nevertheless, the broad thrust of theory and research on ethnic minority groups in education in advanced economies other than Britain is explored.

In Western Europe, the demand for post-war labour existed for very much the same reasons as in Britain – the desire to fill employment in industries and economic sectors that indigenous workers did not wish to, as well as 'push' factors within the sending regions encouraging immigration to European economies. Based on an analysis of experiences in France, Germany, Finland, Greece, England and the Netherlands these countries reveal a policy of inclusion and exclusion derived from a historically defined geo-political position (Hof and Dronkers, 1994; Wolbers and Driessen, 1996; Kalekin-Fishman *et al.*, 2002). In all these countries, education policy is relevant to the settlement, integration and adaptation strategies of immigrant groups. All these countries are parliamentary democracies – and the politics of immigration and education have been a function of how groups are seen to constitute a 'problem'. Indeed, most immigrants arrive from 'developing' countries, including Africa and Asia, and what often starts as the immigration of male 'pioneers' soon turns into family re-unification and permanent settlement. A desire to enter, work and live in an advanced European economy has its roots in 'pull' factors. For the overwhelming majority, the attraction is higher wages and a better standard of living. For a limited set of others, there are political considerations in taking the option to migrate – people may fear religious persecution, political dictatorship and so on. Common 'push' and 'pull' factors are reflected in the experiences of many European economies and the differing countries involved in sending immigrants, in the past and today.

In relation to the reactions of host states to immigrant groups, again there are parallel processes that can be extrapolated. First, immigrant groups tend to experience a process of alienation. Here, the immigrant is unashamedly excluded from normal life. Second, the new immigrant has to re-learn to live in the host country – and adapt to norms and values as soon and as well as they can, often with little or no support from state institutions. Third, immigrants are devoid of knowledge in relation to how political processes work, what rights and responsibilities they have or how to access the levers of power. The immigrant is isolated because they cannot easily fit in however hard they try. Fourth, they obtain employment at levels often considerably below their skills, knowledge and experiences would suggest. Severe levels of 'under-employment' [employed in the labour market below their *actual* knowledge and skill levels] and racial discrimination are experienced. Finally, this, in turn, lowers self-esteem, limits aspirations and discourages positive dialogue.

Adapting to host countries is a difficult task as competition for scarce resources means that immigrant groups are required to ethnically commodify their labour or economic activity in niche markets. Further-more, immigrants are at the mercy of white bureaucrats and gatekeepers who might possess hostile attitudes towards them (as has been the case in most European countries, who in the seventeenth and eighteenth centuries legitimised economic expansionism, trade and commerce through the systematic oppression, subordination and exploitation of non-white groups on the basis of their pseudo-scientifically character-ised 'superior' biological status). If accepted by society, this encourages the process of adaptation and leads to integration. Here, diversity is regarded a strength to the host country, ensuring economic vitality and growth. The extent to which groups are required to become a part of society varies between different countries. Some countries, notably France, require an individual to assimilate. The level of absorption is a matter of the host country but one extreme example is assimilation – which is the complete eradication of the traits that characterised the group at the time of its migration. On the other hand, the position any one host country takes will be located on some point on a continuum between complete elimination of the self and the maintenance of extreme separateness.

Unequivocally, immigrant groups were originally incorporated into Western European economies and societies on the basis of their import-ance for the labour market. The assumptions by states and societies were that these workers would return to their sending regions once demand for their labour had ceased. This short-termist view did not bear fruit in reality with many immigrant groups remaining. From the point of view of the host countries, deportation has not been a politically expedient option. As such, in Britain and in France, immigrants from former colonies have special dispensation to permanently reside and receive full citizenship. In Germany, Finland and Greece, recognition of kinship is the basis for the claim. Any notion of inclusion has by definition within it the idea of exclusion. This excluded other can exist by virtue of language, religion and culture, as an historical absence which sets local indigenous people apart from immigrant groups. Exclusion from the labour market means that people have an insecure relationship with the state, heightened by a lack of expression in native languages. In relation to education, more specifically, an important issue is raised. What are the schools to do in dealing with a non-white non-host language speaking pupil intake? It is clear that educational policy is a direct way of achieving integration and therefore remains an important tool in the 'social engineering' of immigrants and their adaptation. Essentially, schools serve an economic and social func-tion. Economic – as education provides a ready supply of variously technical human labour. Social – as it generates the next generation of the bearers of cultures, identities and aspirations. What different European economies did for immigrants entering their schools was, to be sure, quite similar. It was a strategy for either controlling numbers or using the education system to integrate children into the host society. This appeared in all Western European economies in one guise or another.

In North America, even though there were considerable improvements in race relations in the 1960s, ethnic inequalities persist in education as they do in the rest of society. Ogbu (1997) argues that although in certain liberal and middle-class quarters social class is regarded as the major reason for the consistent underachievement of African-Americans in education and not 'race', 'race' remains a key explanatory factor. He observes that while all ethnic minority groups start lower than their white peers in the early grades, Asians (South East) improve and then even surpass their white colleagues. For African-American students the converse is true. It is African-American men who fair worst in education – relative to other ethnic minorities. For Ogbu (1997, p. 772), the school-performance gap 'was created by the forces of racial stratification: white treatment of blacks in the educational domain and black responses to schooling. The gap remains as long as these two forces remain'. For Ogbu, majority society treats African-Americans as an inferior *caste*, and they, in turn, internalise these negative attitudes which has the impact of making the positions of African-Americans in the education system even more precarious as they fail to perform in education through the fear of having to act 'white'. Ogbu supports school personnel in better understanding the 'culture of poor black students', while at the same time encouraging African-American communities to play a stronger supporting role in the education of their children (Berube, 2000).

In the current thinking that exists on the various theories of *capital*, potential merits of the different concepts in understanding the experiences of South Asians in the English education system emerge, given the positions of South Asians within society as a whole and how a lack or possession of economic, cultural and social capital impacts on their education. In particular, cultural capital theory considers the micro-processes at work, as pupils engage with parents, teachers and the system itself. Social capital theory elaborates the importance of networks, associations and 'connections', and here too, the education of South Asians can be interpreted as a function of how different ethnic minorities mobilise certain class and ethnic resources. The notions of cultural and social capital are useful theoretical positions. Subsequently, they emerge valuable tools in the analysis of the empirical data to stem from this study.

These discussions lead to a synthesis of the main strands of empirical research in the educational achievements of British South Asians in the post-war period.

3
Empirical Research on British South Asians in Education

Based on the principles of meritocracy, the Education Act of 1944 was intended to provide a system of education for every child in British society. But as early as over four decades ago research first began to question the reasons for differential educational achievement among ethnic minorities. At the time, the education of different working class and ethnic minority groups was considered a function not only of their 'innate capacities frustrated or encouraged by their material environment', but also of 'culturally conditioned attainments, attitudes and aspirations of the ethos of the educational institutions to which they have access' (Floud and Halsey, 1958, p. 184). As discussed in Chapter 1, from assimilation, integration to cultural pluralism (multiculturalism), at a time when central government policy was increasingly shifting to the New Right, a major ideological attempt in the form of antiracist education was made by the Left-radicals. A variant that might be dubbed antiracist multicultural education is seen in some schools at present. The position of South Asians within existing class structures not only dictates their norms and values towards education but also governs their motivations and aspirations, which are also affected by teachers and schools. As such, research indicates that ethnic minorities underachieve because of 'intellectual capacity, family structures, cultural differences, disadvantage and social background, language problems, low self-esteem and racial prejudice' (ibid.), which has its genesis in an earlier period of post-war education policy and practice.

Ever since the post-war immigration and settlement of ethnic minorities, sociological research on educational inequality has found educational achievement to be strongly associated with social class (Halsey *et al.*, 1980; Heath and Clifford, 1990; Goldthorpe, 1996). In addition, there is convincing evidence to suggest that parent education levels are also important factors to consider, especially in relation to higher education entry (Burnhill *et al.*, 1990). As such, there are certain implications for British South Asians: not only do they occupy different economic and social positions in society compared with ethnic majority groups (Modood *et al.*, 1997), but also certain South Asian parents tend to be less educated (Ghuman, 1980; Bhachu, 1985), in particular certain South Asian Muslim parents (Joly, 1989; Gardner, 1992). It is important, therefore, to review some of the pertinent *processual* research carried out on South Asians and ethnic minorities in education over this period. Relevant studies from the 1970s onwards, concerning South Asian educational achievements, including an interpretation of the Rampton and Swann Reports, both extensive central government commissions published in the early 1980s, are examined. The interest in *school effectiveness* research throughout the 1980s and early 1990s, the roles and functions of teachers, and research on how South Asians experience further and higher education in the current period are all considered.

First generation research

A North of England-located study of school-leaver examination performance found that considerations of social class did not entirely explain why Indians and Pakistanis performed as well as they did. They did well not because they were necessarily middle class but that they had '[internalised] middle-class educational attributes' (Taylor, 1973). It was also established that the encouragement from parents was directly related to educational success. South Asian economic migrants were thought to have brought with them the 'baggage' of trying to achieve educational success for their young. The aspiration of high educational achievement for their children is ingrained, and exists had they migrated to another country apart from England or not at all (Taylor and Hegerty, 1985).

Another early study used a comparative white group to examine South Asian educational achievement processes and further attempts were made to learn more about the apparently close link between educational achievements and parent support levels (Gupta, 1977). It was found certain South Asian groups had 'unrealistic aspirations', which remained ultimately unrealised resulting in eventual 'under-employment'. Furthermore, proportionately more of the young South Asian men and women wished to remain in education beyond school leaving age, replicating Taylor's (1973) findings. The reason for the greater tendency was thought to originate from the 'South Asian psyche'. There were in addition other reasons provided. Greater continuity in education may also have been associated with a fear of discrimination in the labour market.[1] At the time, the direction for research was to propose that an instinctive desire to move economically and socially upward was the reason for the high importance placed by South Asian parents upon their children to do well in education. It was not because of their middle-class status *per se*, rather a middle-class orientation towards education. Much of the early research, on the whole, identified educational underachievement to be restricted, in the main, to the disadvantaged sector of the ethnic minority community, characterised by rural-born and poorly paid South Asians living in homes in substandard inner-city areas (Robinson, 1980).

After the immigration and settlement phases of the early 1960s, ethnic minorities began to be regarded more and more as a problem, 'the British views both of themselves and the colonial "other" coalesced to create an image of an "alien threat" facing British schools and British society in general' (Blair and Cole, 2002, p. 64). Furthermore, the idea of 'underachievement' came to take hold on ethnic minority education discourse rather than to focus on systems, schools, teachers and overall standards (Troyna, 1984; see Fine, 1991 on North America). More pernicious was the representation of different 'ethnic minority educational problems'. South Asians were characterised in compassionate terms, passive but not studious while at the same time not presenting disciplinary problems for teachers. This idea of the 'passive' South Asian was placed alongside the 'aggressive' African-Caribbean. The latter became a 'stick to beat the West Indian pupil with' (Tomlinson, 1984). Generally applied to the young South Asian women, the idea of passivity was to suggest their cultural subordination by South Asian men too (Brah and Minhus, 1985). Clearly, by the late 1970s ethnic minority parents were finding that their children were not receiving the education that they had hoped for – from obtaining the performance levels required to progressing favourably in education. At the same time, state institutions regarded that the underachievement of ethnic minorities in education stemmed from the group rather than the structure and functioning of the social world.

Education and the state: early responses

The Labour government of the late 1970s commissioned an investigation into ethnic minority educational underachievement to look initially at

African-Caribbean groups. After the publication of the Rampton Report (1981), Lord Swann became the chair of the committee with the remit widened to explore South Asians, eventually publishing the five-year study, the Swann Report in 1985. Planned to explore the educational experiences of African-Caribbeans, the Rampton Report (1981) was criticised for not being an adequate assessment of the factors contributing to their educational underachievement. It was questioned, 'if West Indians are underachieving, are they doing so because the education service is generally inadequate for all children or because it is particularly inadequate for West Indian children?' (Reeves and Chevannes, 1981, p. 36). The Rampton Report (1981) specifically focused on African-Caribbeans in education but due to political influences it became clear other ethnic minority group experiences of education required a more lucid understanding. The move led to the publication of a further report in 1985 but there were criticisms, however, made of the Swann Report (1985) too. For Rex (1987, p. 11), it was seen 'as an exercise in multicultural education discourse. Even the name was changed to "Education for All" as some teachers in certain LEAs would see that it was no concern to them'. It 'cultivated difference through the maintenance of a core set of common political values'. It attempted to develop an *education for all* so that pupils in largely white schools did not become the 'racists like the generation before them'.

It was argued that the Swann Report (1985) diluted many ideological perspectives. Of the members of the committee, the Left advocated an antiracist agenda putting to question economic and social structures. The Right demanded identification with a common white-Englishness, with the quality of the school mattering most. The Liberal view believed the early socialisation periods of children were crucial to their educational achievement. The committee, nonetheless, was unable to capture aspects of both antiracist education and multicultural education. As a former member of the committee put it, 'the terms of reference were not neutral ... [They were] ... informed by what I might call a social-democratic view of the nature and causes of the educational underachievement of ethnic minority children' (Parekh, 1989, p. 231). Furthermore, it is argued and suggested that the Swann Report (1985) did not contain any reference to eradicating racism in society or to educating against racism. It confirmed the multiculturalist belief in the 'perfectibility of existing educational structures' and the importance of integration into them. Essentially, the factors of underachievement were thought to originate from an adverse domestic environment not conducive to learning. The Swann Report (1985) was thought not to have considered adequately the factors of ethnicity, social class or gender. It was a 'multicultural manifesto' that attempted to create social cohesion and consensus. The approach to education by central government conformed to the politics of privatisation, deregulation and competition – as part of a general shift towards the New Right.

The effects of schools

During the mid-1980s, as New Right in education gained ascendancy, the educational inequalities of individuals and groups began to be increasingly measured at the level of the school. In particular, it used multilevel and multivariate logistic modelling of 'hard' examinations data which incorporated specific background characteristics of candidates.

The School Effect by Smith and Tomlinson (1989) was a study of 18 urban multicultural comprehensives in four LEAs; two in the South East, one in the Midlands and one in the North of England. The study aims were to measure differences between schools based on outcomes achieved by pupils at 16, taking into consideration differences in attainment over a five-year period (1981–1986). The study found ethnic minority pupils were achieving relative to the national average at the time. There was a strong association between social class and examination achievement such that on average children from professional and managerial families were up to eight times more likely to attain the higher grade passes than those from families belonging to the disadvantaged and underprivileged (where neither parent had a job in the five years before the study was carried out) (Smith and Tomlinson, 1989). The study concluded that the school a child attends makes the greatest difference to examination attainment than any factor associated with ethnicity (Tomlinson, 1992).

There were other statistical research carried out in the mid-1980s, based on the analysis of examination results by ethnicity with other quantifiable variables, provided by the Inner London Education Authority (ILEA) between the years 1985 and 1987, and statistically modelled by Kysel (1988) and Nuttall *et al.* (1989). Examination results in 1986, of 17,058 pupils from 106 schools, showed East African Asians and Indians performed well with Pakistanis performing above average. The Bangladeshis achieved well below average. It was argued that limited Bangladeshi performance was due to 'poverty, social class and lack of fluency in English'. Factors within schools included 'negative stereotyping and low expectations' on the part of the teachers of particular ethnic groups, 'lack of relevance of the curriculum' and 'poor communication between the school and the parents' (Kysel, 1988). In 1987, 87 per cent (121 of 141) of the schools responded to the study (18,314 pupils). On this occasion, it was found that 'all ethnic groups perform[ed] significantly better than the ESWIs [English, Scottish, Welsh and Irish]', except those of African-Caribbean background who performed slightly but not significantly worse' (Nuttall *et al.*, 1989). Young women performed best of all. When the governing bodies of the different schools in the ILEA-funded study were asked to respond they offered broad-curricula factors as the reason for difference which would be corrected through 'rigorous monitoring and high quality language support'. Nuttall and Varlaam (1990) argued that social class was the primary factor thought most significant outside the control of the individual school.

There have been more attempts to carry out similar research but they raise more questions than answers and begin to lend themselves to different methodological approaches. A larger-scale study in the early 1990s examined the effects of ethnicity, gender and social class on educational achievements over a nine-year period. Samples were selected from primary school and progress measured until pupils left schools with their GCSE results. Eight factors were determined to statistically impact on results: eligibility of free meals, large family size, one-parent family, semi- or un-skilled manual occupations of parents, ['under-employment' and] unemployment, behaviour, fluency in English and 'ethnic family background' (Sammons, 1995). Haque and Bell (2001), in their recent multilevel analysis of educational outcome of Bangladeshi school pupils, using GCSE examination results data from 12 schools, found that educational performance is strongly correlated with social class but outcome is also based on background variables such as parental occupation and education and how recently the group arrived into Britain. In all these studies however, the use of 'hard' data an analysis of *processes* is lost, as it is *inputs* and *outputs* that are considered. It is not possible to understand the different processes that impact different ethnic groups in variously different educational settings. It is not apparent how these background variables interact with outcomes at the everyday level. It is not clear whether structural or cultural factors are significant and why (Aitkin and Longford, 1986). As such, it provides opportunities for further, albeit, more qualitative research to tackle to these questions. The entirely statistical approach to measuring performance differences by ethnicity, social class, gender and other variables is critiqued.

The notion that there is a fair and accurate method to compare one school with another is questioned by Gray *et al.* (1986). Differences between pupils at the level of the home are not easily identifiable such that 'comparable opportunities' open to pupils cannot be measured in easily distinguishable statistical terms. Variations in examination performance used as the benchmark for how 'better' or 'worse' schools are judged appears to be a limited concept and yet comparisons between secondary schools have largely been confined to their results in public examinations. The use of aggregated results has led to an inadequate view on the processes because 'individual data are collapsed to the school mean-level' (ibid.). Moreover, examination performance variability year on year affects the development of longitudinal analyses and models incorporating measures of prior-secondary school attainment provide almost completely different results from those that do not (Gray *et al.*, 1990). There is limited indication to show how far school factors are effectual in relation to factors outside the control of the school (Coe and Fitz-Gibbon, 1998). The most significant flaw appears in identifying the processes of educational achievements by ignoring the economic and social context in which schools and their pupils find themselves (Plewis, 1988). As a result of school effectiveness research, the relationships between schools and their communities had been largely overlooked until very recently (Gibson and Asthana, 1998).

On the whole, the school effectiveness research project lost much of its momentum by the end of 1980s. Apart from methodological problems and issues that are raised there are also questions of how far school effectiveness research has been playing to the 'tune of government rhetoric'. Goldstein and Woodhouse (2000) argue that school effectiveness research has been systematically 'abused' by governments over the last two decades and the oversimplification of the concept has met with a focus on league tables and outputs *per se*. It is considered important for school effectiveness research to be removed from direct governmental association and mediate its relationship with 'school improvement' research such that this new area might be termed 'educational effectiveness' or 'institutional change' research.

Institutional racism = the attitudes of teachers?

Antiracist educationists propagate the idea of teacher racism in education, regarding teachers at the centre of educational underachievement. The idea of teacher racism and institutional racism in schools, on the other hand, is certainly not new. *Rampton* related ethnic minority underachievement to the failures of 'bad teachers', 'a lack of responsiveness' and 'bad practice'. Indeed, even earlier on, research on teacher attitudes towards ethnic minority pupils suggested that they had failed to recognise 'differences in culture' (Brittan, 1976).

A fundamental aspect of the problem is whether teachers *actually* act in a discriminative way. Teacher attitudes are thought to affect pupil 'setting' (the ways in which teachers select different pupils for different level examination groups based on perceived ability). Consequently, some ethnic minorities are prepared for examinations below their natural abilities might otherwise indicate (Troyna, 1978). In general, teacher racism is thought to affect African-Caribbean groups the greatest. The tendencies are for South Asians to be regarded by teachers as possessing high technical ability but being socially conformist too, in comparison to African-Caribbeans who are thought to have low ability *and* potential discipline problems (Mac an Ghaill, 1988). In other similar studies, comparable patterns emerge. A study of 13+ subject choices conducted in the mid-1980s found that African-Caribbeans did not make the additional effort to improve themselves educationally because they believed teachers would not eventually move them up into the higher sets (Wright, 1986, 1987). In one ethnographic study of a Midlands school, it was discovered that because of the negative perceptions of white teachers, African-Caribbean boys 'had to fight harder to retain their high status choices' (Gillborn, 1990, p. 139; see also Eggleston, 1986; Hurrell, 1995).

In the case of South Asians, research has shown parents have a propensity to agree to GCSE subject choices based largely on teacher determinations; 'most of the process is pre-judged'. In one study, it was found Bangladeshis, Pakistanis and African-Caribbeans were the most disadvantaged with GCSE subject choices. East African Asians and Indians were considered as having 'high science potential'. It was the 'white, male middle-class pupils from a two-parent family' that were the most contented with subject choices (Tomlinson, 1987). It is apparent, therefore, schools can adopt their own system of channelling individuals based on perceived ability. The effect is seen clearly in the individual concerned and in the examination results they ultimately obtain (CRE, 1992). As such, it is repeatedly found that white pupils are more likely to be entered for the higher-grade subjects than ethnic minorities (Tanna, 1990). Ethnic minority pupils tend to be under-represented in the higher sets and are more likely to be over-represented in those containing children with 'learning difficulties' (Troyna, 1992). Research conducted on teachers and their attitude towards ethnic minorities has consistently revealed the importance of being placed in certain GCSE sets for eventual examination outcome. Working class and ethnic minorities are found to be worse off and ethnic minority young women are often 'compartmentalised by teachers' (Tomlinson, 1987). Furthermore, recent research has also continued to show the extent to which young African-Caribbean men are far more likely to be excluded (expelled and suspended) from school because of racism and discrimination. Gillborn (1998) ascertains that these repeated research findings provide incontrovertible evidence of racism in schools and how teachers can be directly associated with the educational underachievements of certain ethnic minorities.

Throughout the 1990s, an intense debate enraged on the nature of teacher racism; its origins and/or whether it could be adequately proven at all (Foster, 1990, 1993; Wright, 1990; Connolly, 1992; Gillborn and Drew, 1993; Troyna, 1993a,b). The question is, are teachers deliberate in their actions, thereby firmly placing the onus of underachievement onto them and the schools? Or, alternatively, is it the particular social and the cultural norms and values of certain ethnic minorities that inhibit their achievement, such that teachers and schools are only *party* to the process by reacting in a negative way towards ethnic minorities? Rather than evaluating the structure and mechanisms of schooling *per se*, multicultural educationists tend to regard under achievement to be a function of the nature of ethnic minorities. It is argued by some that they are part of a 'wider project' to deny the existence of structural educational inequality, especially in the light of ethnographic research of the late 1980s and more recently (Mac an Ghaill, 1988; Gillborn, 1990; Basit, 1997a; Haw, 1998; Bhatti, 1999), which has unequivocally emphasised the extent of prejudice and discrimination experienced by ethnic minority school pupils and further education college students alike.

The debate over teacher racism is never ending (Pilkington, 1999). The presence of teacher racism is one that is deemed sensitive and remains open to further research. It is quite the case that teachers make a tremendous difference to the way in which ethnic minorities educationally develop in the end. This discussion adds to the wider criticism teachers and the profession have been receiving in recent times, in particular by OfSTED (1997), largely because of 'a lack of professionalism' on the part of teachers. It led to the present Labour government to become determined in encouraging new entrants into the profession by providing them with the opportunity for fast-track career development linked to performance-related pay (DfEE, 1998).

South Asians in further and higher education

In the analysis of the educational achievements of South Asians there are discernible patterns that emerge based on attempts to explain variations in performance. Particularly in relation to examination results research, on average, South Asians are thought to perform better than African-Caribbeans and are far more likely to continue in education after compulsory school leaving age, compared with all groups. Early research identified this trend and urged that a mixture of higher aspirations combined with added parental involvement encouraged young South Asians in their educational endeavours. It is important to look now at further (16–19) education and higher education entry (18+) research on South Asians to discern the extent of advantage and disadvantage for different groups as they progress beyond their compulsory schooling.

Possibly the largest study of ethnic minorities in education and the labour market is the Youth Cohort Survey (YCS) based on individuals periodically sampled from a town in North West England. It is still collecting and analysing data today (Demack *et al.*, 2000). Statistical results have robustly established a high rate of universal participation for 16–19-year-old ethnic minorities in education (Drew *et al.*, 1997). The findings are especially pertinent given the social class and gender of South Asian respondents. There are, however, complexities to this broad-sweeping generalisation. Further analysis of the YCS by Drew and Fosam (1994) has found South Asians use the 16–19 period to improve upon GCSE scores, proceeding to take 'A' Levels a year on. Three explanations are provided. First, there is an apparently greater commitment on the part of ethnic minorities and their families, which helps to ensure success combined with a cultural belief in the inherent importance of education and that removal from it would be detrimental. Second, there is greater motivation on the part of certain ethnic minorities to ensure they have the best possible qualifications before formally entering the labour market. Third, ethnic minorities may continue to stay in the education system to avoid racial discrimination in the labour market. These patterns are repeated elsewhere in other research.

At the beginning of the 1990s, analyses of 1991 'traditional' universities and 'former polytechnics' [in 1992, the systems were merged to form Universities Central Admissions System (UCAS)] entry data were undertaken (Modood, 1993; Taylor, 1993; Connolly, 1994). For the first time, detailed information on ethnicity, gender and 'A' Level scores was made available. It was found ethnic minorities applied to read degree subjects that were popular with candidates who had relatively high 'A' Level scores, resulting in greater competition for the more prestigious degree courses and thereby making them more difficult to get onto them *per se* (Modood and Shiner, 1994). In the need to make repeat applications, universities and higher education colleges were likely to ask for higher grades or to not make offers at all. African-Caribbeans and Pakistanis were less likely to gain admission to university, with the Chinese and Asian-other significantly more likely to have done so. In addition, young ethnic minority women were more likely to have gained admission than men. Those from higher social classes were 'significantly' more successful than those from partly skilled backgrounds in gaining entry. Candidates applying to local universities were significantly more likely to be admitted. Nevertheless, important issues remained. Why were the Pakistanis and African-Caribbeans less likely to obtain entry, particularly to the 'traditional' universities [which remains to this day]? It was speculated at the time that lower expectations of Pakistanis and African-Caribbeans might well have affected these groups, especially during earlier periods in their educational life-cycles. In addition, the 'former polytechnics' may have been more appealing as they tend to offer vocationally driven degree courses. Furthermore, students may have expressed a desire to remain near other ethnic minorities with shared ethnicity, religion and culture, especially if that was their experience in school and is in the wider social world. Continued analysis of secondary higher education entry data suggests that although many young ethnic minorities are now entering the sector in larger numbers they do so to the 'new universities'. This has subsequent impact on labour market entry. Biases in education and the labour market help to create a cumulative negative pattern of ethnic disadvantage (Shiner and Modood, 2002).

Recent research by Ball *et al.* (2002a) looks at the experience of higher education 'choice' by ethnic minorities. It suggests that social class remains the strongest explanatory factor in the higher education choices of ethnic minority students but an element of ethnic identification with certain higher education routes was also occurring. That is, ethnic minority students are being more considerate of the 'ethnic mix' of the higher education institution they wish to enter. Decisions are made on the basis of whether the chooser is *contingent* or *embedded*. Contingent choosers know little of their intended universities but make a decision on the basis of practical constraints balanced with positive criteria. Embedded choosers are more informed of the different types of universities and courses on offer and are able to take a more 'educated' decision based on discussions with parents, family and friends. Here, the ethnic mix of the institution does not matter in the same way as it does for contingent choosers.

Synopsis and the way ahead

Research conducted on the education of South Asians in the 1970s and early 1980s largely expressed concern with their adaptation. Studies of examination performances showed the higher rates of achievement of South Asians in comparison to others. Reasons for this revolved around the accelerated upward social mobility aspirations of newly settling immigrant groups. They were nevertheless considered incongruous to the social class positions they occupied in reality, although little attention was being paid to differences at the sub-ethnic minority level. Research on setting in relation to subject choice has found cause for genuine concern, particularly in relation to how teachers are thought to be 'labelling' some pupils with having more potential for success than others, particularly young South Asian women. Unquestionably, the whole idea of teachers who are racially prejudicial towards ethnic minorities is an exceptionally sensitive area with vociferous views from those who agree and disagree on both the potential and measurement of it. Related to questions of the placing of different ethnic groups into different subject settings by teachers is the overall effectiveness of the school itself. Various attempts have been made to identify a strong statistical relationship between pupil, school, background and outcome, however, not entirely satisfactorily. And, research on routes of entry into higher education suggests that ethnic minorities are present in numbers greater than their proportion of the relevant population would suggest. Then again, the differences within South Asians, for example, are often greater than between them and although social class, ethnicity and gender are recognised as being important how they are actually played out within the lives of different South Asian groups is less well understood.

During the 1990s, central government funded research reviews further elaborated upon some of the issues in ethnic minority educational inequality. The Office for Standards in Education (OfSTED) (1999a) reported on a follow-up exercise emanating from the 1996 review of educational inequalities in English schools (Gillborn and Gipps, 1996). It was found that the performance of Bangladeshi and Pakistani pupils during the early years remained a concern. Underachievement, however, was found to disappear once a sound command of the English language had been acquired. The fact that so few Bangladeshis and Pakistanis achieved the high GCSE grades remained a cause for concern nevertheless. Many of the secondary schools highlighted by OfSTED had already implemented broad-ranging equal opportunity policies. Although a number also collected precise ethnic minority data on achievement few were seen to be using it effectively. Where children had particular language difficulties the use of bilingual home-school link-workers was felt to be essential. The OfSTED (1999a) report highlighted that a great many LEAs had still not effectively implemented policies to tackle the educational underachievement of certain ethnic minorities.

The Runnymede Trust Commission on the *Future of Multi-Ethnic Britain* (2000) acknowledged the ongoing inequality issues facing ethnic minorities in education. It is argued that there has been no systematic funding of social research into educational inequalities since the implementation of the Education Reform Act of 1988. Education has become a market with resources allocated to schools on the basis of student numbers and with parents choosing those very schools based on reputation and standing. Anecdotal evidence from North America, which has experienced a similar development in education, suggests that ethnic segregation increases in certain schools. Given the already strong class-orientated structure of education in Britain, increased 'marketisaton' only helps further to increase polarities and subsequent ethnic and social divisions (Tomlinson, 2001). Furthermore, the issue of *triage* is important to explore. Pupils continue to be entered for different tiers of an examination system on the basis of potential for success. It has the impact of placing certain ethnic minorities in lower groups than higher. It is essentially a function of schools and teachers allocating on the basis of perceived potential often two years or so before examinations are taken. The result can be harmful for certain ethnic minorities because of the negative expectations and stereotypes schools and teachers are likely to possess.

Apart from *capital* and *social class*, gender and ethnicity are also important considerations for new research. Although the factors of social class and parent education levels may well help to explain a level of variation between South Asians it is argued there are additional factors which help to explicate distinct differences between groups. They are observable along religious and cultural lines. The *processes* underpinning the educational achievement of South Asians are made up of a complex web of factors, including social class, the effectiveness of schools, gender, teacher ethnocentricity, wider institutional racism, the role of parents and the continually changing nature of the education system. This research takes as its central point of departure the need to explore achievement for distinct South Asian groups in the context of the British education system (with all its extremities). This is carried out through an analysis of the different *processes* for different South Asians in different institutions of education linked to the class structure. Within this framework, an exploration is made of the cultural and social capital that different ethnic minorities generate, maintain, develop and invest to proceed through education.

The economic, social and cultural relations of South Asians not only affect the kind of educational institutions they attend or how effective they are – at the macro level – but also their motivations and aspirations that are, in part, affected by teachers and schools – at the micro level. Questioning racialised and gendered disadvantage in education requires an assessment of every aspect of education, as it is important to distinguish, for both theoretical development and policymaker relevance, between the view that *all* South Asian high achievers are ethnic minority successes and that *all* South Asian underachievement results from cultural and institutional racism. The middle class hold on education is something that has not been challenged in recent periods – both by state or academe. The fundamental result of this phenomenon is the continued exclusion of working-class white and ethnic minority people from the realms of elite higher education. Within this paradigm, the division between high achievers and lower achievers in education continues to widen. The experiences of South Asians and other ethnic minorities exist with the wider framework of class-bound educational outcomes. Some South Asians are clearly at the 'bottom' of the education pile while others are very much the 'top'. The reasons for this are contained in the reasons for the many but there are additional influences both endogenous and exogenous to certain South Asian groups that impacts on their education. A focus on the different *processes* of education illustrates the ways in which primary, secondary and tertiary socialisation processes materialise for different South Asians groups. Using Bourdieu's notion of *cultural reproduction*, it possible to see how certain South Asians might proceed in education because of their social class as well as 'ethnic resources'. For some, class and cultural advantage generate access to other spheres in which their social and economic positions are improved. For others, underachievement in education perpetuates a cycle of poverty and disenfranchisement.

This study aims to provide further insights into the processes of educational achievement for South Asians. Questions asked include, are the educational achievements of South Asians a function of social class or the school effect alone? How is the effectiveness of an institution a determinant of achievement? What impact do South Asian parents have on the education of their children? What roles do religion and culture play? In addition, how do teachers affect the education of South Asians? What are the perceptions of teachers? What is the effect of anti-racist multicultural policy in schools? The empirical chapters discuss the essential findings to emerge from the in-depth qualitative data in this research. They are organised so as to explore processes chronologically, from leaving primary school to entering university, specifically looking at the point of entry into selective education, the reasons for differential subject choice throughout and the potential routes to higher education. There are specific discussions in relation to the importance of the home and the school and, finally, teachers speak openly on their perceptions and experiences. It is very much the case that ethnicity, capital and class structure are poignant features that emerge important in the educational achievements of South Asians.

The following chapters contain the analysis of interviews and surveys with school pupils, college students, parents and teachers. Examples of the typical responses and those relevant in the development of grounded theoretical, empirical and conceptual discussions are presented in the following chapters in the form of extracts from the interview data and descriptive statistics from the surveys. Case studies are also highlighted. Further details on the sampling of the data, descriptions of the interview and survey responses, analysis of the interview process and secondary analysis of GCSE and 'A' Level examinations data from the study schools and further education colleges are found in the Appendices.

4
From Primary to Secondary Schooling: Selection of the Few

Studies conducted on the nursery (3–5) and primary (6–11) education of immigrants and ethnic minorities in the 1970s highlighted inconsistencies in performance and educational outcome. These studies concerned the performance of white and ethnic minority children at the end of their primary schooling. It was found that the 'reading age' of pupils was on average one year lower for ethnic minorities. South Asians born in Britain did as well as white children. There was reason given to suggest the British-born South Asians faired averagely by the time they left primary school even if they required catching up during the later years. Local education authorities varied in their attitudes towards finding a solution with some more prepared to tackle issues directly and others far less demonstrative (Little, 1975; 1981; 1986).

According to OfSTED (1999b), the standards achieved by ethnic minority primary school pupils have been rising in recent years, although the performance of Bangladeshi and Pakistani pupils in the early years of primary schooling still remains limited. Once they are 'proficient in the English language', their attainments often match or exceed that of English first-language pupils from similar backgrounds.[1] For example, the OfSTED (1996) report on the teaching of reading in 45 inner-London primary schools showed that Bangladeshi pupils achieved lower standards at the age of six compared with any other ethnic minority group. They subsequently made good progress, and by the time they were ready to leave primary school at the age of 11 their performance was similar to other groups. White pupils from disadvantaged backgrounds performed less well overall compared with all the other groups. These observations follow general findings in this area which tend to show a slow start followed by a gradual improvement on the part of poorer ethnic minorities in general and on the part of Bangladeshi and Pakistani primary schoolchildren in particular. The importance of primary schooling certainly cannot be underestimated for South Asians – a recent study on ethnic minority primary schoolchildren confirmed that the primary school a pupil attends has a significant impact on their progress during their early years in secondary schools (Strand, 1999). It seems that the educational underachievements of the past remain to the present day. Furthermore, this secondary analysis of outcome data masks subtle processual understandings which are evoked through different methodological and epistemological approaches.

It is important to explore views towards and aspirations of the South Asian pupils, students, parents and teachers in the study in relation to primary schooling experiences (although the focus of this study is not on primary schooling experiences in any significant detail). A particular concentration is on the process of gaining entry into selective schools by middle-class South Asian parents and the different experiences and perceptions of working-class South Asian parents in relation to this course of action.

Experiences of primary schooling

Pupils, parents and teachers were asked to speak of the importance of primary education in scholastic development and how pupils were being 'equipped' for secondary school entry. For the most part, primary school leavers proceed to carry on their compulsory schooling in secondary modern comprehensive schools. There is the possibility of taking selective school entrance examinations which permit pupils to enter grammar (selective) or independent schools (selective and fee-paying). Respondents talked of the various experiences affecting them.

Answers did not vary significantly between South Asians when asking selective school pupils about their early schooling. Statements made suggested unproblematic interactions with teachers. As one 17-year-old East African Muslim woman at Rosebud School stated, 'you don't even see colour then . . . do you? [Not] when you're that young'. Another 16-year-old Sikh woman at Rosebud School accepted that her time in primary school was positive, and she formed constructive relationships with her classmates of all ethnicities. It was said of her preparatory school,

[There were] very few Muslims and Hindus – a few Muslims than anything else . . . In the nursery, the new children coming in were more Hindus and Muslims – higher up where I was when I left there were mainly Sikh . . . Because the classes weren't very big, everyone was friends with everybody really. I mean my best friend was Kerry, she was a white girl and then I used to go around with a black girl called Natasha. We were quite close, all of us.

Of the comprehensive school pupils, one Pakistani 15-year-old young woman at New Heath School acknowledged that the primary school she attended was helpful and felt that she had made good progress. She said, 'I actually got on quite well with all the teachers...I loved sciences. I loved English especially.' The overwhelming tendency was for both selective and comprehensive school pupils to evoke positive experiences in their earlier relationships with teachers and with other pupils in their primary schools.

Further education college students were asked if they had been to nurseries. Fifty-five per cent [60/109] said they had and 45 per cent [49/109] said that they had not. Of those that did attend nursery, 97 per cent [58/60] started nursery at the age of three or four. For those who have not been to nursery there were a number of interesting observations. Eighty per cent of Bangladeshis in the sample [12/15] had not been to a nursery [all eight of the Bangladeshi boys and four of the seven girls]. A great deal can be explained by the fact that some stated they had received most of their early education in Bangladesh and consequently began late in the English education system. An 18-year-old Bangladeshi man wrote down on his survey return, 'I didn't attend nursery because I came late into this country', noting down further that he did not enjoy his junior school, 'because I couldn't speak English'. Forty per cent of the total Bangladeshi sample [6/15] in the college student survey was Bangladeshi-born. When asked about satisfaction with infant and junior schooling, relatively consistent patterns emerged. In relation to the infant years (3–5), 76 per cent [76/100] of students agreed that it was either, 'very enjoyable' or 'good'. In relation to junior schooling (6–11), 73 per cent [77/106] of students agreed that it was either, 'very enjoyable' or 'good'. Not a single college student expressed an explicit aversion towards their infant or junior years (aged 3–11), and only a small number [4/106] stated that they had not considered it in anything less than a favourable light. The findings from further education college students' survey cohere with those from the interviews with school pupils, who generally considered their early schooling positively. A written statement by a 17-year-old Hindu woman from James Watt College is typical of this sentiment, 'I really enjoyed J and I school where my environment was very multi-cultural and happy'.

South Asian pupils from both selective and comprehensive schools felt pleased with their primary schooling. For the further education college students, responses were similar. It was found from the survey, however, that many of the Bangladeshis were not British-born and because of later entry into the English schooling system they were at an acute disadvantage. There is a clear Bangladeshi difference in relation to the other South Asians in this regard. These findings confirm the general understanding of the 'delayed start' faced by certain ethnic minority and South Asians in the primary education system. As a result of later immigration, settlement and the development of ethnic communities, certain South Asian Muslims are particularly disadvantaged. Once in the education system, they not only improve but even exceed their expected performances. They are generally satisfied with their experiences of primary schooling.

Certain middle-class South Asian pupils had the experience of education in preparatory schools before entering their selective secondary schools. These schools are privately funded institutions that routinely send children to selective secondary schools. It is the experience of this transitional process to which attention is now drawn.

Routes to selective school entry

It is important to explore the ways in which pupils are 'prepared' for selective school entry and how it differs from the experiences of pupils from comprehensive schools. Questions are raised about the processes of gaining entry into selective schools by means of supplementary tutoring and with the general support of their specific primary and preparatory schools. Responses are presented in terms of the issues involved in the change from primary schooling to selective schooling taking into consideration ethnicity, gender and social class.

School pupils

In terms of ethnicity and gender, of the 30 young South Asian women in the selective schools in this study (six Pakistanis, 14 Indians, seven East African Asians and three Bangladeshis), only 12 were Muslim. Not a single young Bangladeshi man was in the sample of 12 from Psi Grove School and only one young Bangladeshi woman entered Rosebud School after passing the 11+ (selective school) examination. The two other Bangladeshi girls at Rosebud School entered the sixth-form to take their 'A' Levels (16–18). Altogether, 16 of the 42 in the selective were Muslim. The remainder were Sikh, Hindu or Muslim Indians and East African Gujarati-speaking Hindus or Muslims.

Only a handful of the pupils in the selective schools stated they received little or no preparation for the 11+ examination [6/42]. The vast majority reported they had spent a considerable time in training before the tests [30/42], anything from 'four years' at one extreme end of the spectrum to 'two months' at the other. The use of tutors employed outside of school time was widely stated although the extent of the tuition varied between pupils. It would seem that some tutors were adding to the final stages of preparation with parents taking a considerable lead in this respect. Furthermore, the facility of certain preparatory schools to help train pupils acted more as part of their general organisational structure. An 18-year-old Sikh young man at Psi Grove School stated he received 'outside help' two months before he took the 11+ examination, and had been confident of his success. His professionally employed father had tutored him for two years. Another 16-year-old man, a Hindu, at Psi Grove School added, 'I wanted to pass it obviously. I'd been working so hard so I thought that I might as well go for it'. Both these respondents felt able to take the tests and maintained the desire to pass them. Respondents from the girls selective schools also indicated that a certain element of preparation had been the experience. A 17-year-old Sikh young woman at Rosebud School said that during her time at preparatory school,

> Everybody did the 11+...I had some extra tuition from one of my teachers at school – we went to her house after school every hour. This was for a term really...Four came here a couple went to ['Omega High' Boys and Girls] and I think four or five boys passed.

She added that her parents also helped in a number of different ways. They were able to provide her with the 'resources' she needed in order to generate maximum potential educational opportunity. She said,

> My parents got me these 11+ books. I liked working at that point, I don't know why. Because a lot of the stuff we did at school was quite 11+ orientated, like doing similes and all this in English – I mean it wasn't totally different to what we had been doing in classes – it was just like extra work.

Similarly, a 17-year-old East African Muslim young woman at Rosebud School affirmed how she was coached for entry into selective school.

She stated she had a tutor to assist her training for the 11+. The period of tuition lasted, 'I think it was about three or four months' before the examination, she said. For selective school pupils, the use of tutors was widespread.

In contrast, the pupils from the comprehensive schools expressed a lack of interest shown in selective education *per se*. To be generally apathetic and misinformed was the overall tendency. Selective schools were considered to exist for a certain social class of people and, for these working-class South Asians, such an education was considered unattainable. Most of the selective school pupils had tutors to help ensure entry – even those who might be characterised as 'upper' working class. Not possessing the class consciousness or being able to take advantage of the social and cultural capital of other South Asians suggested a clear division taking place. A 16-year-old Pakistani young woman at Longlake School said, 'I didn't want to go to grammar school. I don't like going to far places and grammar schools are usually very far'. There is visualisation of selective school education in the form of distance away from their point of origin and zone of interest. A 16-year-old Sikh young woman at Longlake School stated that she took the 11+ examination while attending an inner-city primary school, 'I went through books and things but I didn't have a tutor...my dad got like books on English and Maths and Science specifically for the 11+ and I just worked on them'. Although she took great pains to prepare her efforts were to no avail in such a hotly contested market place. For many South Asian pupils from comprehensive schools a certain degree of apprehension was felt towards selective schools. For this respondent the choice of Longlake School was definitive. Asked about her feelings towards grammar schools, she added, 'I knew what it was but I didn't really want to go to grammar school... I just didn't want to go'.

Remaining in close proximity to same-ethnicity friends and relations is an important factor in the decision not to opt for selective school entry. A 17-year-old Pakistani (*Shia*) young woman from New Heath School felt that her preparation for selective school was not an automatic response to potential opportunities. Her view was that she needed to remain in a mixed-sex educational environment as the world of work contains all sexes. Although she recognised that a girl's school would probably help her to obtain higher grades she also recognised certain important socialisation experiences that may benefit her later on in life might be lost. She argued, 'my dad was considering it but I considered going to a girl's school (selective) [and] I was totally against it. Because, I think ahead, there are not many universities when you get a chance for single-sex education...so when I work with males it would be much harder. So I thought I would learn at an early age'. Her argument is a simple, well-made and liberal one which considers the need for women to experience socialisation with men in order to successfully compete with them in the market place. In many other cases, pupils stated they were aware of selective schools but did not wish to attend because they preferred to go to schools with their friends and that these *other* schools were too far away or physically beyond their reach. A small number of the overseas-born young Bangladeshi men and one young woman said that they were not aware of independent or grammar schools at all and, as such, had not prepared for entry.

It can be seen therefore the extent to which different South Asian pupils enter different types of schools and the processes that lead to them. The strength of selective schools, their reputation, ethos and standing were essential in how middle-class South Asian children were 'prepared' for selective school entry. With the use of private tutors, middle-class South Asians were able to attain a high degree of access. Middle-class positions in life and the professional employment of parents ensure that not only a high value was being placed towards education but that parents were prepared to go to most lengths necessary. It is *not* true that all of the pupils in the comprehensive schools did *not* possess a class interest in selective schools or made some preparation for them in some way or another. What they did not necessarily possess is the same level of cultural and social capital compared with their middle-class peers. Furthermore, their class interests were defined by their social interaction with others like them in their own communities. Being able to 'speak the same language' was a factor in keeping ethnic minority groups together.

College students

College students were also asked whether they were coached for selective school entry, or were involved in the 11+ examination process in any way. It was interesting to note the high proportions of both Indian and Pakistani respondents who had sought selective school entry. Indians were far more likely to have taken the tests and Bangladeshis the least. The Bangladeshis were also most likely to have 'wished they had done this' [6/13]. By religious classification, given the sample was small, Hindus were more likely to have opted for independent schooling with Muslims (Bangladeshis and Pakistanis) more likely to indicate that they 'wished they had done this'. Those that had taken the 11+ examination and had not succeeded [42/109] were asked to elaborate upon how their parents had been involved. Eighty-one per cent [34/42] said their parents were either 'highly motivated' or 'enthusiastic'. However, 40 per cent of the Pakistanis said they were 'not assisted at all' [8/20], whereas half of the Indians in the sample had a sibling or a relative to help them [9/18].

South Asian parents

South Asian parents were questioned about their roles in determining the nature of their children's secondary school entry. Closely involved middle-class parents were unambiguous about their motivations towards selective schooling. Middle-class South Asian parents in *petty bourgeoisie* and professional employment positions were better able to condition their children for selective school entry. Hindu, Sikh and Muslim Indians and East African Muslims dominated the more advantaged positions in this educational transition.

A middle-class East African Bohra[2] (Shia Muslim) father [8][3], who had sent his two sons to a preparatory school reflected on the considerations he was making when determining selective secondary education for them. One school was highest on his list as it is arguably the strongest boy's selective and fee-paying school in the city [Omega High for Boys]. He said that he 'knew of the school...and the school was not far away. We did think that perhaps our children would be better off because the staff–pupil ratio would be more helpful'. Asking the father whether he had made any extra effort in preparing his children, he said,

> I mean we did have one or two schools in mind that we would like them to go...and the tests for those schools. The tests were rather old fashioned...and we prepared them.

Both sons successfully passed the common grammar school entrance *and* independent school examinations. The father said he chose to send his sons to the fee-paying selective school when there was the option to send them to a state-funded grammar school. They did so because of its strong reputation and record of achievement. The father added that paying the fees for his two sons was 'sometimes a little difficult', but he also stated that the facilities were outstanding and music and sporting opportunities were impressive.

Other reasons for deciding on selective schooling at the age of 11 included the belief that state schools were unable to provide an education sufficient to their children's academic development. Parents stressed the importance of 'standards'. They considered that the class interests of the social group entering 'sub-standard' schools did not meet with their individual expectations. To legitimate their class attitudes towards schooling, the idea of standards is raised to suggest a genuine platform for their perspective. Ultimately, the parents wish to secure high social class positions for their children, as they have done for themselves and they regard it important that the 'best' is achieved every time. A comment made by a professional Hindu mother [21], with two daughters at Omega High School, was characteristic of this sentiment, 'there is no standard in the comprehensive school...children won't get anything at the end'.

A successful self-employed Bangladeshi father [4] living in an outer-area of Birmingham did not consider independent schooling for his three 'mixed-race' children. This father, like some other middle-class parents, was instead keen to make certain grammar school entry, and used the services of tutors to reinforce his children's chances (who were, at the time of the study at Psi Grove and Rosebud Schools, one of which was interviewed for this study). This respondent was adamant that he would only exploit state-funded selective education and would not have to consider having to pay for his children's education beyond his taxes. He stated,

> I'm a bit funny in that respect. I sort of see myself...that...why should one pay for these things. We pay enough taxes and all these things and I just didn't believe in it. I just thought we fight until we get our place. But because the children got in [Rosebud and Psi Grove], I just didn't come across it [having to pay for selective education]... But I don't think that I would have sent them to private. It has its own ethos and its own politics. Somehow, I just don't subscribe to that.

On the need for tutors, he further clarified,

> They started very early. They started about nine. I would say about half an hour a week, that's how they started. Generally, as time progressed, it sort of increased in quantity and amount of practice. Tutor came about a year before, once a week. The whole thing was so hush hush because Birmingham City Council's policy was that 'No Tutoring!' But it happens, they will not sort of confirm or encourage it, they prefer to sweep it under the carpet rather than confront the problem. So as a result, all the headmasters were instructed 'No Tutoring!'... and to discourage telling parents what books to buy...

> You either have parents who know how the system is working. And there are a group of parents, they don't know until their child sort of

just about gets ready for 11+ exams, then they realise they should have done this and they should have bought that sort of book. It's too late then you see. It's a total fog, so mystified, the whole system – the veil of secrecy is absolutely incredible ... The alternative was to find a good comprehensive school. If we hadn't managed to secure one then obviously selling the house and moving to another place where they have a good comprehensive school. Yes! Education, you know, is top priority.

This father expresses clearly the issues that exist for parents and their children in the race to determine places in selective secondary schools. He also describes the differences between those who are likely to succeed and those who apparently lack the prudence to think ahead.

For parents originating from working-class backgrounds, experiences were different in a range of ways. Restricted class interest and existing lower social class levels were the main barriers in parents not considering selective education. An unemployed Pakistani father [17] of four (three sons and one daughter) talked of his eldest son's experiences at a Roman Catholic nursery when seeking his transfer to the infant school. He was informed that 'there was no place for his Muslim child'. The school was reputed to have told him, 'we give priority to Roman Catholic pupils'. He believed the education provided at the school was of a high quality status and this attracted other South Asian parents. He talked of the experiences of his South Asian Muslim friends who had received similar notices telling them their children were no longer wanted as priority was given to Roman Catholic children. His justification for wishing to keep his children in the school rested on the idea that it was a good school because of the largely white make-up of its intake. The extension that 'failing' inner-city schools are a function of the 'failing' schoolchildren who attend them is the internalisation of the belief that it is the ethnic minorities dominating such schools who constitute the 'problem' and not the system itself. He stated, 'where there are more white children and less Asian children ... education there is going to be better' (*translated from Punjabi*). This Pakistani father is illustrative of many who possessed this class-consciousness. He continued,

I think that for most of our people; where there are less of our children and more of white children {obviously} the education standard there will be better. Where there are many of our children there is going to be a problem of language {Right!}. They try to speak in their own language, whether they speak Punjabi, Urdu, Gujarati, Bangla; our own people when they get together speak their own languages and some come home swearing.

Translated from Punjabi { } indicates original use of English

In other cases, South Asian parents whose children had been to their local primary schools were generally content to send them to their local comprehensive schools. A part-time employed 'mixed-race' Pakistani mother [23] of three, said in relation to primary schooling, 'I was thinking of like the nearest to home...and that...but they did swap around a few times because I wasn't happy...' The reasons for the changes, it appears, were because other pupils had been calling her children 'racist names'. Her moving them around was to find a school that provided improved 'standards' but also accepted her 'mixed-race' children. This mother alludes to a certain class-consciousness but is limited by direct racism and socio-economic disadvantage. Eventually her children settled at a local primary school, invariably with a higher concentration of ethnic minority pupils than she might have ordinarily wished. She added on the current school, 'I'm not really happy with the schooling around here at all actually – for infants...but Thorpe Park [primary school] was the best one I could think of...like locally...I wasn't too keen on it at first, cos' then they came home with a lot of swearing'. It was asked of her views towards selective schooling and what if any role she played or might have wished to play,

> I would have liked them to do the 11+ and go grammar and all that. I couldn't see it happening financially. I wouldn't have been able to do it...with grammar school you need a lot of back-up I suppose, like they do extra tuition and all that lot, and there's not one close by, and there's travelling but it would have been nice...cos' children wanted to do it...I think.

An unemployed Pakistani father [14] of five with two sons at New Heath School adds a comparable observation. Grammar school entry was seen to exist for the privileged few and he argued that under-privileged people like him would not fare positively in the market for places. He said,

> Not every child can go to a grammar school. This is a concern for all parents. For that you need to have tutors visit your home. I am uneducated myself. I have no money to pay for tutors because I am

unemployed. Those that enter grammar school are children with parents who are educated, who can support, who can provide tuition themselves; some are doctors, some are engineers, some are managers, some are whatever. It is the children of these parents that get tuition in the home and it is they who go to grammar school. {Third class} people like us, we are happy if our children make it to college. At the age of sixteen, either it is children that want to leave school or it is parents that remove them. The future of our children is quite bad, many are in gangs, they wander the streets, they smoke cigarettes, they do this, they do that...and if you cannot look after your children closely, there are so many traps that they can fall in.

Translated from Urdu { } indicates original use of English

Views towards and experiences of selective schooling by working class, 'under-employed' and unemployed South Asian parents were largely conditioned on their social class positions and overall perspectives based on their individual experiences in the social world. Some poorer South Asian parents alluded to selective education but it appeared to them as 'worlds apart', and it is unequivocal some of these norms and values were likely to be transposed onto their children.

Teachers

Teachers were asked to provide their views on the processes leading to selective education for some South Asians. Passing the 11+ examination was a highly sought after commodity and it was argued South Asian parents often go to great lengths to try and ensure success. A senior Indian Psi Grove Schoolteacher [14][4] described it thus,

I come in for the 11+ tests and there is a very large number and there are a lot of Asian kids. You probably need to speak to senior management...but I think it's probably...it wouldn't surprise me if its something close to 40–50 per cent, so it's a very large number but I think a lot of times the Asian parents put their children in without really realising that their kids can't cope, they just think lets go for it and the preparation is an aspect, more and more people are beginning to use private tutors outside.

Reinforcing the point made above, a teacher [3] from an inner-city comprehensive school believed South Asian parents made every effort to get their children into selective schools but were often unsuccessful because of lack of preparation,

> That's right … the whole idea of the various activities, the tests that they have to do, the prep schools are from a very early age training their pupils to do this 11+ but if you go to ABC [inner city] primary school none of the children there would have ever seen a past paper or previous verbal reasoning test and if a child in ABC gets entered to the exam because the parents want it, they're gonna sit there and think, 'Ah, what's this?' Whereas someone who's been practising for five years already knows what's gonna be expected.

Teachers were confident that parents were not only overeager for their children to enter into selective education but that they did not always possess the means – economic, cultural or social capital – to do so.

Discussion

Selective schools have never been more important in the demarcation of class than today (Adonis and Pollard, 1997). Middle-class South Asian parents are aware that their children will perform better in the selective education system which can lead to elite university entry and professional careers (Power, 2000). Competition for places is intense particularly at times when the future of grammar schools is uncertain (Crook *et al.*, 1999). Selective schooling provides South Asians with accelerated upward mobility, given also that the economic and social divisions between rich and poor, or rather between white and ethnic groups, are wider than ever. Of the one thousand that were in existence in 1965, the 164 grammar schools that remain today contain about four per cent of the secondary school-age population. Approximately eight per cent of all secondary school-age children are in selective schools (fee-paying and selective), although it is clear that there are regional concentrations of both the schools and the middle-class pupils that enter them (Edwards and Tomlinson, 2002).

It is apparent that parents value the education their children receive in selective schools. Even though government statements might suggest otherwise a closer examination of 14–16 performance data indicates that pupils perform stronger in grammar schools compared with comprehensive schools (Prais, 2001). Parents have always been aware of this and it is no surprise that aspirant middle-class South Asian professional parents wish selective education for their children. The findings in this reflect other similar studies which explore parents' knowledge of their children's education. South Asian parents were found to be differentially knowledgeable (cf. Thomas, Vass and McClelland, 1997) and equipped to access selective schooling, in all of its various forms, for their children (cf. Ball and Vincent, 1998). Parents from working-class backgrounds were far more reticent about their children entering grammar or fee-paying schools. It materialised that parents from lower social class backgrounds had the inclination to proceed with selective schooling but did not always possess the social and economic capital required (cf. Reay and Ball, 1997; 1998). It is unambiguous that the way in which South Asian parents are able to put their children through selective schooling is by possessing the capital, insight and the resources acquired through their occupational, residential and social class positions.

In general, pupils that managed to enter independent schools largely came from higher social class families, although this was not the case for all grammar school pupils. Some affluent and higher educated South Asian parents are able to achieve their aspirations for their children's education by sending them to selective schools, whether as an extension of the family's status and its aspirations or through the utilisation of the appropriate efforts in correctly preparing their children. A crucial factor is the role of parents in preparing their children for entry into selective schools. The experience is also reinforced by the school pupil interviews, many of which highlighted certain instances of direct positive parental involvement in ensuring entry into the selective education system at an early age. Furthermore, some aspiring middle social class parents, irrespective of South Asian ethnicity, felt ordinary comprehensive school education would neither be suited for their children or possessed the 'standards'. Aspirant parents originating from poorer economic and social backgrounds felt the most favourable type of schooling for their children would be found in schools with mainly white children. Other poorer South Asian parents felt obliged to send their children to local schools. They also felt, however, they had no real choice in the matter as they believed certain types of *other* schools were reserved for the privileged few from higher social class backgrounds. Neither did parents seemingly possess the economic resources to put their children through the selective education system even though they may well have had the intention. Attitudes of exceptionally poor South Asian parents were mixed, from the notion that ethnic minority children constituted the problem in schools to complete disenfranchisement with the education system and the social world in which they exist.

It is important to look now at the issue of subject selection in detail, exploring the impact of gender, ethnicity and social class.

5
Subject Selection: Critical Perspectives

Setting approximates to the ways in which apparently brighter pupils are placed in different subject sets to others – both in different year forms and subject classes. It has implications for the ways in which pupils are allocated subject choices and the eventual tier of the GCSEs they eventually sit. Certain subject selections have implications for the type of further and higher education courses that are ultimately taken and the type of employment and sector they eventually enter.

In an early study on the effects of setting in schools, Troyna (1978) found ethnic minorities were likely to develop educational aspirations in direct congruence to their set positions. African-Caribbeans in the higher sets formed an identity that helped to shape their eventual high-status educational and occupational positions, shedding a 'colour' identity and expressing behaviours and norms reflecting their peers in the same higher sets. Conversely, African-Caribbeans located in the lower sets formed relationships with other African-Caribbeans that were also concentrated in the lower streams. The interests of these African-Caribbeans subsequently emerged antithetical to the interests of those in the higher groups. Individuals located in the lower sets were more likely to form different social and cultural friendship-networks with those in the higher sets as well as acting in direct opposition to them (see also Hargreaves, 1967; Willis, 1977; Ball, 1981; Weis, 1985; Abraham, 1989).

In recent studies on the selection of GCSE subjects at 13, science subject choices made by young South Asian men were thought to be unexpected given the limited exposure they may have had of 'science knowledge' compared with their white peers. The overall considerations in research on the desire of South Asians to attain 'high science' educational goals and their good performance in science suggest they are based on a positive orientation towards education in general. It has been found that young ethnic minority women select subjects at 14 and 16 based largely on cultural factors, with parents expressing certain educational aspirations but at the same time permitting daughters the freedom to decide (Kelly, 1988). Other research on 13+ subject selection by ethnic minorities has shown that different groups have different perspectives based on their importance for future careers (Woodrow, 1996). It seems that ethnic minorities are potentially taking subjects inconsistent with their social class and experience of certain subjects to some extent (although in these subjects they performed comparably in the end). What remains apparent is the long-term vision of eventual employment in professional or technical fields.

It is important, therefore, to explore the way in which South Asian school pupils select their GCSE subjects at 13. Specific issues relate to questions arising out of setting, subject selection at 13, the role of parents and teacher perceptions of South Asian parents and their children during this process. It is an attempt to discover whether initial setting has the potential to influence eventual educational outcome.

Setting and GCSE subject choice

School pupils

For most of the South Asian pupils in selective schools they were not immediately separated into perceived potential ability groups. In year nine, different Mathematics and English ability groups surfaced formally in many of the selective schools in the study. Selective school pupils were asked about the factors that motivated them to take the portfolio of GCSE subjects they eventually did. For this 17-year-old Hindu young man at Psi Grove School, his choices were determined by how useful and appropriate the subjects were for his further and higher education plans. He said, 'first, friends were out of the question...I knew that what I am going to do is going to be different from everyone else. At the end of the day, I wanted to do what I enjoyed first'.

In other instances, it appeared that there existed little formal choice beyond a tightly bounded set of subjects deemed suitable by the national curriculum and the overall academic strength and direction of the schools. A 17-year-old Sikh young man from Psi Grove School iterated, 'most of the subjects I wanted to take were already compulsory... sciences and maths. I took two languages because I enjoyed them'. A similar response was provided by an 18-year-old East African Muslim woman at Rosebud School. She stated that there was little explicit choice as the structure of the school timetable and the available curriculum was strictly specified. She said, 'there wasn't any pressure from my parents. It was what I wanted to do. There wasn't all that much of a choice. It was either Geography or History. There wasn't an influence from anyone really'. Likewise, an 18-year-old Sikh young woman at Rosebud School indicated that many of the choices were predetermined by an inclination towards the science subjects. She said,

> The only choice I think you really got was whether you did French or German ... or whether you did history or geography ... or double award sciences. I wasn't really bothered ... but I have always been orientated scientifically so straight away I decided I wanted to do a double award.

A 17-year-old East African Muslim young woman at Rosebud School commented on what motivated her selection of GCSE subjects. The statement below is representative of many South Asian Muslims from selective schools. In this case, there was also a wish to study Islamic Studies at GCSE level. The latter was influenced by forces outside of Rosebud School. She expressed,

> I did separate sciences, French, history, geography and classics. Yeah, my parents wanted me to do the sciences because my dad is a pharmacist and my mom is a radiographer. And so, they wanted me to try something in the sciences, you know medicine. So they say, 'you do the sciences'. But I was going to do it anyway and ... Yeah ... I want a career in medicine so ...

> Every teacher wanted me to do their subjects ... well most of them ... and so it was difficult to choose. Because I thought that some of the teachers would say that, 'no don't do this', because you won't be able to cope with it or something. But they've all said you'll be able to do it ... able to do it fine ... which sort of made it more complicated, if you see what I mean.

> I am also doing Islamic studies out of school and I might do Arabic as well. I'm doing the coursework. I don't know whether I'll take the GCSE. I sort of go to the Sunday school thing. It's not much. One lesson a week, couple of hours a week. We all do the work in the class so it's okay.

A 16-year-old East African Muslim young woman at Rosebud School, affirming the general consensus on the selection of her GCSE subjects, said 'there wasn't any pressure from my parents . . . it was what I wanted to do and . . . there wasn't all that much of a choice. It was either geography or history . . . so I chose history . . . and things like music, business information systems, things like that. But, my friends did mainly things that I did, there wasn't an influence from anyone really . . . I chose general studies as an extra. I would have preferred to do geography and history but that wasn't an option'.

The three comprehensive schools in the study, St Aiden's, New Heath and Longlake Schools adopted an *apparent* setting-free policy for the first two years of secondary schooling. Although schools stated that no setting policy was in place it was clear 'informal setting' was prevalent. Distinct differences emerged in mathematics and English. In terms of GCSE selection, comprehensive school pupils tended to concentrate just as much on science subjects but were also driven by more vocational subjects rather than the traditional academic science subjects preferred and chosen by their selective school peers. For example, subjects such as art and design were likely to be taken by young South Asian women and business studies and information technology by young South Asian men.

General National Vocational Qualification (GNVQ) subjects, at various levels, were likely to be taken in conjunction with other GCSE and 'A' Level subjects in all the comprehensive schools in the study. Some pupils were found to be sitting additional GCSEs in Islamic studies or a South Asian language (Gujarati, Urdu or Bengali in the main) inside or outside of the schools. Pupils who did not take additional modern language or religious studies subjects were at least familiar with the possibilities of taking them. Pupils who had started in the higher sets tended to remain in them throughout their schooling, ultimately achieving very well. Some of the young South Asian men and women from the grammar schools felt they were able to move up after extra effort believing they had at first been placed in sets lower than they believed they ought to have been.

There were distinct differences between the opportunities the different types of schools present. Pupils in the selective schools normally sat a minimum of 10 GCSEs with greater depth in the sciences but pupils in the comprehensive schools invariably chose up to eight subjects with vocational courses supplementing GCSE subjects.

College students

Further education college students were asked questions in relation to their experiences of setting. Almost half of all respondents [54/109] recognised their setting had taken place in secondary school. In terms of how their parents felt towards their setting just under half stated their parents were 'happy with it' [26/54]. The South Asian group with parents least satisfied with setting were the Bangladeshis (although cell sizes are small). The majority of Pakistanis and Indians said their parents were satisfied.

Students provided fervent written responses to the question of setting in secondary schools. A 19-year-old Pakistani student from Cherrywood College emphasised his feelings on the system of setting and related it to the way in which it can sometimes impinge on further academic development. He wrote in some detail,

> I don't think pupils should be placed in sets or bands at secondary schools because I found that many of my friends who were placed in the lower bands, lacked motivation and the highest possible grade that they could achieve was a D due to them being entered for the foundation paper. This did not give them a chance to get a grade C or above (some were capable of getting a C at least). I also think the Double Science Award should be changed (scraped) by the exam boards to Single Award, because the content of Chemistry, Biology and Physics is very limiting and basic, especially Chemistry. In Double Award the concept of the mole is not covered at all making it harder for students who study chemistry at 'A' Level, who haven't a clue about the mole. This makes it very difficult for them to understand the basics of chemistry. This is also true of Biology as well. Students should be well prepared for 'A' Levels, because GCSE to 'A' Level is a very big jump, if not the right material has been studied at GCSE, the first year of 'A' Levels can be very demanding and stressful.

> Also greater amount of time should be spent on maths, because the per cent of retakes at colleges is extremely high. Teachers should make sure 95 per cent of the pupils obtain their GCSE Maths at school.

> I think relevant and useful work should be studied at GCSE as I personally have experienced problems with aspects of my 'A' Levels, especially by Science Subjects.

> I think colleges should take people who have achieved excellent GCSE grades ... They should have strict entry requirements, e.g., maths must be passed before they start 'A' Level courses. Colleges should stop thinking about the money they receive for each student they let on the course and should put money to use by getting more

things (e.g., learning resources centres). They should also concentrate on getting the highest possible grades for each student in the college and getting the pass rate above 95 per cent.

Further education college students were asked which of the reasons presented to them in the attitudinal statements described best their motivations in selecting certain GCSE subjects at the age of 13 or 14. Seventy-five per cent [69/106] of students took subjects on the basis of 'those subjects that they were good at' or their 'favourite subjects'. Seventeen per cent [18/106] said they had 'long term career goals'. Only seven per cent [7/106] said either 'friends' choices' or 'favourite teachers' influenced them. Two Pakistanis stated that it was 'parental pressure'. College students were asked whether they had to 'keep their parents happy with the choices made'. Sixty-three per cent [63/100] of the respondents stated 'yes'. Subjects were chosen based on those 'most liked' and those they felt they were 'best at'. Pakistanis were more likely to say that they had 'to keep parents happy'. Most respondents agreed the advice that they received from their teachers was not indifferent to that received by other white pupils. Given the opportunity, Indians were least likely and Muslims (Pakistanis and Bangladeshis) most likely to take additional GCSE subjects. A number of further education college students claimed that they did not realise they had been set at all. Most of those who believed they had been set stated parents were aware of the situation and were generally content. It is important to take into consideration, nevertheless, that effectively all of the students in the survey comprised of former comprehensive school pupils (89 per cent). Those in the lower set placements were more likely to be young Bangladeshi and Pakistani men and it was this South Asian Muslim group who were also more likely to express some concern with teacher expectations.

In the processes leading to subject selections, a part of the analysis here is the extent to which choice is seen to exist at all. The type of secondary school affected how subject choices were structured. Core curriculum subjects were a given, and less prescriptive choice was limited because of timetable and teacher resources. This applied to both selective and comprehensive schools.

South Asian parents

It was stated by parents from middle-class backgrounds that the strong points of selective schools had the greatest power in influencing the educational paths to be taken by their children. Educational achievements were well proven and parents had a predisposition generally not to question decisions made by them in these schools. A professional Muslim father [8], with two sons at 'Omega High for Boys', spoke of the importance he gave to the general strength of the school and its potential influences upon his children's education in his decision to send them there. He said,

> To be honest, we thought they were taught what they were taught. They had found out what they were interested in and they chose their subjects: the both of them. Although the second one tried to advise my younger one that some subjects would be more difficult but he chose the ones he wanted. We left it because we thought if we do interfere and they were not happy it would be two factors. At least it was their choice and then they didn't feel that we had pressurised them or anything.

There is a general tendency by middle-class South Asian parents to regard the effectiveness of selective schools as fundamentally important in their aspirations to put their children through them. Parents were of the view that in the final analysis investment in selective education would pay ripe dividends.

A professional Hindu father [21] was able to send his only son to an independent school from the age of eight to 18. He added that ensuring his son obtained the most from education meant having to 'make sacrifices'. The consequences of not succeeding were presented to his son as resulting in potentially lower sector employment status. A clear description is being made on the part of this father to present education to his son as an advantage in class terms, when reflecting on a conversation he had with his son, who at the time was a young boy,

> I would leave home at about a quarter to eight in the morning – he wouldn't get home until six half-six at night – because I would pick him up and drop him off – and he would say to me, Dad, 'you know, I'm working all these hours, and all the kids in the street, they're playing out', etc. And I said well that's fine but what you have to think about is that in the future, if you make the best of what you have in terms of opportunities, then these kids are the ones who are going to be manual labourers or have mediocre jobs. What you could do is go to the top and he seemed to accept that; it wasn't a forced issue it was an explanation! For every decision to make there is always a negative side to it – that was the negative side for him.

A discussion about the nature of his son's fee-paying selective schooling developed more openly. He was asked how the intellectual expectations generated by the school affected family life within the home and what roles and responsibilities were required in order to meet the demands placed on them, economically, culturally and socially, in the process of successfully developing his son's education. He elaborated that in,

> In the year that he took his GCSEs, he came number eight in the country. What I will say is that, it is not sufficient to put a child in a private school. That will not help them as much. You need to create the right environment at home. It has got to encourage – and discipline if necessary. You have to take an interest in what they are doing, you yourself have to be able to answer some of the questions that they are going to put to you – because they learn very very fast in these private schools – and somehow we managed to get the right balance at home so that he had the best opportunities to make the most of what he had.

The idea of parents 'managing' their children's education was emphasised further by a middle-class Bangladeshi father [4] whose children were at Rosebud and Psi Grove Schools. He indicated how easy it was for parents to relive their own high educational aspirations through their children which would not necessarily be the right attitude to take. He said, 'I don't want to relive my ambitions through them. I don't want to go into that trap. I give total freedom to my children'. One of the reasons for these attitudes among middle-class and upwardly mobile working-class South Asian parents is said to be a result of the experiences of the British in India. He added that notable figures in the history of India, who were influential in changing the political map of the world, had all been educated in elite English schools and universities, 'Gandhi was a barrister, Nehru was a barrister...' and these were all positive influences on the South Asian psyche in relation to education.

In contrast to the middle-class South Asian parents, on the whole parents from working-class backgrounds expressed a level of involvement distinct in its orientation towards 13+ subject choices. Parents were likely to take a far tighter hold on both subject choice and general academic direction. An elderly unemployed Bangladeshi father [7], with children in comprehensive schools said, 'well, before they chose, we discussed the thing and then we decided which they should take and which subjects they should not take. We went through a discussion'.

One parent felt he had to be more direct with the selection. An unemployed Pakistani father [14] of four told of his influences upon his eldest son,

> I told him, especially the big one, to pick those subjects that are {the main...because you are going into medicine...} this was my wish. But then I saw that he didn't want to know. He said that, '{as a training doctor you have to work long hours and so on. And that all Asian people want their son to be doctors and nothing else}'. For this reason, I stayed quiet. I suppose this was fine. I tell the others do something with a scope that is {worldwide} in approach. We'll see what the others do.
> *Translated from Punjabi { } indicates original use of English*

Findings concerning parental influence on 13+ choices echoed those from pupils and students. Working-class South Asian parents tended to exert as great an influence as possible on subject selection whereas middle-class parents were more prepared to let their children in conjunction with schools to determine the eventual choice, although not always as the views of teachers testify.

Teachers

In the selective schools, teachers believed that parents had developed certain expectations of the education system and their children that were unrealistic. Parents, in the position of having their children in selective schooling, were thought to possess overly-ambitious aspirations that were unachievable. A senior Indian teacher [14] at Psi Grove School iterated that irrespective of the general academic orientation of the school, parents placed an overwhelming emphasis upon pursing a career in 'the professions', predominantly medicine and thus the GCSE and 'A' Level subjects required to pursue these paths. He stated,

> I think there is a lot of pressure on them [South Asian boys] from the parents themselves, the parents feel that my son is at a grammar school and because he's got into a grammar school he's got to become a doctor or something high powered like that and they've got such high expectations. Just because of that they force their kids to try above their ability really, to reach levels which obviously they can't so a lot of kids who don't do well it's because of this extra burden. If the parents were relaxed a bit and let the kids go with the flow, still encourage them – encourage them rather than pressurise them – they would actually, probably do better.

The headteacher [17] at Rosebud School emphasised the point. She felt that certain South Asian parents 'pushed' their daughters towards particular forms of higher education entry because it improved their 'marriage potential'. This headteacher believed the young South Asian women in her selective school developed particular academic goals for specific purposes – based on parents regarding the education of their daughters in selective education in terms of future 'marriage market' capital. She said of South Asian parents,

> I think there is all the while in the [South Asian] families, there is this desire to enter professions which are socially and upwardly mobile. I still think there is the marriage factor, you are more 'marriageable' if you are in a profession, you'll get a husband who is similarly placed . . . that outlook as well . . . I think that is happening. The worry I sometimes have is that girls are pushed into those subjects against their will but I would say there is almost no evidence of that happening and we try if that is true to say to the girls lets talk to the parents, lets look at alternative things. I have only come across one in the whole of this year. I think I would be aware of it either through staff telling me or girls telling me directly . . .

An understanding of how significant medicine as a profession appeared to be for young South Asian women was also reflected in a comment made by the head of sixth-form (16–18) at Rosebud School [16],

> Oh absolutely, yes they are going for what jobs are carrying the status in the community. Apart from medicine, my impression is that nothing else compares very much, but also to be a lawyer, doctor, dentist, pharmacist, perhaps. They don't always look at the arts subjects and they don't always believe there are the jobs at the end of it.

The headteacher at Omega High School [13] reaffirmed the position that certain South Asian parents placed far too great an emphasis upon medicine and it affected potential outcomes for the young South Asian women who would perhaps find more success in other fields.

> I understand there might well be a sense of social insecurity and that the medical profession is seen as a very safe option in a whole lot of ways but I find that we have got girls, South Asian girls, who shouldn't be doing science 'A' Levels, who are incredibly gifted in other ways and yet the family pressure to take sciences and then do

medicine...not even to consider a pure science research degree...is very very strong. Now I find that difficult to deal with because the parents clearly feel that the advice the school is giving is not right, they think they know better than the school, lots of parents think they know better than the teachers and that's a phenomenon that one is used to...What I've linked with that is that when these girls perhaps don't look as if they're going to get top grades that they need, I sense much more of a sense of dissatisfaction with the school than I do from white parents. So the South Asian parents will come and say well this isn't good enough, what are you going to do about it, and that's quite hard again because the answer to that is well we are doing everything we can, we're working with your daughter as hard as we can but we have kept saying we don't think she's going to get [grade] As and we can't manipulate the university system, it's as it is, and that's hard to know. I feel as if they feel that we've let them down in some way and I suppose I don't know whether all parents do see it in quite the same way.

It was agreed by many of the senior selective schoolteachers that some South Asian parents expected a great deal from the school. South Asian parents from higher social class positions whose children had gained entry into selective schooling often placed pressure on their children to perform above realistic levels and in subject areas that were not ideally suited to them. Realising the potential of high status selective schools, these parents felt their children ought to perform exceptionally but in the event potentially damaging the prospects for some or limiting the opportunities for others. The notion that South Asian parents are educationally ambitious for their children but sometimes overly was well supported by teachers. Teachers agreed South Asian parents co-operated with the schools. Interestingly, teachers did not feel parents were directly critical of them. It suggests, although parents can sometimes be disappointed with the schools their children attend, in cases of under-performance or dissatisfaction they do not view teachers with derision.

The reasons for the overall tendency on the part of South Asians to pursue higher education in the sciences and in such subjects as law were because of its significance to the 'immigrant mentality', as argued by a senior lecturer at St Margaret's College [20]. It was suggested that for ethnic minorities and South Asians it was important to raise their social, economic and cultural status in a society that exhibited racism and discrimination towards them. Education is firmly rooted in the awareness of South Asians, and through their parents, it is apparent the extent to which they regard its importance and take part in it successfully. He said,

> I think that where you've been an immigrant community you will have suffered racism, institutional or whatever as we know from the Stephen Lawrence. You will have suffered racism that racism may well have extended to job opportunities. Therefore I think it becomes very very important as an immigrant community that you do 'worthwhile' degrees and that means doing a professional degree, it means that you quite rightly but maybe overvalue degrees in medicine, dentistry, pharmacy. We know the liturgy, ophthalmics has been discovered by wider communities and so there is very clear demand in Birmingham from the ethnic minority communities for science 'A' Levels.

Teachers from the inner-city comprehensive schools were positive that South Asian parents encouraged and supported their children but they also felt that some lacked the necessary resources to meet the educational needs of their children. The point of view was endorsed by a teacher [3] from an inner-city comprehensive school,

> Some [parents] are very supportive. Some have got amazing aspirations for their children and you know that they are not going to achieve them. The child can barely read and write and the parents think that they are going to be a pilot or an astronaut or whatever. I think that a lot of parents have very high aspirations but I think that some of them have got limited recognition of their own child's ability. Parents sometimes think that it's just gonna happen, no sort of clue about what's involved...

Other teachers from the comprehensive schools reported the extent to which poorer South Asian parents were being closely dependent on the school. There was an expectation on the part of parents that the school would take all the necessary steps to ensure positive educational success without their own direct involvement. It was suggested that parents possessed a general unwillingness to engage with the school as well as they could. By doing so they did not maximise the learning resources available to their children. The deputy headteacher [11] of Longlake School said,

> There is still a general attitude amongst parents that the school takes responsibility for children and that hasn't really changed as time

progresses, there are rather more of the second generation – third-generation parents coming along who do take more ... Having been here as long as I have it's nice to see people that I taught when I first came coming back with their children, and their attitude is obviously slightly different because they have an understanding of what goes on here, they know what the expectations are in terms of parental support so for those people it continues to be a moving target. But they are a relatively small proportion of the population that we service but, by and large, its' still, 'well it's your business, you get on and do it'.

An Indian teacher [8] from an inner-city comprehensive school also re-emphasised the belief that some parents lacked the 'educational resources' to assist their children. The basic foundation could be traced back to the impoverished economic and social conditions found in the sending regions before migration to England. He said,

Now our 'Hindu group' is diminished to almost nothing, we still have a large number of Sikhs and Muslims whose parents tend to be least educated, they've come from rural backgrounds. Our Muslims are mainly sort of Mirpuris and our Sikhs sort of sons and daughters of ex-Punjabi farmers. Although they value education highly and they do want their children to aspire to educational success, I am not sure that they have the mechanism and the knowledge of how the system works for them to encourage their children and support them enough.

Teachers from the inner-city comprehensive schools were positive that working-class South Asian parents were taking an active role, certainly not inactive compared with white parents, and as active, in some senses, as middle-class South Asian parents with their children in selective schools. What is discerningly different about working-class and poorer South Asian parents is their lack of knowledge of the processes, their disengagement with the school and limited scholastic support mechanisms for their children within the home, as argued by the teachers. A combination of a lack of economic, cultural and social capital was thought to be found in these South Asian groups.

Discussion

All the pupils in selective schooling expressed that not only were parents encouraging but also keen to ensure eventual success. It was reinforced by the academic orientation of the schools. Subjects were chosen on the basis of availability, interest and class orientation. Middle-class South Asian parents were more likely to take a firmer hold on subject selection and the overall direction of academic study. Working-class South Asian parents were less able to direct necessarily, although not exclusively, but were far less likely to know of the most advantageous ways to proceed. In the former case, some South Asian parents were likely to be overly engaged and in the latter some South Asian parents were thought to be under-engaged with the school. Resources available for selective school pupils, both with the home and the school, were considerably greater than that for South Asian pupils in comprehensive schools. Here, parents possessed low educational qualifications, worked in low occupational positions and resided in inner-city housing. Parents were nevertheless highly positive about their children's schooling and remained optimistic about their chances – although they lacked the appropriate information, knowledge and 'contacts' as well as wider economic, cultural and social capital that their middle-class South Asian counterparts possessed in abundance.

The ways in which secondary school pupils and further education college students perform in their GCSE and 'A' Level subjects and what they hope to do in higher education follows.

6
Higher Education Choice: Ethnicity or Habitus

Various studies have shown that South Asians have a propensity to remain in further education at far higher rates compared with their white peers (Taylor, 1976; Gupta, 1977; Craft and Craft, 1983; Penn and Scattergood, 1992; Drew *et al.*, 1997; Lightbody *et al.*, 1997; Demack *et al.*, 2000). The view is that South Asians elect to move on to further education for the purposes of gaining further educational qualifications, attempting to overcome educational disadvantage by 'topping up' (Tanna, 1990) or wishing to remain in education because of fear of racism in the labour market and the need to be better prepared for it. Research findings continue to suggest that the 16+ choices that ethnic minority pupils make are largely a function of parents, teachers, friends and their own judgement. Certainly there is little reliance, if at all, on the guidance of official practitioners (Kidd and Wardman, 1999). Hence, it is essential to look at the research findings in this study in relation to experiences of GCSE and 'A' Level examinations taken and the processes leading to and aspirations in relation to different forms of higher education. The views of pupils, students and teachers are used to illustrate the ways in which the educational achievements of different South Asians diverge.

School pupils

Pupils from the selective schools scored highly in their GCSE examinations often leading to a desire for entry into the elite universities and/ or their colleges. Young South Asian women as well as men expressed marked aspirations to study science, with medicine, dentistry and engineering (as well as pure sciences) being popular choices. In addition, law was another popular option. Pupils from the selective schools were also inclined to be more articulate about their potential educational futures. This was observable in their general attitude and approach. It could be seen in their dress code, language, social etiquette and overall confidence levels.

All the respondents from the selective schools chose to remain in their respective sixth-forms. The high educational success rates of these schools were fundamental in retaining pupils. Various rudimentary explanations were offered for why pupils chose to stay on. Two Indian (one Sikh and one Hindu) Psi Grove schoolboys typified the responses from the selective schools, 'I have chosen to stay. It is a good school and I can relate to the teachers well' and 'it would have been a lot easier to stay here and carry on'. For South Asian pupils in selective schools remaining in the school sixth-form was almost universal. The choice of further education institution is informed by a myriad of factors. Individuals make their decisions on the basis of spatial realities, 'choice is both enabled and constrained' by the complex interplay of 'material practices (e.g., housing patterns, transport, social networks)' and the perceptions and imaginings of 'space (e.g., mental maps, the "friction of distance", familiarity and fear)' (Ball *et al.*, 1998, p. 171).

Setting aside the motivations for certain types of further education institutions and courses it is essential to elaborate upon the precise achievements that various South Asians in selective schools attain. A 17-year-old Hindu woman at Rosebud School took 11 GCSE subjects. She obtained four grade A*s and seven grade As. This person was reflective of the vast majority of all young South Asian women in the selective schools. Her achievements were determined by the strong academic orientation of the school and her desire to perform highly, supported by her family and the home. She elaborated first on the precise grades she obtained and how she felt about them in relation to others. It can be seen the extent to which exceedingly high performance is something that both pupils and the school expect. She said,

It was kind of like what I wanted. It was what I expected as well. I didn't want any Bs. It sounds really daft. It seems really odd when I went to get my results – well did I want them – do I deserve them or what?

The highest result in the year was eight A*s and two As...There were 15 of us that got all As. And then there were people that got five A*s and above. They got a prize and they got a little medallion thing...and there were seven of those...and there were many people that got one B but many more A*s than me. Out of the fifteen, two or three were Asians.

This young Indian woman was in the first year of her 'A' Levels in Chemistry, Physics and Mathematics at the time of the study. She expressed the wish to read medicine at university and explored the different options available to her in carrying out her academic pursuits.

> I want to go to Birmingham [University]. It's near and I've been there and I've looked at the course and everything...and I just think that I like it there really...I don't particularly want to move away from home very much either...Also my mom doesn't want me to be out of Birmingham, she wants me to stay here.

In making up her mind, she also considered other universities. These universities are not necessarily any stronger or weaker than her desired choice but there are important spatial issues to consider. Her wish to enter Oxbridge was tempered by her belief that it was not the class 'snobbery' that she might or might not wish to engage with but more the issue of the required grades. She said,

> Birmingham, Manchester want ABB at 'A' Level and London want AAB. Oxbridge want 3 As. I know its kind of a stereotype that they are all snobs there...but I know they're not. I don't think I am going to get in for one...because I haven't got the ability really. I learn things but sometimes I can't apply them properly or I am usually a few percentage points off a really high score...I've had that all my life and it's really annoying...but I get used to it.

Many of the other young South Asian women in the selective schools performed exceptionally well both in GCSE and 'A' Level subjects (see Appendix B). For the most part, these young women wished to maintain their current levels of success at the school. Similarly, a 16-year-old Sikh woman at Omega High School for Girls also revealed her high-status ambitions. She talked about the way in which her educational paths would be determined by how tactically she selected her 'A' Level subjects. She also faced limitations. Although in a prestigious selective school it is apparent that setting does dampen pupil's motivations, and consequently become demotivated by the fact they there are structurally limited to what they can ultimately achieve. This has ramifications for further academic development. She said,

I want to be a Pharmacist or something like that. [As to 'A' Level subjects]...It would be Chemistry, Biology and something else. Maths would be an advantage...but I can't do that because you need to get an A [at GCSE] to do the 'A' Level. And because I am doing a lower paper, I can't do that. I don't think I'll be able to get it anyway. I think that Physics would be another advantage. I really don't feel that I understand a word but in tests I get good marks so...

A 17-year-old East African Muslim woman at Rosebud School articulated her intentions for study after GCSE examinations. This individual, by having achieved a long string of A and A* grades at GCSE, realising that to read medicine at university three A grades at 'A' Level would be her least requirement, still believed that this field of study remained her most appropriate option. She was also cognisant of the potential of other medicine- or science-related subjects that were available to her at university. She exclaimed,

I don't mind staying in Birmingham...Birmingham will ask for 3 As. If you resit everybody wants As then. You can get into other universities but I'll have to get As and Bs to even think about doing... optometry...or pharmacy then.

Her aspirations to study medicine originated from a reading of the improbabilities of success in other employment sectors. It can be seen the extent to which both South Asian parents and teachers in schools shape these perceptions and, in effect, what pupils might regard as their most or least favoured educational options are actually framed by others. She added,

I wanted to go into journalism but it's too competitive and there's not a guaranteed job whereas sciences are fine. You are more likely to get a job, I think, it's a wider field you can do a lot more with it.

A feature that has been revisited on a number of occasions in the research findings from the selective schools is the demand to study medicine at university, primarily among the young South Asian women compared with men. It is discussed why this aspiration was so prevalent from the point of view of an 18-year-old Sikh woman at Rosebud School,

It's 'cause of the parents, they want the best for their children. I wanted to apply for medicine since the age of ten. I think that Asian parents are more determined to get their children somewhere then white people are and some black people. I mean that some black people are but I mean white people just tend to let their children do whatever they want. Whereas I think the Asian parents encourage or pressure their children more than others. I mean there are five or six new girls [South Asian] that come [into the sixth-form]. Four of them are doing the sciences, and all four of those want to do either medicine or dentistry.

A number of the young South Asian women from the selective schools said that attending Aston and Birmingham universities were high-ranking choices for them. The wish to live at home while studying at university was a feature of many young South Asian women and some of the men too. Nevertheless, both young South Asian men and women in selective schools chose high-ranking universities and subject courses as the norm. These decisions were a reflection of the high performance they achieved in their GCSE subjects and their desire to enter the stronger universities through the advice, information, encouragement and direction of the schools, teachers and parents.

Pupils from the comprehensive schools exhibited certain similarities towards staying in their schools for further study. Many of the pupils move to their school's sixth-forms to study their 'A' Level and GNVQ subjects, although it was less likely among the South Asian women compared with men – a function of gender, religion and space. There were a number of examples where the young Bangladeshi and Pakistani women were less convinced of the advantages of travelling away for further or even higher education. A 17-year-old Pakistani woman at New Heath School is typical in this regard. She said,

> You can get good grades wherever you go, it just depends on whether you wanna work or not. You can go to a really good sixth-form and really fail everything or you can go to like a really bad one and pass them.

Nonetheless, a 17-year-old Pakistani woman at New Heath School [wearing *Hijab*] expressed the wish to remain at the school sixth-form simply because of practical reasons. It seems that some of the South Asian Muslim parents were taking a more active role in this respect and considered remaining close to home advantageous because of the relative strength of the school, the limited travelling time and the comparative security of remaining within the socio-cultural realms of the inner-city areas in which the educational institution is located and where they live. She said,

> I rebelled so much against my parents...that I wanted to go to college...that I wanted to...you know...become independent and learn stuff. So here, I know the teachers...smaller classes...closer to home...you don't have to pay for bus passes. There are more ticks than crosses.

This young South Asian Muslim woman felt confident that with the assistance of her father, employed as a laboratory technician, her educational life course was already predetermined to some extent – at least in that it would remain in the sciences. In relation to her views on university entry, she said,

> I think I would give medicine a miss...because I am not sure that I could achieve the grades. So my next bet is on endocrinology... something that is medical related...My dad said that you can do what you want as long as you get the grades.

In the 1980s, the trend for higher educational research suggested that young Muslim women did not participate at rates on par or perform as well as the men (Afshar, 1989; Siann *et al.*, 1990). In the last decade, however, this situation has been completely reversed, with all young women achieving better than all young men, irrespective of ethnicity (Osler and Hussain, 1995; Ahmad, 2001; Abbas, 2003a). It is related to the changing cultures experienced by the young Muslim (Bangladeshi and Pakistani) women, who are increasingly challenging existing patriarchal norms and values and asserting themselves through educational advancement by 'negotiation' (Singh, 1990; Basit, 1997a; Debnath, 1998; Haw, 1998; Haque, 1999, 2000).

In this study, for some of the young South Asian Muslim women in particular, the question of staying at home and attending a local university was a delicate one. Those wishing to stay at home were aware of some of the benefits; namely, the strong reputations of both Aston and Birmingham, the saving on accommodation costs and reliable sources of support. In the end, however, the final choices for young South Asian women were considered to have been strongly influenced by parents, and especially fathers.

College students

Some students, however, were critical of their parent's support in their education during this process. Three young Indian women from St Margaret's College wrote the following separate entries on the self-completed surveys. They refer to the ways in which parents are inadvertently placing a great deal of pressure on them to perform well but did not always have the appropriate levels of understanding, support and guidance to help them within the home. The importance here is to appreciate how, on the one hand, South Asian parents are highly aspirational but, on the other, their actions and behaviours can sometimes be deleterious.

[A] Doing 'A' Levels is equally hard as running around the world in 80 days especially if you have no help or guidance – and this means working twice as hard. On top of all this there comes colossal, I mean colossal, pressure from your parents. My parents unfortunately have no English education and what really gets me is that they think it's so easy to pass with A*s and get degrees. I think that we (I) are very unfortunate to be living in England because we are all the time facing an immense culture clash.

[B] I have been estimated BBB at 'A' Level and because I had many As and A*s at GCSE, my father feels this is not good enough. My parents always put me down – saying your work is deteriorating, not realising that 'A' Levels are so hard. I think if they had supported me more instead of telling me I'm stupid, I may have done better. Being an Indian 'girl' in particular has also meant that my parents were against sending me to university. They felt being a girl, I'd not be able to survive on my own. My education is really important to me and I had a really hard time explaining to my parents that no bad would come of me going to university. I think parents make it really difficult for Asian girls to study – I know they did for me anyway.

[C] Parents strongly pressure children to study and achieve what they themselves never could for various reasons. This can act as both motivation, yet a hindrance, as they are pressuring the children without realising it.

Students were asked about their educational and occupational intentions on leaving. The vast majority of all South Asian students wished to pursue an academic route into university, although the Bangladeshi groups

were least likely to be committed to this path. Certainly, 43 per cent
[6/14] of Bangladeshis said that they were going to 'look for a job'. Indians
were more likely to want to attend university than any of the other
South Asian groups [25/36].

Teachers

It is clear both South Asian school pupils and further education college
students perform in education in relation to how effective schools
are and how well South Asian parents are able to assist their children
successfully – through combinations and permutations of social class
and cultural capital. It is manifestly born out in relation to GCSE and
'A' Level grades achieved and how South Asian pupils and students
select certain degree subjects and institutions. In their attempts to gain
entry into higher education and the differences that emerge between
the different South Asian groups of interest, it is important to explore
the views of teachers towards South Asian pupils and students.

Focusing on the move into higher education, the headteacher [17] at
Rosebud School felt that young South Asian women are generally
confident of the educational paths they take. She said that,

> There is a very strong desire to go into higher education. It will be
> rare that an Asian girl (a) doesn't stay in sixth-form and (b) doesn't
> go into higher education and they of all the groups are the ones that
> if by any chance something goes wrong with 'A' Level and they don't
> get in I can guarantee they'll try again another year and will get
> there. They will often go to sixth-form college to do special re-take
> courses, we don't take anybody back.

Similarly, the deputy headteacher [15] at Psi Grove School felt new
South Asian entrants in the sixth-form display distinct interests in the
science subjects rather than in the arts or humanities, whereas the South
Asian pupils moving up the school were likely to take them from
a wider range of different subject options. He said,

> Generally speaking if an Asian boy comes into us from a sixth-form
> we're really surprised if he wants to do arts subjects, if he's gone up
> through the school . . . In other words they do the subjects they feel
> like doing whereas if they're coming from outside the school, they tend
> to want to do the science subjects. The stereotype is that they want
> to be doctors and do you want be doctor, no, no, no . . . The priority

would be to those who've gone up the school anyway and we're putting new buildings up for space ... To say we look at the colour of their faces when they come, that is not true, we do not.

The viewpoints suggest some of the South Asian pupils in the selective system are perhaps being overly narrow in their educational directions and in making the best of the various opportunities presented to them. The headteacher [13] of Omega High School stated that the young South Asian women in her elite school were perfectly capable of performing well in 'A' Level subjects. However, the issue singled out was the over-aspiration to read medicine at university and how it potentially damaged the occupational life chances of the individuals in question,

> I think the fact is that a lot of the girls of all backgrounds could probably do whatever subjects they wanted to at 'A' Level and do perfectly well in them but there are cases where there is no doubt with some of the South Asian parents that the girls probably would have got a string of A's ... and they have struggled through the sixth-form and not particularly enjoyed their science 'A' Levels. I mean they are doing well by any standards but I don't know.

> Yeah. And I mean this is a separate issue but I have reservations about whether medicine is such a good career for women. I actually think that people are wrong in not seeing that. Actually, it's a particularly bad career for women!

A senior teacher [16] at Rosebud School commented on a particular situation in relation to a father of a young East African Muslim women and her educational direction. The father was considered to have been over enthusiastic in his educational wishes for his daughter. It is an example of how a South Asian parent is considered to have behaved irrationally in relation to higher education entry for his daughter and, in that respect, is reflective of others. She said,

> We certainly do have one Asian girl at present in the upper sixth year who has applied for medicine against our advice, who is not going to get the grades and got a rejection. I had a long talk with her father who will not accept the situation and said she's going to get in regardless of the fact that there's another girl with a stronger academic ability in the upper sixth year who has applied for medicine and was

told by her father to apply for medicine who doesn't want to. Again wondering how to proceed, now her father says she'll go and do retakes until she gets the grades until she gets to medical school. I think we tend to deflect them a little if we can see that in the lower sixth they are not going to make it. We just say look go for dentistry, optometry, something along those lines, which they have done, one or two have.

The assertion that South Asian parents are overly asserting their children to read the highly sought after subjects such as medicine was also noted by the deputy headteacher [15] at Psi Grove School,

There is still a high percentage that still wants to be doctors and they get quite disappointed when they don't meet the UCAS grades criteria and we actually find that they try a second time. Their parents are still pushing them, when they leave the school, if they haven't got the 'A' Level grades here they tend to go to these tutorial colleges just so they can go into that particular field.

Apart from the subject areas South Asian pupils and students were thought to be enthusiastic about, discussions with teachers were concerned with where South Asians preferred to study for their degrees after taking their 'A' Levels. The headteacher at Rosebud School emphasised how young South Asian women tended to stay at home for higher education. The headteacher believed that doing so provided both rewards and penalties,

With all groups, yes there will be a desire to have Birmingham, possibly Aston depending on the subject and have a higher priority in their choices. For all groups that is becoming an important thing and the good thing in Birmingham is that there are three universities in Birmingham and there is Wolverhampton. They can also go out to Warwick, Coventry, Worcester, so there's quite a group of good local universities so living at home doesn't neces- sarily mean you haven't got a good choice of university. You're networking into some of the best universities in the country which in itself poses a problem because the grades that certainly Aston and Birmingham are offering are terrifically high, and Warwick, and they're so high so that in itself creates a problem with staying local.

Teachers in the inner-city comprehensive schools noticed similar experiences in how their South Asian students made their higher education choices. Where in selective schools, certain choices are characterised by the strength and standing of degree subjects and universities, in the comprehensive schools and further education colleges students were choosing to go universities that were relatively close to their homes. Although the issue here has less to do with universities demanding high 'A' Level grades, it is more about questions of geography and, in some instances, gender. The most significant factor, however, appears to be the increasing costs to the individual in higher education. The deputy headteacher [12] of New Heath School noticed the preference of his pupils to attend local universities. He said,

> I would say that 99.9 per cent of girls go to local universities, Birmingham, Coventry, Leicester, Wolverhampton and indeed many of the boys too strangely enough, one or two are escaping further a field, I'll remove that word 'escape', one or two are looking further a field ...

The type of further education courses that are taken in inner-city schools and further education colleges are not always those considered the 'gold standard'. Pupils can often take alternative routes and in due course gain entry into higher education. The deputy headteacher [12] at New Heath School added that students entered, 'Derby, Leicester, UCE (University of Central England), Coventry, the new universities around the area and following on their studies into subjects because of their choices at GNVQs or A Level, carrying on doing things like business studies, law ...'

Echoing the explanations provided by some of the headteachers and senior teachers, a lecturer [23] talked of the destinations that South Asian students took from St Margaret's College,

> The destination of university students for the last two years is on the map of the English Isles. Asian students are overwhelmingly in the West Midlands and in and around London and a lot of students do want to go to Birmingham or failing that UCE or Wolverhampton or Warwick or Coventry or perhaps Stoke. I haven't found that students are particularly concerned whether it's a new university, in fact they do tend to see the old universities as better so Warwick and Birmingham are the best. But Warwick of course is more difficult than Coventry because it's the other side of Coventry, it's more difficult to live at home and go there. But in the last couple of years there's been

a change here because all the stuff about fees. Now we're finding that white students are copying Asian students and now far more white students want to go locally where you can live at home which you can pretend doesn't cost money because it's not yours and you can keep your part-time job. So there's been a drop overall in the students this year in the number of students applying to university and there have been far more people applying to local universities, overall for the college as a whole.

Attitudinal responses from teachers to a series of statements in relation to the educational and occupational subject choices made by pupils and students found that 65 per cent of teachers [40/62] agreed with the notion, 'I would be deterred from encouraging a pupil/student to select a subject if they were not thought good enough.' In relation to the question of the type of subjects that are chosen, 66 per cent [43/65] of teachers agreed with the sentiment, 'Asian parents and students strongly favour science subjects'. A further 42 per cent [27/65] of teachers believed that, 'medicine is far too much a popular choice for Asians in higher education'.

Discussion

Research conducted in the 1980s found that South Asians were more likely to study medicine, science and engineering at university compared with their white peers. South Asians were found to re-take examinations to improve upon grades and, as such, the South Asian students were often older when starting university (Vellins, 1982; Ballard and Vellins, 1985; Tanna, 1990). Research based on 1992 UCCA and PCAS admissions data found that the inequalities of pre-university entry remained when moving into higher education (Modood, 1993; Taylor, 1993; Connolly, 1994). In relation to the degree subjects that were significantly more popular, such as medicine and law, the various elite university and higher education college systems were relatively neutral in the treatment of ethnic minorities. The elite universities offering degree subjects requiring lower 'A' Level grades were less likely to be impartial. Young Pakistani men and women were significantly under-represented in traditional universities and over-represented in the 'former polytechnics' (Modood and Shiner, 1994). There is a trend among South Asian students entering university to read subjects at prestigious institutions requiring the highest 'A' Level grades, while on the other, there is also a pattern for some to attend 'former polytechnics' or pursue certain subjects, which can lead to comparatively less well-paid work.

Despite the overwhelming preference for subjects such as medicine, research evidence shows that certain medical schools have repeatedly discriminated against ethnic minority applicants. It is important to take this into account given that so many of the South Asians, and particularly those in selective schools, expressed a strong pull towards the discipline. The CRE (1988) investigation found that St George's Hospital Medical School in London was biased against ethnic minority applicants and especially women (it was found that a faulty computer program had unwittingly created the problem). Further analysis of wider medical school entry data has found that, given 'A' Level grades, ethnic minority applicants are more likely to be discriminated against in comparison to their white peers. The difference, furthermore, tends to be greatest between white and African-Caribbean groups (Esmail *et al.*, 1996). It is because of the determination of a certain social class of South Asian parents and their children which continues to be resilient in the face of adversity that permits this determination. Medicine, as a degree subject, carries real economic, social and cultural importance for many South Asians but it is only a handful that are ever able to make it, and it appears a great many of those who wanted to may have well been hindered because of factors related to racism in the application process.

The findings from the current research support the notion that South Asians are far more likely to aim for the most demanding degree subjects (in terms of the 'A' Levels) in the stronger, 'traditional' universities than in the 'new'. Certainly, the South Asian pupils and students were aware that they were selecting the most sought after subjects in the most desirable of universities and were inclined to overlook those subjects based on offers of relatively lower 'A' Level grades within the same institutions. Other South Asians were increasingly likely to opt for university education nearer to their homes in an effort not to be heavily impacted by the costs of higher education. In terms of the actual career choices made, the sciences were definitive for young South Asian men and women in all the schools and colleges, in both 'traditional' and 'new' universities. Social science and humanities degrees were less popular with the exception of law. In the selective schools, the demands made by South Asian parents, especially from fathers, for their daughters to read medicine were considered to be over and above realistic expectations.

Much of the findings generated here can be grounded in the sociology of education on social class, Bourdieu's cultural capital and *habitus* theses and the more current re-workings of social capital theory. South Asians of different social classes are internalising a range of values towards education based on their individual experiences and aspirations. These aspirations are formed by the knowledge, information, 'connections', networks and associations that various South Asian groups have access to or are a part of. The educational institution has an important function to play helping to frame and bound these aspirations. The embodiment of this *habitus* is considered to be 'social class "in the head"' (Ball *et al.*, 2002b). In addition, for ethnic minorities and South Asians, other reasons emerge in the attractiveness or otherwise of certain higher education institutions and these are linked to the immigration, settlement, racialisation, ethnicisation and, in some cases, radicalisation of certain South Asian groups. They are also a function of the educational institutions people attend and the overall level of opportunities that exist within them. They are also based on how 'knowledgeable' parents are and the effectiveness of the support they provide to their children. In all these instances, both the home and the school are important in relation to outcomes, and it appears that it is the balance of these forces that remains important in the lives of many South Asians as they pursue their educational objectives. What makes this more pertinent is the role and function of ethnicity.

It is necessary, therefore, to evaluate the attitudes of pupils, students and parents in relation to the role and function of teachers and schools compared with that of the home in order to explore the dichotomy of whether it is ultimately the school or the domestic environment of South Asians that impacts most on the educational achievement processes for different South Asian groups.

7

A Question of Responsibility: The Home and the School

Research has continued to show that parenting is an important part of the educational achievements of pupils in secondary schools (Feinstein and Symons, 1999). The efforts that South Asian parents make in their children's education are recognised as being highly motivated. With current changes to the education system, parents are *apparently* provided increased opportunities to become further involved with schools. Not every parent, however, is able to take advantage of this, largely due to economic and social exclusion. At the same time it has been found that teachers can sometimes relate to South Asian parents without taking into consideration their economic and social circumstances; 'parents' perceptions of teachers as superior and distant is reinforced by teachers' own stance' (Crozier, 1999, p. 327).

It is crucial to explore how the South Asian home *and* the teachers and the school effect the education of South Asians and in which particular circumstances. The essential questions here seek to determine whether the causes of achievement or underachievement reside in the home or in the teachers and secondary schools and further education colleges that South Asians attend. Pupils, students and parents were asked questions in relation to teacher ethnicity, the role of the institution in supporting South Asian pupils and students and how the various South Asian religio-cultural behaviours impact on the lives of South Asian pupils and students and their education (Abbas, 2002b).

Teachers in schools and further education colleges

Teachers in England have received much public criticism in recent times, particularly at the end of the 1990s (OfSTED, 1997; DfEE, 1998). The popular image of teachers has deteriorated, which is reflected in current central government efforts that encourage applicants to take education degrees and teacher training courses. In relation to a politico-ideological explanation of the educational achievements of ethnic minorities, antiracist educationists consider the overwhelming influence of the teacher and the nature of the teacher–pupil relationship as critical. Multicultural educationists argue that a dependable environment within the home coupled with resources and knowledge are the necessary factors for achievement. Invariably, a combined effort is often needed and successful attempts at developing home–school partnerships provide illustrations of ways in which to deal with this issue (Tomlinson, 1984; Vincent, 1995).

School pupils

School pupils were asked whether they would consider themselves or their teachers if they felt they had underachieved. In addition, pupils were asked to determine whether their attitudes would change if teachers were of South Asian or of other ethnicities (cf. Ghuman, 1995). Here, sensitive issues are explored in relation to the conspicuousness or otherwise of 'teacher racism' (Foster, 1992, 1993; Troyna, 1993b; Short and Carrington, 1996, 1998; Cole, 1998a,b). The aim, nevertheless, was to explore the impact of ethnicity on teacher–pupil interaction – with an essential objective to discover whether attitudes towards teachers alter with change in skin colour or other visible markers of difference.

The discussions with South Asian pupils in selective schools were informative. A 17-year-old Sikh woman at Rosebud School commented that the ethnicity of the teacher does not matter, she said, 'I don't think it makes any difference personally'. Some South Asian teachers were thought to disassociate themselves with other teachers of the same ethnicity.

> I've noticed that. My mom is a teacher and she says that you do get Asian teachers who are more with whites than they are with Asians, they just fob them off and slag them off!

Nevertheless, there were very few South Asian teachers within the selective schools and, as a result, pupils did not have a wider perspective on the matter to permit them to effectively discern issues in the demarcation of ethnicity and class. A 16-year-old Hindu man at Psi Grove School, in relation to the small number of ethnic minority teachers in his boy's school, said, 'I'd like to see a lot more than two

Asian teachers...If the white teachers wanted to understand I am sure they could'.

A comment on the ethnicity of teachers from a 17-year-old Sikh man at Psi Grove School was symptomatic of many in the selective schools. The view suggested that it was the ability of the teacher, irrespective of their ethnicity, which made the greatest impact. He also articulated that his relationship with mainly white teachers was largely perfunctory. Talking about how the South Asian pupils get on with the white teachers, he said,

> We get on alright. I might not like them; but it's just because of the way they teach. But I've never disliked them. There have never been any bad words or anything. [A good teacher is] somebody that actually teaches the class rather than turn away to the board and keeps writing away. There is usually one person in the department who turns away and writes on the board...and in the sixth-form...you have to make up by asking other teachers to help you...outside lessons...to compensate.

He added further on the fact that Psi Grove School contained only two ethnic minority (South Asian) teachers at the time of the study. He suggested that because of their ethnicity he was able to form more constructive relationships with them. He said,

> Mr Khan ['mixed-race'], although he is Asian, it doesn't really show. Mr Singh is like purebred Asian. He's got all the Asian traits...the Asian accent. They're both okay I mean. I reckon I do get on better with them...'cause when we do meet it's more personal – between five or six of us...you just tend to be more relaxed.

An 18-year-old East African Muslim woman at Rosebud School commentated that, irrespective of ethnicity, teachers are important in the development and maintenance of positive relations. She said,

> I think the relationship was the same as with any other teacher [of different ethnicity]...It wasn't really different in any way at all... I don't think it really makes a difference as long as they know how to teach those subjects to those pupils. The teachers knew a lot about all the faiths, different religions...and they accepted that and they tried to help where they could...really...and I think that was a positive thing to do and it worked really well.

In essence, the generally high academic standards in selective schools and an aspiration to achieve exceptional GCSE scores, year on year, lead teachers to be committed to improving standards. Although, in the grammar schools, over a third of the pupils at both Rosebud and Psi Grove Schools are ethnic minorities, teachers are required to consider the achievement of all pupils *per se*. This is born out from the statements made by the selective school pupils.

The perspectives of pupils in secondary schools towards South Asian teachers are also contemplated. A 16-year-old Hindu woman at St Aiden's School said, '[South Asian] teachers give other Asian pupils a bit of time...I think they [pupils] would feel better if there were more Asian teachers in school'. A 15-year-old Pakistani woman at Longlake School was especially positive about the potential benefits of same-ethnic teachers, stating, 'all the Asians [pupils] are very happy to see that the Asians are now coming in to teach. It makes them feel proud to see that the Asians can do something'. The majority of the young Bangladeshi and Pakistani women highlighted the potential additional benefits of same-ethnicity teachers. The comment below by a 16-year-old Pakistani woman at New Heath School was representative of many. She expressed belief in the importance of same-ethnicity teachers when certain school issues require a more culturally sensitive understanding and approach. The perspective is unique as it suggests that there are potential limitations to the current practice. Pupils may well require an added dimension to existing pupil–teacher relations precisely because of ethnicity. She said,

> I don't think that it's got anything to do with the colour of your skin. I think it's the quality of your teaching. But, I suppose it is a bonus that they are Asian. I think it is good on a cultural basis because, if say you have a girl that has got a problem at home...and it's an Asian problem say...then she can relate it to the Asian staff I think.

Although distinctions exist between different teachers because of their ethnicity there are other qualitative facets deemed important in evaluating the appropriateness of teachers. Judgement is based on the ability of the teacher to be effective *per se*. This individual talked further about an experience in relation to one white teacher. Her observation at the end of the quotation is indicative of the prevailing attitudes of most pupils from the comprehensive schools. She said of some of the white teachers that behaved peculiarly towards her,

It is the way they talk...there are actually one or two teachers. It's just their tone of voice...the way they project their opinions. There is one teacher...you can tell...he's got a picture of the queen on his wall and he actually told us once, when the bell went and we all got up to leave, 'What do you think you are, American kids?' Presumably [North American] kids lack discipline and are difficult to control and I think this is what he meant by that. [In general, the teachers] most of them treat us quite equally...and if they didn't, I don't really care...as long as I get my grades.

Overall, pupils from the selective schools ascertained the appropriateness and acceptability of teachers based on their capacity to teach adequately regardless of ethnicity. In the comprehensive schools, pupils considered same-ethnicity teachers for same-ethnicity reasons but, again, considered the overall effectiveness of the teacher as the most significant factor.

College students

Further education college students were asked how well they related to their teachers at secondary school. Eighteen per cent of the South Asians observed that they did not get on well with 'only one or two teachers', and nearly one-quarter of all respondents stated 'there were some teachers that did not like me for some reason'. Only four per cent [4/106] agreed to the statement, 'I did not get on well with the vast majority of my teachers'. There was no difference of opinion between the South Asians in relation to the above statements. Respondents were also asked who they would hold responsible if they did not do well in their education. Of the three South Asian groups, Pakistanis and Indians were more likely to be critical of their teachers, with 51 [27/53] and 42 [16/38] per cent agreeing to the words, 'yes, some teachers were simply not that good'. Nevertheless, 46 per cent of students [49/107] agreed with the notion, 'no, I would only blame myself for not working hard enough', interestingly, with Bangladeshis half as much more likely than Indians and 16 times more than Pakistanis to agree with this sentiment.

The students were sure that they were central to their own educational achievements but went on to emphasise that they believed racism existed in the education system and that some pupils and students were potentially more disadvantaged than others because of it. The two open-ended statements below are quoted verbatim from the survey returns. These young Bangladeshi and Pakistani women argued that they experienced surreptitious as well open racism in their schools. The first quotation is from a young Bangladeshi woman at James Watt College and the second from a young Pakistani woman at Cherrywood College.

[A] I very strongly feel that last year at college I was let down by my GCSE English Tutor because from my point of view he only took note of the white students on the same table and whenever we asked for help the teacher came for a while then went off again to the other desk where there were white students asking for help and he would spend quite a lot of time with them. Due to this I could have passed my GCSE English but I ended up with a D.

[B] I believe that if I had gone to a better secondary school I would have done better in my 'A' Levels. I did biology, chemistry and English literature and didn't get the grade I needed in biology. I re-took my biology and did one year intensive psychology and am now waiting for my results. The sixth-form I went to was excellent, except for my English teachers who were very negative . . . My English teachers in college I felt were racist and very negative and I tried very hard to get the grade in English literature that I neglected my other subjects a bit. But my English teacher told me I would never get into university into a good degree. I think that affected my education.

An 18-year-old Pakistani man at St Margaret's College put in writing the importance, in his mind, of teachers and in the process vociferously expressing his own experiences. He believed that it was crucial to develop a mutually respectful relationship between South Asian pupils and white teachers based on trust and commitment. He wrote,

The presence of a teacher in a student's life is profoundly important. Teachers by students are seen as a representative or microcosm of the whole society, if not the country. It is not unrealistic to say that the feelings carried by a student of a particular teacher can decide the direction of his/her life in the world.

I carried my disdain for teachers into college, where not only my feelings, but life was to change. It is all down to one female English teacher. It was either through literature or the caring personality of the teacher that a change to my thinking was made. The teacher and literature are indistinguishable for me. Through literature and the help of the teacher I have come closer to humanity, understanding and religion. Most importantly I have found some identity in the society for which we had been treated as 3rd class citizens; thus in preparation for 'good jobs'.

I am not saying that the 'beauty of literature' or my 'English teacher' will change the lives of all black students. But, there is 'something' and a 'particular teacher' somewhere that can change your life. I have been blessed that I had found the things to change my life. Now out of love of literature and love for and credit to my teacher, I hope to also change lives for the better by teaching.

The teacher's power to control the student's life is what is frightening. If the teachers guide and help discover the talents of students, rather than shove 'knowledge' down throats, we will have an epidemic of 'lives changing'.

A 17-year-old Sikh woman at St Margaret's College wrote about her wider educational experiences. The comment is indicative of the type of realities experienced by South Asian students in an intensely competitive educational environment. Having spent a period in the independent education sector she identified the differences between two necessarily different modes of education. She wrote,

I would like to make a disturbing comment from personal experience that there is more prejudice/racism in private sector education and in sixth-form colleges because this is a critical time where there is a race for university places.

I have found that white students are often given more assistance by teachers and that they tend to offer college resources first to white students in a subtle manner. Maybe this is because I have never attended an institution with such a high proportion of students from ethnic minorities. I have also noticed that in a classroom white students sit on one side of a classroom with black students on the other side. This illustrates the intense competitive atmosphere at this level of education.

I have found these experiences quite shocking and more defensive as a student coming from an ethnic minority.

A final comment from an 18-year-old Pakistani woman at James Watt College is on how the perception of religion by teachers affected her time at secondary school. She wrote that she felt isolated and eventually insecure about her academic abilities,

Teachers are not able to understand the concept [religion]. Most had a secular feeling towards religion, this was reflected in the teaching.

My religion has meant I am always stereotyped mainly negatively, I feel this has strongly influenced my lack of confidence in classwork.

The above statements evoke the significance of the teacher–pupil relations based on popular perceptions of the *other*. Students were divided as to whether they would hold themselves or their teachers responsible for underachieving, although Bangladeshis and Pakistanis were least likely to have related well with teachers – with some statements made by college students that were fairly critical of teachers.

Parents

The views of South Asian parents towards teachers tended to vary based on social class. It is not surprising, therefore, to discover differences between the views of South Asian parents at one end of the socio-economic scale, involved in elite, independent education compared with South Asian parents who live in the more deprived areas with children in less effective comprehensive schools. The comments below originate from parents with children in selective fee-paying schools: the first from a professional Hindu father and the second from a professional Hindu mother.

[2] I think that by and large we were very happy with the teachers he had at school, as is evidenced by his results.

[21] If the other children are okay in the class, you can't blame the teacher.

Parents felt a degree of faith in selective school results and that the values, codes and ethos of schools would be positively impressed upon their children. Middle-class South Asian parents were asked where they would lay the responsibility of educational underachievement if it were found to occur. The first response is from a professional Hindu mother with daughters at Omega High School and the second from an East African Muslim professional father with sons at 'Omega High for boys'. Cleary, the emphasis is on the individual more so than the schools.

[21] If she didn't do as well as she wanted to, then, I wouldn't blame any one part of the system. There has to be contributing issues... with her own ability perhaps to an extent... with teachers not

understanding her...meaning perhaps I didn't create the right environment.

[8] I personally feel from my experience that quite a fair amount of learning has to be done on your own. And, I think, actually, I mean I wouldn't blame the school in the sense that obviously – like all pupils and temperaments are different.

South Asian parents from lower social class backgrounds maintained that the school was principally responsible for educational achievement. This view is largely based on the experience of *underachievement* as opposed to *achievement*. The broad distinction between these two sets of parents is epitomised by the following observation made by a middle-class Bangladeshi father [4] with children at both Psi Grove and Rosebud Schools,

In my mind, I think that parents are in two different camps. One sort of parents they seem to know the mechanics of the system and they have got knowledge and expertise to make the system for their favour. And then you have the other set of parents they leave everything to the teachers or to the schools, sort of lay back...sort of wait until it is too late, until they find there is nothing that they can do. In terms of percentage, I find 75 per cent probably lay back and suddenly they wake up.

Further considering the impact of social class on attitudes and perceptions, a working-class Sikh mother [26] stated that many South Asians underachieve because they lacked high 'expectations'. It is based on the idea that weaker students need more attention from teachers and so take it away from the stronger students in the class. She said,

I don't think it's a case of bad teachers...You're going to have lower levels of expectations because the type of children that are in there. Children, who are naturally gifted, they are not going to be pushed enough because the attention is directed at the children of lower level learning.

This Sikh mother viewed the higher 'expectations' of certain South Asian pupils to be crucial and regarded the family as decisive in its development. She elaborated on how she felt the lack of 'expectations' hindered the educational potential of certain South Asian children. She stated,

Expectations would come from the home in the first instance – and then from the school. The school is there to teach a child. Ideally a child should be able to come in to the school and want to learn as opposed to a child who wants to come into the school and disrupt the whole damn class. You know! They should have a child willing to learn; the will, the self-motivation has to be within the child. That will come from their surrounding community, their home in the first instance. Our people are too busy, especially ladies, gossiping about each other, picking fault at other people, instead of looking at their own situation.

Some of the working class and unemployed South Asians were directly critical of school systems in the inner cities. Disapproval was expressed in relation to some of the primary schools and their teachers. In discussing the context of South Asian Muslims in inner-city schools, parents were more likely to suggest that it was the schools that were responsible for ensuring educational success, as they themselves were making all the efforts they possibly could. A working-class Pakistani father [9] said,

Children are sent to school to get educated and if they come out with nothing, who's to blame? I wouldn't lay my blame onto anybody, the results are there, and you are talking about thousands. In the last ten years, not many have faired well and this is your future community ... future nation.

[What in his mind caused the current problems to arise?] There weren't enough places in nurseries and the education in primary school is poor. If you don't lay the foundations right, if they don't get nursery places, they don't get educated from the start at that age at three or four then they will fall back and then they aren't pushed enough in primary schools. When they move into secondary schools they say these children are two years behind, three years behind. What can we do with them? So it's a vicious circle ... If the child is not doing well at school he's not going to be interested in school is he? He's stuck in a science lesson, he can't do it. He is not going to be interested in going to school. It's motivation at the end of the day. Why aren't the children motivated by the system? It's the system that is failing the children. Parents aren't. You talk to any parent they want their child to do well, they want their child to go on into further education, they want the best for their child. Blaming the parents is one of the things that the system does, it's the system that's failing the child.

Language issues were raised by teachers in a number of the schools. Many regarded it as one of the key reasons for educational under-achievement (see Chapter 8).[1] A number of the Muslim parents felt sure that it was paradoxical to put forward that English as a second language was a direct feature in the educational underachievement of, in particular, ethnic minority and South Asian inner-city schoolchildren. An unemployed Bangladeshi father and school governor of a local primary school [6] propounded that policymakers consistently showed 'different attitudes towards inner-city schools'. He elaborated,

> What has happened, always, they're using the inner cities for experiments and this sort of thing, but they're not telling the truth. This is the main fact. They say 'well we are this, we are that...' Actually this is not the case because United Kingdom is a multicultural and multi-racial society. They are saying it in word. But they do not maintain it honestly and sincerely, they are not using it in action. And, then in inner-city school, they always say, English is the second language. That's why they are not doing better. But I think this is to make excuse...because...when the inner-city children go to the outer-circle, there are no complaints at all. They're doing a lot better than European children. The main point is this: it is the attitude of the teacher. It is the aim of the teacher. This is the thing.

Other comments made by working-class South Asian parents were on the whole more balanced. Respondents felt sure that parents and teachers could not be considered in isolation as they do not work independently of each other. An unemployed Pakistani father [14] with children at New Heath School, on the question of who to consider the most important in educational underachievement, said,

> You can blame the teacher and you can also blame the child – if the child does not do any homework, or hesitates going or plays truant, then you are going to blame your child not the teachers. If the child attends regularly, and if there is still some problem, then it must be the staff...Sometimes I do blame school sometimes I do blame children because well...It is a difficult question again, if a child complains

you just cannot throw it away, at the same time you cannot challenge the teachers.

Translated from Urdu

Parents were also asked about their views towards South Asian teachers. A relationship was established such that South Asian parents from working and lower social class backgrounds were more likely to be approving of South Asian teachers necessarily because of their ethnicity. These parents noted that same-ethnicity teachers were of greater importance because they were thought to be knowledgeable of the discrimination faced by ethnic minorities. They were also felt able to communicate positively with pupils because of shared history, religion or culture – as well as being able to speak in an array of South Asian languages and dialects. As such, working-class South Asian parents viewed same-ethnicity teachers favourably (whereas parents from middle class and higher social class backgrounds expressed a desire for more effective teachers *per se*, irrespective of ethnicity).

In reality, it was found that working class South Asian parents had two broad approaches to English education. First, South Asian parents viewed English education based, in part, on the residuals of a colonial education system experienced in Bangladesh, India and Pakistan before migration (pre- and post-1947). Second, as economic immigrants in Britain, the universal acclaim English higher education has throughout the world results in the adaptation of middle-class values towards education by working-class South Asians. The dynamic for South Asian parents here, as it is for other ethnic minorities and disadvantaged people, is the extent to which education is used as a tool to rise up from the disadvantage and discrimination they experience in their daily lives or the necessary development of a continuing investment in education.

Religious and cultural relations within the home

It is argued that as teachers in differing types of schools can affect South Asians of varying social classes, an analysis of circumstances within the home permits the exploration of issues pertaining to religious observance and culture maintenance that may also affect their education within schools. To precisely measure the effect of religion upon education is difficult as it is determined by a myriad of factors. Nevertheless, it is meaningful to conceptualise the relative importance that religion has among South Asians and its influence upon educational achievement more qualitatively.

School pupils

In evaluating the experiences of selective school pupils, interviewees were asked to elaborate upon how they thought their religion and associated cultural characteristics affected their education at school. An 18-year-old Hindu man at Psi Grove School felt his religion was 'less strict' than Islam, for example. He said,

> My parents have always been religious as such. I am religious. I go to the temple. I pray at home whenever my parents do. That isn't a problem for me. I participate in all the religious activities as such. It's like which is more important right now. Let's say if I was a Muslim, I am not allowed to smoke or I am not allowed to drink. I must admit I have drunk before and have smoked: if I was a Muslim all that peer group pressure that is there, from home, you shouldn't do this or you shouldn't do that. My religion is less strict.

Another selective school pupil stated that her home contained many religious symbols and artefacts making the impact of religion a persuasive force. This 16-year-old Sikh woman at Rosebud School expressed that her religiosity was not as acute as it ought to be, however. She said,

> [Religious?] Yes, quite. My grandmother is very and so is my granddad... my mom is kind of going that way now. My Aunt is. We don't go to the Gurdwara often...even though it's only five minutes down the road. I know I should go...but I just don't because I am lazy. We have photographs of Gurus and everything. Yes, we are quite religiously orientated.

Compared with the Hindus and Sikhs, South Asian Muslims often related cases of added involvement with the religion of Islam. A 17-year-old Pakistani (*Shia*) woman at Rosebud School talked about her extensive religious activities,

> I go to the mosque a lot. There are youth clubs there... and I go out with my friends... visit the cinema together. I really don't have time for anything [else]. I just go to the mosque a lot and I am involved in so many meetings there. I haven't got time for other clubs and stuff...I don't wanna go out anyway.

> At nine I started doing it properly all the time [being committed religiously]...but before that I'd now and again...or most of the time or whenever I've remembered.

In close similarity to the pupils in selective schools, pupils in the comprehensive schools were also conversational about religiosity and in particular the experiences within the home. Furthermore, there were marked parallels. An 'upper' working-class, 16-year-old Bangladeshi woman at New Heath School believed that she was not as devout as she should be but believed in the religion nevertheless. She said,

> I don't pray like five times a day or anything. I believe in it. My mom is like the most religious in the family. My dad's not really into it. He only goes to mosque on Friday because my mom makes him go... I used to go to this place and like this teacher used to read Arabic and that but... that was it. It was a two-hour thing... going after school and at the weekend. I am not really that religious. My mom was like that you have to do it and that and my dad was like at the end of the day it's up to you.

For the vast majority of all South Asian Muslim pupils, the religion of Islam carries real importance in their lives. But what is also clear is the extent to which the younger generations are taking the opportunity to re-learn the religion and re-shape their experiences in Britain because of it. Many of the pupils felt there were genuine issues of interpretation and practice that negatively impacted them, particularly the young South Asian Muslim women. A 15-year-old Pakistani young woman at New Heath School articulated her feelings on the nature of Islam and how it was affected by living in Britain. Her outlook was holistic and concerned a wider view of the religion. She said,

> I think a problem is that some people get culture and Islam mixed... and they think that you are not a Muslim if you don't wear *Salwar-Kameez*. Now *Salwar-Kameez* is just a style and they see that as part of Islam and it's not.

> I don't have to show externally that I am a Muslim though. It is obligatory to wear a *Hijab*... which I will do soon. I have to make sure my intentions are right before I do anything.

> I am only seventeen... but I mean my parents want me to have a stable education... we've been brought up in Britain... obviously we are going to be influenced by the Western society.

Muslim pupils and students were inclined to be far closer to their religion such that they felt it broadened every aspect of their lives.

It involved a specific adherence to their faith, requiring both time and energy for religious observance. Here, young South Asian Muslim women appeared to be more devout than young Muslim men.[2] In addition, young South Asian Muslim women stressed the patriarchal culture of home life which was based on cultural variations of Islam practised by South Asian Muslim parents (cf. Robinson, 1988). As one 16-year-old Bangladeshi young woman at New Heath School put it, 'culture is the problem, not exactly the religion. Like...our parents they do not really believe in religion, they think about the culture'.

Factors in relation to *Izzat* (respect) and patriarchy are likely to affect the perceptions and attitudes of young South Asian women towards education (cf. Wilson, 1998; Basit, 1997b; Haw, 1998; Ahmad, 2001). It is argued that certain negative religio-cultural practices increase the likelihood of a negative impact upon schooling and that this is especially true for Bangladeshi and Pakistani women. It has also been argued that other South Asian religions, for example Sikhism and Hinduism, affect their adherents less in this way. That is, it is argued that to be a 'good' Sikh or Hindu is not as demanding as being a 'good' Muslim (cf. Stopes-Roe and Cochrane, 1987, 1990) and, consequently, religion can get in the way of formal education, especially if it is loaded with patriarchy and various other misinterpretations of Islam. For most young South Asian women, however, religion is considered a positive force, especially when combined with positive efforts on the part of the parents, as articulated by the college students in particular.

College students

Further education college students were asked how they felt about their religion. Of the 106 [of 109] that responded to the question, 50 per cent, including 25 out of 50 Pakistanis, agreed with the statement that 'my faith is my guiding light'. Forty-nine per cent [34 out of 70] of all Muslims in the sample agreed with this sentiment. Similarly, respondents were asked whether they thought their particular religion has an overtly cultural feel to it. Muslims conveyed greatest variation with their particular practice of religion with many of the Hindus stating that their religion was 'meant to be cultural'. It was further asked of students whether they thought their religion or culture had in any way disadvantaged their studies at school. Nearly half disagreed [51 out of 106]. In terms of religious classification, 44 per cent of Muslims, 50 per cent of Sikhs and 58 per cent of Hindus answered 'no' to the question.[3] Three-quarters of the Muslims had been through supplementary schooling in comparison to approximately one-third of the Indians [11/16 Bangladeshis; 35/53 Pakistanis compared with 11/37 Indians].[4]

A range of comments made by Bangladeshi and Pakistani South Asian Muslims on the nature of religion within the home are elaborated upon. They highlight how Muslims considered the religion critical to their educational and spiritual development. An 18-year-old Pakistani woman at James Watt College put in writing,

> I would like to point out that religion does not hinder but in fact promotes education for both males and females. Though I must stress that these days parents are encouraging children to get an education, not necessarily for job opportunity but for personal achievement, especially girls.

The following comments originate from two young Bangladeshi women (aged 17 and 18). The first at Cherrywood College and the second at James Watt College. They both contain strong links to strict Islamic perspectives that view duty and devotion to the faith with the utmost of importance. They wrote,

> [A] Although I am not particularly religious, religion I feel plays an important part in my education. I feel that without Allah's help and guidance, I would not have achieved so much.

> [B] I personally feel that religion comes before your studies because you may be a manager in this world but you could be unemployed in the next when you die. But this isn't to say that you shouldn't study because my religion points out that you should try your best in whatever you are doing or are going to do.

Students also elaborated on the nature of religion and how it affected wider social relations. For this individual, it was felt important to develop a sense of independence, an education that furnishes her with the necessary tools to operate in society and to move away from outmoded considerations in relation to young women. A 16-year-old Pakistani young woman at James Watt College wrote,

> My parents encourage us to do well in education because they feel we will have a better life, but I think it is also connected to status in the community and of course marriage.

> I personally think it is very important for a girl to be independent especially in Asian families which are patriarchal (headed by the

authority and ruled by men). Basically I think our culture stinks and has nothing to do with religion, because women are too repressed within their own families. My parents are very understanding and broad-minded therefore I have no problems but many of my friends experience this. They are not allowed to do many things but their brothers are which is unjust and unfair, and it really annoys me! Islam is a beautiful religion which respects women, and honours women, but people especially men make rules which suit them and disadvantage women in many ways. Most Asian parents do not realise that in India and Pakistan people are 'modernising' their ways, and Asians in Britain are 'left behind' holding on to 'old' traditional values, which are not important.

The extent to which young Bangladeshi and Pakistani women have been negatively affected by the way in which the religion of Islam has been distorted to subjugate women was repeated in many transcripts and written statements. The statement below from an 21-year-old Pakistani woman at James Watt College, who was at the time returning to education after a break from it, is especially pertinent in its evocation of the compounded nature of the religio-cultural norms and values practised by some South Asian Muslim parents and how some in education are adversely affected by them. She wrote,

It is difficult to go through education if you are born of a generation who have immigrated to this country. You are torn between two cultures. In my culture, women are regarded as being of marriageable age as soon as they are 16 years of age. That is when the most important part of the education starts. My parents got me married at 19. I did not get any kind of qualification to get a job. All you hear is 'you can't do this' and 'you can't do that', 'the religion does not permit it', or 'the culture does not permit it', or 'what will people say'.

I felt torn between cultures. I even hated my religion, my culture, parents. But they (the parents) were only like that because they had been brought up like that. Girls are restricted so much that some rebel against their parents. But I gave up and did what they wanted me to do.

Now after all these years I have the opportunity to further myself and it is a great feeling.

College students were asked to determine the religiosity of parents. Mothers were far more likely to be perceived as being religious compared with fathers. Seventy-five per cent of Bangladeshis [12/16], 64 per cent of Indians [23/36] and 60 per cent of Pakistanis [31/52] agreed with the statement that mothers were 'very religious'. In relation to fathers, 47 per cent of Bangladeshis [7/15], 49 per cent of Indians [17/35] and 50 per cent of Pakistanis [25/50] agreed they were 'very religious'. Interestingly, 13 per cent of all mothers [14/104] and 15 per cent of all fathers [15/100] were thought to, 'believe, but not practise [their respective religions]'.

Many of the South Asian Muslim college students, although sometimes critical of their parent's practise of Islam, because of its strong cultural associations, offered positive written remarks on their religion, their culture and relationships with parents. For these respondents, their parents, Islam and values towards education were intertwined. It appears where patriarchy is minimised and where parents are actively working together with their daughters, especially, educational opportunities are enhanced. It also appears that these sentiments also carry with them more developed notions of social and cultural capital. An 18-year-old Indian Muslim woman at St Margaret's College noted,

> I feel that I have been encouraged to achieve an education from my parents. They have always wished that I have a good education. My teachers at college have been fully supportive in my work. If I had any difficulties they would always be willing to help me overcome my difficulty.

> I think that my religion has given a positive side to my education, as religion advises you to gain an education, and my parents and I respect this advice and follow it. My culture, I feel, has supported me in achieving an education, because most people in my family have had educational achievements.

A 17-year-old Pakistani man at James Watt College wrote an analogous sentiment, but felt that it was also important to be pleased with possessing such important and useful religious values. He wrote, 'I feel perfectly comfortable with my religion and culture, in fact I am proud, and believe that no-one should ever feel ashamed of their own religion'.

It is apparent that parents shape the religious and cultural orientation of homes in many differing ways. All South Asian Muslim students viewed their religion, on average, with greater commitment than many of the Hindus and Sikhs. Some of the South Asian Muslims, especially young Bangladeshi and Pakistani women, were more likely to suggest that the type of patriarchal religion and culture practised within their

homes generated increased pressures. Nevertheless, for the vast majority, when interpreted and practised pragmatically, Islam was regarded as
a positive force in people's lives.

Parents

Parents were questioned about the role of religion and culture within
the home and how it influences education within schools. A professional
Hindu mother [24] with daughters at Omega High School talked about
the Hindu religion and culture in relation to other religions. The mother
described in her own words the nature of difference between the various
South Asians. It related to a perspective based on her middle-class status.
She said,

> We are Hindus. But we are sort of you know not as religious as I suppose
> Muslims in the same class. I mean they would still be coming to the
> school, in the evening going to the prayers and going out to the
> Madrassas and things like that. So it's more built into them. They
> [the daughters] went to Church of England so obviously they learnt
> more about Christianity, though in RE they learnt about all the
> religions. I mean they [the daughters] don't know much about their
> religion, their own religion like we don't know as much. Whether we
> were Christians, Hindus, Muslims, Sikhs whatever, I don't think it
> [impact of religion on education] would have made any difference.

In contrast, a middle-class Muslim father [8] with sons at 'Omega High
for boys' talked about the positive impact of Islam within the home. It
was asked of this parent what effect religion had on the educational
achievements of his sons. He said,

> I am quite a bit lapsed in my practice and my wife she prays and she
> fasts and observes the *Majlis* (gathering) and everything. I am quite
> surprised, both of them [his sons] but particularly the older one without
> any compulsion certainly...I mean he does not see an example set
> by myself, this is my wife doing it...both of them without any com-
> pulsion do Ramadan.

The middle-class South Asians were typical of other parents in their
social class. Religion was there as an option, it was not mandatory and
nor would it in any way get in the way of a strict education. In exploring
the views of parents from working-class backgrounds, the question of the
role of religion within the home was asked. Here, responses presented

a closer association with the religion, particularly on the part of the South Asian Muslims. A part-time employed 'mixed-race' mother [22] with daughters at St Aiden's School said that Islam was a binding force,

> Well there is standards and respect and that, I think that it does help. Yeah, 'cos a lot of children without religion haven't got that respect that you should have.

An unemployed Pakistani father of four [17] commented on the religiosity of the individual and how it affected the educational achievements of some Bangladeshi and Pakistani children. His view was characteristic of many Pakistani fathers adamant that religious instruction would be developmental rather than restrictive,

> I think that it makes no difference on education, the reason being, this Islamic teaching that they learn, I know of children that have recited the whole of the Qur'an and {they are still going to university and going to college, they are very bright...very very bright}...If it was going to make any difference, obviously they would be behind, but this is not the case.
>
> *Translated from Punjabi { } indicates original use of English*

For South Asian parents, religion carries differing importance in their lives based on social class and ethnicity. Middle-class South Asian parents were less strict and relaxed about religious practices *per se*, irrespective of the religion itself. For working-class South Asian parents, religion was seen to be important, particularly by Muslims.

Discussion

Issues in relation to the experience of teachers and schools and whether they can be regarded as central to the educational achievements of South Asians were widely discussed. There was a general agreement on the part of both middle class and working class South Asians that the ethnicity of the teacher did not matter as much as their effectiveness, save for the occasional need to deal with same-ethnicity matters or when in instances of being in same-ethnicity teacher–pupil settings some of the pupils and students felt more comfortable around them. Nevertheless, there are a number of examples indicating acute racism and discrimination on the part of teachers as perceived and experienced by South Asian pupils and students.

Middle-class parents were of the view that teachers could not be considered central to educational achievements as there are a whole host of wider factors to take into consideration. They were adamant that if they are able to provide a strong and supportive learning environment and that if they encourage their children over-zealously their children would perform well. On the other hand, working-class and unemployed South Asians were more likely to consider the teacher and the school. The reason for this is a function of the severe under-performance on the part of many South Asian Muslims in some of the inner-city primary and secondary schools children attend. Efforts to try and improve matters were often to no avail and so many South Asian Muslim parents came to the simple conclusion that it was poor teachers with lower expectations of South Asian Muslim children in poorly managed schools that was the more significant issue. Clearly, therefore, there are a number of concerns at the level of the school that do impact some South Asians more than others – that is, it is the Bangladeshis and Pakistanis who are more likely to perceive a negative experience. This is argued to impact strongly on their potential educational achievements.

Nevertheless, there are questions at the level of the home which need to be evaluated and they are considered in terms of how the social, cultural and religious lives of South Asians impact on them in schools. Given that it is the South Asian Muslims that underachieve and that the schools and teachers are partly implicated in this, it is not unimaginable that the home environment is potentially lacking in some areas too. Acknowledging their often lower social class positions, encouragement on the part of South Asian Muslim parents towards their children's education is strong but it appears that apart from factors associated with diminished levels of cultural capital there are wider religio-cultural issues impacting on the Muslim groups and they need to be fully elaborated upon.

Studies carried out in the 1980s on the education of young South Asian Muslim women showed that progressive attitudes towards further and higher education were found in all the South Asian groups; however, there was still concern on the part of some Muslim parents that their daughters might go 'astray'. Other studies on choosing certain educational paths found that it was only the 'uninformed [South Asian] fathers' who insisted their Muslim daughters not to carry on with education (Shaikh and Kelly, 1989). Overwhelmingly, 1980s research on South Asian Muslims in education, and the impact of parents, found some reticence in permitting daughters to continue in education after a certain age. In this study, it was found that the young South Asian women were as likely to be encouraged to achieve in education as the men, if not more. Throughout the 1990s, in an increasingly competitive educational environment, young South Asian women have accelerated ahead of the men in all subject areas and at both GCSE and 'A' Level.

As a result of a distinct cultural orientation towards education, studies of Sikh mothers have shown a strong aspiration for professional status occupations for their children. Sikh women have been established in English society much longer than their South Asian Muslim peers, and based on different economic and social distinctions Indian women as working mothers provide a more positive influence (Bhachu, 1991). Furthermore, because of certain caste differences, the *Thekedhars* may be more employment orientated compared with higher caste Sikhs for whom educational success is seen to be of greater importance. Further research in this area has found that young Sikh women do indeed pursue education for the purposes of 'marriagability' (Gibson and Bhachu, 1988; Berrington, 1996). Religious codes of practice and behaviour, on the other hand, compel Muslims to Islam. It results in extra demand to ensure that children learn the basic systems of Islamic belief, and if deemed appropriate, in religious supplementary classes after school (Joly, 1989; Parker-Jenkins, 1995; Osler and Hussain, 1995; Ghuman, 1997). In general, the views of parents reflect their social class, education levels and take-up of religion. Muslims generally tend to be stronger adherents of religion irrespective of social class or school effect. Most Hindus and some Sikhs are often less religious irrespective of social class or the effect of the school. As such, there are particular implications for South Asian Muslims in schools and colleges in the city of Birmingham.

The desire to succeed in education is in part determined by the influence of parents who, it seems, have different levels of access to knowledge of the way in which success is best acquired. Many Muslims enter their local schools in the inner city. These schools are under-resourced and teaching tends to be significantly inferior in quality in comparison to the selective schools (though comprehensive schools make up 92 per cent of all schools). It could be said that the reason for Muslim educational underachievement is founded on a range of factors. That is, it is not just their prevailing economic and social circumstances but the educational disadvantage is also based on the way in which the religion of Islam and its followers have been 'demonised' in society. It has the effect of making everyday British Muslims become increasingly regarded by majority society as a threat or distinctly hostile to western norms and values. It has implications for the ways in which British South Asian

Muslims are perceived and how they relate with individuals in the host society such that more recently formed negative perceptions based on religion add to and reinforce the pre-existing ethnicisation and the emergence of an increasing radicalisation of some South Asian Muslims.[5] The experience is part of a complex form of cultural and structural racism affecting Muslim groups in wider society. At the same time, debate on what it means to be British and/or English is at the fore.[6]

In determining whether it is parents or teachers that are the most significant in the educational achievements of South Asians it was found that the outcome depended on the type of South Asian group in question as well as the effects of schools. All South Asian groups wished for success but it was apparent that there was a clear divergence between the experiences of Muslims (Bangladeshi and Pakistani) in relation to Indians (Hindu and Sikh). This foundation rests on cultural capital and social class differences between South Asian groups, considering too the ways in which religion and culture affects each group. Hindus have largely integrated into society, whereas South Asian Muslims in British society have been increasingly regarded, particularly since the early 1990s, as the outsiders-within. Ethnicity and cultural capital impact on the education of South Asians *within*, the effects of schools, the impact of teachers and social class impact the education of South Asians *without*. It is important to explore these and other wider issues from the perspectives of teachers so as to develop a holistic picture of experience and perception.

titudes and Behaviours of Teachers

The way in which teachers perceive pupils and students and behave towards them is critical to education. Teachers, based on their norms and values, form a perception of the *other* through a process of characterisation. Relations, however, have been found to be compounded at the level of the ethnic minority pupil and the white teacher (Wright, 1986; Gillborn, 1990; CRE, 1992). It is important, for this reason, to determine how the teachers in this study see South Asians, work together with them and where issues emerge develop appropriate home–school links to improve communications between pupils, parents and schools ultimately raising the academic performance of pupils and students.

Findings from research have revealed that the educational development paths of young Bangladeshi and Pakistani women are often divergent from men, in essence because of factors associated with the religio-cultural norms and values of certain South Asians and the negative perceptions of teachers. It is important, therefore, to explore the areas of difference between young Muslim and non-Muslim men and women in education. In essence, the reasons for the diametrically opposed experiences of young Bangladeshi and Pakistani men and women compared with Indian Sikhs and Hindus, in particular, as seen through the views and opinions of teachers.

Gender, culture and British South Asian Islam

The policy at Psi Grove School is for young Muslim men to be provided every encouragement to pursue their religion, particularly at times of calendar activity. The ability of young Muslim men to be in a position to practise their faith was thought to be celebrated by the school. A senior Indian teacher [14] at Psi Grove School spoke on the matter,

> With Muslim boys because of their prayers, etc., you might find that they go off as a group on Friday lunchtime to do their prayer at the local mosque but I think as a school in general we try and encourage them to talk about their religion and the school does provide facilities for them. Muslim boys can go upstairs into a room and say, 'I want to pray'. If a particular group had problems then the school in general would speak to the parents and say look this is interfering with your son's education, etc., and to a large extent, I find that parents back up what we say ... Yes, we are sympathetic to individual groups.

At Longlake School, it was felt that both the young South Asian men and women were achieving on par with others and the school was making positive attempts to work with South Asian parents in reassuring them that the interests of their children were placed first. The deputy headteacher [11] at Longlake send emphasised the way in which South Asian Muslim parents sometimes removed their daughters from school but that it was a phenomenon less significant than in the past. Nevertheless, he highlighted that it was still very possible for some of the young South Asian Muslim women to be taken out of education after compulsory school leaving-age. He said, of the issue,

> I think that's beginning to move. A lot of work goes on, where we do meet that sort of resistance with encouraging parents to accept that actually it's in the interests of their children to move forwards with their own education whether they're boys or girls. I think the issue for us is that the parents for whom that is more of an issue don't send their girls to Longlake in the first place, they send them to all-girls schools. Fall out tends to be 15–16 than maybe post-16, because there are still large numbers of girls disappearing from schools post-15. When I say large number that's just hearsay, I have to be careful of what I say I suppose, but I know from colleagues in all-girls schools that that it is still a significant issue for them.

Furthermore, a deputy headteacher [12] at New Heath School felt that there were specific reasons for the sixth-form's expansion which were more related to issues of gender. The early successes of the school's sixth-form were partly based on the high numbers of young South Asian Muslim women who stayed on to study for their 'A' Levels and GNVQs. He said,

> We have every year increased our numbers of boys even to this year we have a new topic in our IT and that's increased the number of boys wanting to stay with us but I do put that down to a fairly straight forward factor that within the community the only option for our girls is to stay on at New Heath School because parents and family will let them stay at New Heath so they come back to us. If they wish to travel to other schools they wouldn't be allowed to, New Heath School or bust, whereas many of the boys they want to leave the area, they want to travel, they are allowed to travel freely and so they do move out. We are again trying to break a trend, it has been a trend for the boys and many of the bright girls to go to (X, Y or Z) college and they follow trends. But, we have been working hard for the last two years and we are now starting to attract more boys and we are starting to keep some of our brighter pupils so . . .

Where there is disagreement between the interests of the schools in relation to those of certain South Asian Muslim parents, it was felt that matters were improved by 'educating' parents. Attempts were made to bridge the cultural divide separating the religious and cultural norms and values of teachers and schools with those of South Asian parents and their children. This deputy headteacher [12] at New Heath School felt that the withdrawal of some young Bangladeshi and Pakistani women from education was something that was not going to simply disappear. He said,

> We tried very very hard, but I must say with regards the cultural situation of families, I foresee that it isn't until we move into another generation of parents that we may be able to bridge that gap and then I do think that when we've got parents who have been through the process themselves then they will possibly think differently and that sort of different way of thinking will come through to their family. But, they are very honest views that you have to respect . . . and sometimes it's not for us to try and break a very strong cultural view. It is difficult ground sometimes even though our parents and I would attribute this to our success, even though our parents are very respectful of the teachers of this school.

He also spoke about the nature of gender differences in relation to academic performance and explained the underlying reasons for variations. He reiterated that there were real differences between the ways in which young South Asian Muslim men and women were perceived. Specifically, it was argued that wholly opposed social and cultural gender expectations affected individuals. He said,

> I would say that some of the problems we have with our boys are that they approach things in quite an arrogant manner … that they almost feel that they are going to achieve because, 'I want to because of who I am'. I think probably because of my own experiences away from this country as well, it is a cultural situation with some of the boys who were within their families. They are spoilt, looked upon as protégés and leading members of the family. But the girls work, they get their heads down and they work and so many of our girls who aren't even near the ability levels of the boys achieve far better than them because they work jolly hard. One of the main focuses of the school is to raise boys' achievement. However, whatever we do to raise boys' achievements seems to raise girls' at the same time because they respond to any strategies that we are putting forward. They are trying everything now from some single-sex teaching in English, particularly trying to tempt the boys with a different type of literature than the girls; sporting literature and scientific literature which seems to motivate them to stay with a book.

A teacher [8] in an inner-city comprehensive school felt that the behavioural attributes of young South Asian women suggested that they performed better compared with other ethnic minorities. It was stressed that it was due to young women being separated from the specific forms of socialisation experienced by young men. This differentiation, it was argued, revealed itself in the form of outcome variations between ethnicities and genders. She said,

> I mean girls are outperforming boys across racial divides. I mean it's the biggest hot story at the moment and again questions have been asked as to why. I know that African-Caribbean boys are the highest excluded whereas I cannot think of a girl that has been excluded in five years here. So, the behaviour problems don't seem to be there for all girls.

A senior lecturer at St Margaret's College [23] believed that the Pakistani students were especially active in taking certain approaches to issues when they arise. It was argued that the South Asian Muslim students were inclined to congregate closely around the Islamic society at the college. It is maintained that gender differences were being played out, often in the name of religion but, in fact, informed by South Asian culture. She said,

> We have one group of students here who have their own student organisation, and that's the Muslims, and there are two things that have happened here. One is that there is a very active Islamic society, which takes place on Wednesday afternoon and when anything is asked of ethnic minority students they are always very vocal and very well-organised too and in fact students in elections sometimes vote for community groups. But the other thing that they have is that we've got prayer facilities here now and we had a lot of hassle about that two years ago. It used to be very informal. People would ask us if they could use our room and it was rotated and now we have prayer facilities in what used to be a changing room and I have never been in there but students have a certain amount of material in there and as they've got a priority on that area. But, it's not always been terribly satisfactory from the girls' point of view. I have a bit of a problem in terms of my own ideas about gender, e.g., I let students use this room for an Islamic society meeting and I come past and I see that all the girls are at the back, behind a screen. Or the boys told the principal when he came in that, 'it was alright – the girls didn't need any prayer facilities!'

The deputy headteacher [11] at Longlake School believed that there were some concerns with, in particular, how young Pakistani men behaved. There was unease about how they conducted themselves and how they related to teachers. It was stressed that this was a cultural phenomenon and not religious. He disclosed,

> There are still one or two issues with some of the Muslim boys about Muslim women teaching that one might not be too happy with if one were a good Muslim in terms of the level of respect, but I think that's more about culture than it is about religion and that's again something that continues to raise its head. That the kids use a religious tag for prejudices and behaviour traits that are nothing to do with Islam, that are to do with attitudes and behaviour which are social constructs, and that's very disappointing but we continue to challenge those behaviours and try and move people forward in their understanding ...

An African-Caribbean headteacher [7] from an inner-city comprehensive school was in no doubt why there was a recent rise in *all* young women outperforming the men in his school. He had a simple explanation, remarking,

> At the moment, we see girls doing a lot better then boys and this is no accident. Society whatever 'race', culture, background we come from, we have been very sexist in our arrangements and so we will place a tighter reign on our girls, greater control and greater freedom to our boys, etc. I am afraid our boys are beginning to misuse that freedom when they should be working; when they should be compensating and seeking to compensate for the problems which schools present their way. They are exploring, taking advantage of this greater freedom, which they have over girls. Yes, without a doubt, they're not roaming the streets as the boys are doing so, they're at home bored so they turn to their books [laughs] . . . mmm . . . that will be the answer.

In the survey of teachers, a range of noteworthy views on South Asian pupils and students by different genders were discovered. Seventy-one per cent [44/64] of teachers either 'strongly agreed' or 'agreed' with the sentiment, 'fathers are more restrictive with girls and less with boys'. Interestingly, only seven per cent [4/62] 'disagreed' or 'strongly disagreed' with this notion. Forty-three per cent [26/61] 'strongly agreed' or 'agreed' with the sentiment that, 'Asian girls perform better than boys', although 49 per cent [30/61] remained 'uncertain'. Furthermore, 72 per cent [42/58] and 69 per cent [44/64] were 'uncertain' about the statements, 'Indian girls perform best of all' and 'Pakistani boys perform worst of all'. Finally, here, 32 per cent of teachers [20/63] 'disagreed' or 'strongly disagreed' with the notion, 'Pakistani and Bangladeshi girls will be removed from schooling at the age of sixteen' – with 52 per cent [33/63] remaining 'uncertain'.

When questioned in relation to the religious norms and values of different South Asians, teachers largely provided positive answers. For example, 94 per cent of teachers [61/65] agreed that, 'we should respect all religions for their intrinsic values' (A number of statements provided to teachers contained anti-Islamic undertones in an attempt to discern whether teachers might allow themselves to be ensnared. In reality, it appears that teachers were aware of the angle of questioning and conceivably hesitated from answering insensitively. It could also be a reflection of the genuine attempts made by teachers to ensure that the religion, culture, norms and values of different South Asians are respected and valued rather than negated or neutralised.) Furthermore, 88 per cent of teachers [52/64] 'disagreed' or 'strongly disagreed' with the notion, 'pupil religion and culture ought to be left at home'. Similarly, 69 per cent [44/64] of teachers 'disagreed' or 'strongly disagreed' with the notion, 'the domestic situation of all Asians is problematic for effective schooling'. In relation to questions concerning Muslims and Islam itself, however, 68 per cent of teachers [42/62] either 'agreed' or were 'uncertain' about the idea that, 'Muslim pupils/students are more confused about their identity', although 37 per cent of teachers [24/64] 'disagreed' or 'strongly disagreed' with the statement, 'Islam is a particularly dogmatic religion'. Teachers largely disagreed that religious differences between South Asians affected their education and for the most part provided positive views about all religious groups. On the whole, it would seem that teachers remained reluctant about labelling one religious group more or less academically able than another, irrespective of the fact that there were observable differences in achievements by different South Asian groups.

The attitudinal responses from teachers to questions of performance difference between South Asians, based on religion and gender, show a range of interesting sentiments. In some instances a great deal of attention is being paid to the demands placed upon schools and colleges by Muslim students for prayer and organisational influence. In one of the colleges, it was considered that the Muslim students were finding themselves an identity through their college society but also through incidents and situations where there are still issues of integration (both acceptance and adaptation). But the striking observation on the part of inner-city teachers is the extent to which young South Asian women are taken out of education at a certain age. Although, in many cases, it is found that young South Asian women are beginning to make an impact, considering too how their academic performance, in strict terms, is racing ahead of the young men, it is true that South Asian parents and the community structures in which they live prevent a certain number from getting on. In relation to the young men, their attitudes towards the schools and teachers and their behaviour in class caused some concern for teachers. They believed this expression of masculinity was getting in the way of their education. These were specific problems for both the pupils and the teachers in schools. On the whole, teachers were positive or neutral about the religion of Islam itself, separating it from the cultural issues that often impact Bangladeshis and Pakistanis more so.

The attitudes of teachers towards South Asian educational performance show that they largely presented the view that ethnicity did not matter in the educational achievement of individuals *or* groups; rather it was more a factor of teacher enthusiasm and how well schools were equipped. Sixty-eight per cent of teachers 'agreed' or 'strongly agreed' with the notion that 'performance is not a factor of ethnicity, but of the school/college and the ability of its teachers'.

Socialisation and the issue of language: a cultural-deficit interpretation

In-groups, out-groups

An important area of study is the extent to which differences in the social, political and religio-cultural characteristics of South Asian groups reveal themselves in educational settings. The area of focus here is on issues of socialisation, intra-group tensions and language use.

When pupils first start in secondary school, there are limited opportunities for ethnic minorities to cluster together along same-ethnicity lines. It is during later school years that group characteristics begin to take shape and pupils of similar backgrounds and interests come together. Such group formations rest also on extracurricula activities in which pupils do or do not play a part (especially young South Asian Muslim women). It was argued by teachers that some South Asian parents refrained from letting their daughters accompany their white friends to outside-of-school activities.[1] A senior teacher [16] from Rosebud School said,

They [young South Asian women] get round in groups and it's quite obvious, yes, I think that's something a lot of people have noticed. I noticed it in the sixth-form because I see them socialise in the common room but they do tend to sit around in groups. They do tend to move round the campus in groups but then I suppose they are easily identifiable like that and they do have friends from other ethnic backgrounds. I think some of it depends on how restrictions operate on mixing out of school. I have come across that with a girl in the sixth-form where there has been a problem. If they do have friends from other backgrounds but they are not allowed to go out into town with them on a Saturday afternoon so they tend to be excluded from their social [peer] group. So I guess they tend therefore to group with their own [ethnic] group.

At Psi Grove School, it was claimed, however, that the young South Asian men mixed easily with other pupils of different ethnicities. Group clustering along ethnic lines was not considered to be a significant feature as teachers found pupils to socialise in mixed ethnicity settings. The lack of a simple pattern led a senior Indian teacher [14] to suggest seniores variability as the norm. He stated,

> It varies a lot actually. You'll find that one year the Asians tend to stay together in groups, other years you find that they mix quite well. The classrooms in the sixth-form, there are small groups. You do get an Asian group sitting round one table in my physics class but it doesn't mean they don't mix with the others. They get on quite well with the others. It's a friend thing more than anything...

An interesting observation made by one senior teacher was on the characteristics of South Asian pupils entering his inner-city comprehensive school. Through the tight-knit natures of community structures, South Asian Muslims were thought to be culturally disadvantaged in education. It was contended that some families were spatially too closely located and participated in religio-cultural activities deleterious to the educational needs of their children (the 'downside' of social capital). Effectively, it was suggested that the Muslim groups did not possess adequate levels of 'capital' – economic, cultural and social. On the whole, there is a distinct element of wanting to encourage South Asian Muslims to make greater efforts to help with their education. There is less of a focus on school structures and what it could do to alleviate matters from the deputy headteacher at Longlake School [11], however. He said,

> This is not a racist perception. It's a practical view. Children have exposure to learning experiences through visits and things like that, which are simply not part of the cultural behaviour of people within South Asian culture, where family and visiting family and being with family and holidays with family is the focus as opposed to going on visits to places. In the more successful South Asian children, it's changes in their pre-school and family behaviour that's actually making some of the difference so parents are taking them to museums and trips to places to broaden their experience and understanding and have got some of the understanding of what's needed pre-five, because it's the pre-five that's making the difference. So when we have, a significant proportion of our year seven [age 12] in terms of

their behaviour are still seven or eight and it's that child's development. It's almost backwardness...

In the social spaces at St Margaret's College, it was felt South Asians students were segregated from the majority white students. The reason for this largely stemmed from the way in which the college is physically shaped, such that separate spaces are identifiable and therefore easily monopolised by different ethnic minority and white groups regarding the territory as their own exclusive social domains. The vice principal [21] at St Margaret's College elaborated on gender and ethnicity differences between students in relation to how they socialised at the college, but was confident to point out that in class South Asian students mixed well with others. He said,

> Right, sure. I think student socialisation is not perfect. What do I mean by perfect? Its quite good within classes, in a way, it's a bit of my liberal view on that. I mean for starters, in 'A' Level Chemistry, the girls sit on one side and the boys on the other side. I am trying and laughing at that, I thought we'd moved on from the 1990s [laughs] so if I can't even get the genders to mix then...But, it is a great joy in Chemistry that I see on a table white students and ethnic minority students and a mix of genders, I only see it occasionally. Outside the classrooms, we have not got a social mixing of the sort that in an ideal world you would like – so we have two canteens and I hate it but one tends to be a white canteen and one tends to be a black canteen.

A St Margaret's College lecturer [20] felt that there were educational as well as social complexities with a number of the Muslim students. The respondent commented on some of the genuine student dilemmas faced in the college. He felt that 'problems' with the South Asian Muslims did not tend to revolve around scholastic performance but were more because of social divisions. He said,

> It has been known for quite some time that its the Bangladeshi community that don't tend to do so well and the other thing I think I have reasonable grounds for saying is that we do tend to perhaps think more nowadays of the Pakistan or Muslim community, we are having slightly more problems with those now, not necessarily academically but more from the social side of college.

In further discussions on the differing social relations between South Asians, the vice principal [21] of St Margaret's College talked about an incident involving different South Asian groups. The comment below provides an insight into the dynamics of social relationships between students, based here on religion, masculinity and sexuality. He stated,

> At the moment, we do have a very strong Islamic Society in the college – I would think that's right. I think it is a learning process that I am going through for somebody like myself who has decided to reject most of the tenets of any religion. I am still learning how important this is but then it's where we're dealing with quite a difficult situation at the moment whereby a Sikh student having been taunted by a Muslim student over two or three weeks for being gay then made a statement which was defamatory about the Qur'an. It has lead to activities outside the college as well as within and those are difficult situations to deal with, particularly to deal with well and to deal with in ways that show that we respect everybody.

Language issues

Teachers often suggested that a lack of proficiency in the use of English by some South Asian Muslim groups added to their limited educational advancements. Teachers believed difficulties with use of the English language hindered the educational progress of some South Asian pupils. They assumed that it came into being because children conversed in their own South Asian languages and dialects at home or that they do not speak English with their parents well enough (this is a well-worn functionalist argument in relation to the adaptation and integration of ethnic minorities into society – the argument holds as ethnic minorities fully assimilate, discrimination is considerably eliminated and a healthier democracy develops). The headteacher [13] at Omega High School talked about the method of selection for her independent school and referred to certain remarks made by teachers concerning the language proficiencies of potential pupils. She said,

> I sit with my head of maths and head of English who are the two people who spend a fortnight of their time going through every script and I hear the discussions that take place and the only discussions that you could pick up on is where we have a reference from the school that will make a comment about language. Now the nature of the selection is such that the girls we are looking at are fluent in English, full stop. Sometimes there will be a reference from the primary

school saying another language is spoken at home but I mean that is actually discussed in favour of the girl in that if she were a border line girl for a place here and we knew that English was not her first language, if say her English mark was slightly lower than her maths mark, the discussion would go somewhere along the lines of, 'well that's not surprising is it? I'm sure we can work on that provided the rest is very strong'. So, I think any comments that could be attributed to 'race' actually operate positively, but that's my perception as a white person in a white culture.

Teachers from the selective schools were sure that language problems were not confined to South Asians. It was argued that a limited use of English, regardless of ethnicity, was reflective of *all* impoverished groups in society. The first comment below is from a teacher at Rosebud School and the second from a senior teacher at Psi Grove School. They said,

[16] I find talking anecdotally, I am aware of some children coming in the first years...because I teach history in the first years as well...the language is a problem although that's not exclusively true of Asians, it's true for white children...because the selection tests are based on numeracy skills by and large rather than literacy skills.

[14] The school tries; we do have help from outside the school to help kids who have problems with language, etc. I think that applies to whether you are an English kid or an Asian kid, there are English kids whose spelling or written work is pretty poor so they get help just as much as an Asian kid would.

In the comprehensive schools, language issues were considered *a priori* in the educational underachievement of South Asians. An inner-city schoolteacher [3] supported the prevailing view that the reason why South Asian pupils possessed a restricted use of English was because it was not practised within the home at the necessary level or depth. She said, 'a lot of the children don't speak any English at home, they've got satellite TV but they are watching Asian channels and listening to Urdu or Bengali at home'. These are strong behavioural assumptions and they are based effectively on the limited perspective teachers have of young South Asians in their homes. Discovering limitations in the use of English, this teacher argues that a range of cultural and religious activities take precedence within the home, rather than to focus on poverty, social exclusion and economic marginalisation which all create a number of inequalities. Arguments in relation to language are code for differential attitudes towards ethnic minorities based on a considered class-consciousness. All the same, many of the teachers in the inner-city schools were convinced that a lack of English was central in their under-achievement (although strongly disputed by parents and professionals, Abbas, 2003b). The deputy headteacher at Longlake School [11] felt it was important for primary schools to work hard to ensure that, on leaving them, South Asian pupils attain satisfactory levels of mathematics and English to endow them with the vital skills necessary for an effective secondary schooling. The comment indicates the extent to which a limited exposure to literature exposes further disadvantage for certain South Asian pupils. He said,

> There are a significant proportion whose reading age is below their chronological age so again the modal value for reading age is still around nine and, if anything it has continued to drop a little bit, which is quite disappointing really because the context of the amount of effort that's going into reading and literacy in primary school would suggest that it ought to be improving but it's still rocking along the bottom.

The deputy headteacher [12] at New Heath School, moreover, was certain that language issues were central to any potential problems faced by the South Asian Muslim pupils in school. A lack of fluency was considered more the predicament than the perceived limited use of the English language. He said,

> I would talk about fluency here which is still a big problem, which still holds back many of our pupils. Fluency – is something that we are constantly working on – to break down those barriers but it is very difficult. I would say that still 90 per cent plus of our pupils are now speaking English at home, so it's not so much the understanding, it's the fluency of expression... Fluency of English is a problem and it's something that we are aware of, all staff are aware of and people are constantly trying to look at strategies of improving. If you walk around the school now you will see somewhere various English expressions posted up on walls and in classrooms. I think the last one was 'r' in February, so there's always something going on to assist those language difficulties. But yes, it's a major factor.

In terms of how South Asian socialisation patterns were viewed by teachers, in the selective schools it was felt that on the whole all the pupils mixed well, especially in the boys' schools and slightly less so in the girls' schools. In the comprehensive schools, South Asian children were thought to lack exposure to various cultural and social experiences and this limited their development in education at an early age. In the further education colleges, it was thought that there were distinctly observable cases of social, cultural, religious and gender identities being played out. In all these instances, it was regarded that issues arose with the South Asian Muslim students more so. Behavioural and socialisation differences are related to structural and social inequalities compounded by religious, cultural and economic alienation experienced by South Asian Muslims.

Use of English by ethnic minorities and South Asians was considered to be an important factor in almost all the different forms of education in this study. In the fee-paying selective school, the headteacher argued that pre-assessed problems with English would not perturb a more rounded consideration of an application to the school by ethnic minorities. In the grammar schools, language issues were thought to arise in all poor, disadvantaged pupils. In the comprehensive schools, however, significant language issues were considered to have emerged with great efforts being made on the part of schools to eradicate the problem. In particular, an emphasis is made on both expression and fluency of language.

For teachers in this study, one of the main ways in which South Asians differ, given the social class of respondents and the type of school, is in the way in which groups manage to acquire the necessary language skills. Most inner-city schoolteachers argued that they understood the multiple-disadvantage that certain pupils, invariably South Asian Muslims, were 'bringing with them to schools' and, over time, they believed they were working hard to alleviate insufficiencies through proactive measures. Nevertheless, it is also apparent that there is a particular focus on language issues which remains a cause for concern. Attention is being paid to apparent 'deficiencies' in group characteristics rather than to the structure of schools and the functioning of teachers.

Teacher ethnicity and antiracist-multiculturalism: policy and practice

A wider analysis of how teachers impact on the education of South Asians through school policy is developed. First, it is important to elaborate upon the ethnicity of the teacher to determine how the view *other* ethnic minority teachers in the profession. Second, teacher expectations of South Asian pupils are evaluated to demonstrate the ways in which teachers affect children. Third, the ethos of the school is scrutinised assessing the ways in which antiracist multicultural education policies are implemented and to what precise effect.

Ethnic minority teachers

Much research evidence exists to show the extent to which South Asians apply disproportionately less for teacher training degrees compared with their white peers. Other research has found ethnic minority teachers have been significantly under-represented in mostly white schools (Ranger, 1988). It has also been recognised that some second-generation South Asian teachers experience overt racism from pupils and parents in all-white schools and sometimes prefer to work in inner-city comprehensive schools that contain more ethnic minorities (Ghuman, 1995). This research asked teachers to what extent the ethnicity of the teacher mattered given the high proportions of pupils and students from South Asian groups found in many of secondary schools and further education colleges in this study.

At the time of the study a number of South Asian and ethnic minority teachers were visible in the comprehensive schools. The deputy headteacher [11] at Longlake School maintained that, until recently, teachers from the ethnic minorities were not applying to the school. He felt that over time, however, the trend was in the process of reversing. He said,

> The reality is that as more people get trained, the opportunity to appoint teachers from an ethnic background, that's appropriate to the needs of our kids, becomes more the case and we do have more teachers from South Asian background teaching in school now: in a wide range of roles, from science teachers through to obviously people teaching Urdu. We also have different teachers in maths, English, a whole range of curriculum areas now so things are beginning to move forward there as well.

A senior Indian teacher [14] at Psi Grove School deemed that it was misguided to target ethnic minorities to fill teaching posts – the merit of the individual was considered more important. Almost all the teachers from the selective schools echoed this particular sentiment. It was based on the notion, that in strong schools, effective teachers were more important irrespective of the ethnic make-up of the school or as part of a policy to produce role models for otherwise disadvantaged South Asian or ethnic minority groups. He said,

> People will say that having an Asian teacher is a very good role model for Asian kids here. And maybe we should have a teacher from the West Indian community as well but I think you should only appoint an individual if they are good enough to cope with this kind of atmosphere and teaching environment. You shouldn't just appoint someone because of their colour and I am a firm believer in that, but I believe in equal opportunities, etc. But, it shouldn't just be well we are lacking an Asian because the percentage is slightly low in terms of pupil–teacher ratio, that shouldn't be the case because I think it does backfire on the individual as well. If they can't teach in this kind of environment they'll find it very difficult.

Problems encountered in attempting to recruit from the ethnic minorities were further emphasised by the headteacher [13] at Omega High School. She believed that perhaps out of a fear of teaching in the independent sector or because they did not think that they stood any chance of appointment success some ethnic minorities were reluctant to make applications. She said,

> One must assume that if nobody is applying they must be deterred. Now why are they deterred? There must be difficulty in that I think a lot of men are to an extent put off from applying to an all girls school, full stop...so that's a whole section cut out and perhaps one could argue that in the South Asian community...So you're left with a smaller group in any case. I have interviewed South Asians that have got to that level, they weren't as good as the white women that I saw...probably weren't as good on paper and didn't... [Hesitation]...Certainly, the applications are not there...that makes a difference.

Teacher expectations

A second area where teacher roles are in question is in their expectations of ethnic minority pupils (cf. Brittan, 1976; Hurrell, 1995). The issues here exist more in the sometimes hidden assumptions and unwitting actions of teachers rather than in direct face-to-face racism. One place where it was manifest is in the selection of 13+ subject choices.

The teachers from the inner-city comprehensive schools, where the preponderance of pupils are Bangladeshi and Pakistani South Asian

Muslims, argued that if 'unwittingly racist' teachers were to apply for posts and be selected they would find teaching in such a climate an overly demanding experience. A senior teacher [1] from an inner-city comprehensive school said,

> ['Racist' teachers] tends to happen less in schools like this because the staff tend to be more educated in terms of the area, the needs, the cultural background. They happen to be more understanding. I think it happens more in the typical white middle-class school.

Similarly, some schools had progressed in their rationalisation of the potential impact of negative expectations on the part of would-be new teachers. The stance of the deputy headteacher [11] at Longlake School was characteristic of many of the senior teachers. He argued,

> I think we've now got a body of staff who really do understand... I mean the lives that most of our children live are still a long way removed from the experiences of most of the staff, other than those who come from...well even some of those who come from the South Asian background...because often teachers of a South Asian background come from a very different socio-economic group to our kids. But I think we've got no teachers left for whom it's a completely alien concept and the understanding is most of the staff here or joining us take on board fairly quickly the understanding that they need to understand where the kids are coming from.

This position was expressively reaffirmed by the deputy headteacher [12] at New Heath School. He reasoned that in a vibrant school, which aimed to be progressive in its approach towards ethnic minorities, a positive outlook on the part of the teacher facilitated an active learning environment that remained encouraging for teachers, parents and pupils. He said,

> You go into some schools and you will hear people talking about 'teacher expectations', expecting people to do well, well the expectations of teachers here are natural now, they are high. The culture of this school is that we expect the pupils to do well. That's the culture of the school. No I think that's the big difference between this school and lots of other schools where they will say they expect pupils to do well and they are working towards it but this school has been working towards it for a long time now and I think it's part of

the culture here. It is expected that the kids will do well, it is expected and that's the way the teachers deliver. They demand high standards of achievement, high standards of discipline but at the same time the whole system here revolves around mutual self respect; the kids respected, they respect the teachers, its not a prison they've got lots of freedom here ... but they are expected to do well.

He remained positive about the general approach taken by the school and confirmed the effect it was having on pupils. It was stated teachers at school were thought to be informed and respectful of all the religions and pupils, and as a result pupils responded positively. Staff numbers also reflected the diversity of pupils. He said,

I would say that fortunately our staff body are also knowledgeable and we do appreciate the situation and yes we do close for Eid ... we do tend to plan our teacher training days around Eid, we do allow our teacher colleagues of whatever culture or religion to have their festivals away from us, whether it be a Sikh, Jewish or Muslim festival we will respect that and give colleagues time to be with their families and it's a natural part of the school ... There is always a deep respect for religion and culture within the school and I think the pupils and the parents respect that very much and although we haven't got a huge majority of staff who aren't from this country we do have a reasonable diversity of staff with us – and staff who have travelled widely and brought with them to the school that level of knowledge of other people and other cultures which is somewhat possibly lacking in this country generally speaking. So, I think we are quite lucky in that respect. In assemblies and tutorials you will always get an appreciation of other religions and cultures ...

Performance-enhancing teachers

An evolving view from teachers was that as teacher performance becomes increasingly measured in output terms it is in the interests of the teacher to ensure success for all pupils as it impinges on the achievements of the whole school. The vice principal [21] at St Margaret's College put the point thus,

Yeah, I hope teachers don't have closed minds but in any community there will be bigots. I think that we question, we hope to understand and I think those are honourable reasons. Cynical reasons: we want a job and if we treated relationships between students in an unsympathetic, unfeeling, clod-hopping way, then the atmosphere in the college would go down. That quickly gets around, applications would drop and we'd lose our jobs. Now that is a very cynical view but it is the self-preservation view.

The views of teachers in relation to attitudinal statements regarding their roles in a multicultural setting, based on the day-to-day educational management issues that arise from working with differentiated ethnic minorities, show the extent to which they are attempting to make a genuine difference. Ninety-five per cent of teachers [64/67] 'agreed' or 'strongly agreed' with the statement, 'the school/college tries to encourage the understanding of all cultures and religions'. In addition, 91 per cent of teachers [59/64] 'strongly agreed' or 'agreed' with the statement, 'it is always important to help disadvantaged groups in education' and 78 per cent [52/67] of teachers 'agreed' or 'strongly agreed' with the view that, 'reducing achievement inequalities is an important policy of the school/college'. The above sentiments reveal that the attitudes of teachers towards South Asians are developmental rather than in any way tentative or unresolved (it may, however, have resulted out of a desire to respond defensibly in relation to ethnic minorities and education. This should not be disregarded). The responses, nonetheless, seem to suggest that teachers were cognisant of the economic, social and ethnic differences between the various South Asian groups and aware of the need to positively improve the lot of otherwise impoverished people.

The views of teachers on wider issues relating to ethnic minorities within schools are interesting to explore. They highlight the position that South Asians need to be considered in schools not as potential areas of difficulty but as individuals with needs and aspirations that ought to be met through 'an evolving system of education'. Ninety-six per cent of teachers [60/63] 'agreed' or 'strongly agreed' with the attitude, 'we have to work hard to ensure that inequalities in education do not remain in the future'. Furthermore, the views of teachers towards South Asians as they enter the education system in the future did not suggest disaster, rather the opposite. Seventy-four per cent of teachers [48/65] 'disagreed' or 'strongly disagreed' with the sentiment, 'I think Asian children are increasingly going to be a problem for schools to deal with'. Moreover, 69 per cent of teachers [46/66] 'disagreed' or 'strongly disagreed' with the idea that, 'as the number of Asians increase in school, so will our problems'. The impressions gained from responses to these statements suggest that teachers felt it was important to be aware of the difficulties facing South Asians in school and in society and how schooling can be ameliorated. Indeed, the overwhelming majority, 96 per cent of teachers, agreed with the sentiment, 'we have to work hard to ensure that inequalities in education do not remain in the future'. Teachers largely agreed that ethnic minority applications to teaching posts were limited, particularly in the selective education sector. In general here, the idea of meritocracy was considered more important than appointing on the basis of generating some kind of 'ethnic balance' of staff. In the comprehensive schools, it was considered that 'racist teachers' would (a) not apply in the first instance and (b) not survive the climate. For the most part, teachers argued that they were respectful of religions and cultures and worked as well as they could in a competitive education market.

An evolving system of education

Control at the core

The current structure of the education system is affected by the characteristics of a national curriculum, testing at all ages, league tables and performance indices. The headteacher [2] at an inner-city comprehensive school expressed it succinctly, 'if the national curriculum says that you have to have English history then you have to do English history ... end of story'.

An African-Caribbean headteacher [7] felt that the national curriculum necessarily maintained a Eurocentric bias which required development in the pursuit of a more effective antiracist multicultural education policy. It was believed that there were parts of the curriculum that continued to celebrate the past imperial and colonial history of the British and, as such, remained outmoded. This progressive headteacher talks about how he places aspects of a wider history and worldview into the school timetable, incorporating the successes and achievements of otherwise unrecognised ethnic minorities. He said,

> The actual planned curriculum, even though the national curriculum dictates what we teach, we have to find ways of penetrating that to make sure that it's not purely Eurocentric and that we contextualise whatever it is – European, in with other third-world contributions, in almost any discipline, whether it's maths, science, history, geography, whatever it is. We can find the leadership to parallel anything that white Europe can come up with and we want all our youngsters to be proud of that and to see that they are worth something.

A junior teacher [3] from an inner-city comprehensive school reiterated the idea that a curriculum existed largely to follow a narrowly defined line of content. She alluded to the bias and what are regarded as real omissions to the curriculum. Often, content concentrated on Britain's past and did not reflect the diverse multicultural history or the experiences of present-day realities. The use or non-use of certain literature was an example highlighted. She said,

> I think that the curriculum is *not* particularly unbiased. If you look at history what do they study? A lot is taken from the European perspective not from other countries. You only see the white side really – in the books that are used in Britain. You are not seeing the slaves' perspective of black history or whatever. The history that I suppose that taught us even India in this country, it was the English perspective, not the other side of people going in and taking over. I think that a lot of curriculum has hidden racism. You in England, the literature you look at is Shakespeare, you look at the Bronte sisters, you look at Jane Austin, you are looking at all these traditional great English writers and you're not representing great writers from other cultures.

Marketisation

The limitations faced by South Asian pupils are built into an education system that has become increasingly centralised. Pupils and students select subjects within constraints (see Chapter 5). Examinations taken by pupils and students are also another example of transformation taking place in the education system. The General Certificate of Education 'Ordinary' (GCE 'O' Level) and Certificate of Secondary Education (CSE) systems amalgamated to form the single GCSE system in 1987, while traditional 'A' Level examinations have almost entirely been replaced by modular testing. Moreover, vocational qualifications and alternative routes into higher education have been established through schemes such as the GNVQ and the development of access courses. Teachers also reported that although more South Asian school pupils and college students obtained GCSEs at 'A' Levels than ever, the higher grades were just as difficult to achieve. Nevertheless, pupils and students were likely to regard such alternative qualifications less positively. There remains a fixation with taking the more recognised GCSEs and 'A' Levels. An inner-city headteacher [9] articulated that, 'vocational qualifications are still seen as the "bronze standard" '.

A science teacher [20] at St Margaret's College talked about the changing system of education. He believed that a change to modular 'A' Levels had invariably helped some of the students to obtain improved grades. He said,

> Many more subjects are now modular and that does seem to give the weaker students more of a chance because they can re-take and it also gives them more of an incentive because if they realise they are nearer to a particular grade they can then sort of maybe work that little bit harder whereas if the exams are all at the end of the two years they don't know how they will do. So we think the modular exams have helped.

Another senior lecturer [23] at St Margaret's College noted how the combination of coursework and modular examinations had helped to improve college educational performance figures. However, it was also argued that too great a dependence on the modular approach may well lead to new problems. She said,

> Most subjects now have either course work or are modular. About a third of the subjects here are modular and most of those have good exam results but that's partly because the people involved in teaching here are not only very dedicated in coming during half term ... but also they are quite involved in examining so they have a really good idea about what goes on. And, I think if the college as a whole went modular I'm not sure whether that would work because students juggle their commitments ... So I think it's very difficult to say but there's not so much of the traditional three hour paper at the end of the two years so I think that is better for students and ... we have one three hour paper which is causing students some difficulties.

Teachers also believed that by South Asian pupils taking additional GCSE subjects in one modern language the results of the school necessarily improved. This was something that was being exploited by the schools. The headteacher [9] of an inner-city comprehensive school put it thus,

> One of the things we find and we celebrate is the fact that we've probably got in mother tongue languages tremendously high levels of achievements, in Urdu and Bengali, and that has an impact on children because it gives them confidence in terms of examination performance but it also gives them qualifications, which they receive.

The above claim was further echoed by two senior teachers from two inner-city comprehensive schools. The statement by the second teacher, however, raises another important question. That is, how far do schools use the will and determination of South Asian pupils to succeed in alternative GCSEs as a justification for not achieving in the more mainstream subjects? It was said,

[2] Our success at Urdu over the last few years has been tremendous ... It's actually kept the C grades of the school buoyant. Without so many Urdu passes, ABC school's results would be probably three to four per cent worse overall.

[9] We've got 11 per cent A–Cs but a lot of those are Urdu, Punjabi or Bengali. We're kidding ourselves if those cloud the issues of why kids aren't performing in the same level as other subjects.

Issues exist in relation to the national curriculum with a number of teachers stating that in its current form it was not entirely suited to the needs and developments of ethnic minority South Asian school pupils and college students. Teachers argued that a Eurocentric bias to the curriculum necessarily remained and it was only through direct measures that it would be possible to engage with, for example, a range of different ethnic literatures. The ways in which the examination systems currently operate makes it easier for all students to perform better and it was thought that the ethnic minority pupils and students were also taking advantage of this. The changing education system provides greater flexibility and opportunity for the South Asians whose improvement in performance as a result of changes to the examinations system were equal to, if not better than, their white peers. Furthermore, the study of certain modern languages and religious studies subjects by certain ethnic minorities and South Asians permitted the school to improve upon its overall results. Some teachers felt this was 'kidding' the education system and its pupils. Some teachers did regard this as a potential problem area as schools could use the interest that South Asians have in languages and religious studies to help 'artificially' improve the overall performance of school results.

9
Conclusion

Since the implementation of Education Reform Act in 1988, the changing nature of the education system has led to an increased marketisation of schooling, with the legacy of 14–19 education now in the hands of the New Labour administration set to remain in power for at least three terms. These changes have largely ignored ethnic minorities in the processes of developing policy. Quality schools have become stronger and weaker schools have either been closed down or have been forced to improve in order to survive. At the time of writing, national GCSE results have improved for the twentieth successive year. Although, ethnic minority educational achievements have been improving, currently the best that they have ever been, the gap between successful and unsuccessful ethnic minorities is wider than ever. The aspiration to obtain educational success by both the individuals concerned and because of central government diktats have led to greater efforts being made on the part of *all* pupils, students, parents and teachers. It is without doubt however, that racism does persist in education, particularly in the form of high 'exclusion' rates for African-Caribbeans and the effect of the tiered GCSE examination system which discourages pursuing the higher grades because of placement in lower examination sets. Over the last decade, although GCSE and 'A' Level results have improved for all, it is also apparent that the increase in performance has been significantly lower for various ethnic minority groups, including British South Asian Muslims.

The aim of this study was to explore and analyse the ways in which different South Asian groups perform in different schools and colleges. Based on the evaluation of research into the educational achievements of South Asians in the post-war period as well as the way in which the politics and sociology of research into 'race' and education have been determined, this study has shown how Bangladeshis, Indians and Pakistanis perform because of differences in social class, the effect of schools, religion and culture – permutations and combinations of economic, cultural and social capital. Also fundamental to consider is the overall impact of the schools – their individual *habitus*. Within them, there exist differing teachers with differing aspirations and expectations of themselves, their school in the education system and their pupils. Antiracist education theory suggests that institutional racism, permeated through the actions of teachers and schools, leads to the educational underachievements of certain ethnic minorities and South Asians, wittingly or unwittingly. Multicultural educationists argue that an environment within the home and the educational and social class resources that different ethnic groups possess provides the more relevant explanation for underachievement.

In drawing conclusions, it is essential to identify the causes for differential rates of ethnic minority educational achievement looking at an array of factors inside the home as well as the school based on the data analysed for this study. It is believed that this extensive research and empirical rigour has been both broad as well as multi-layered in determining an understanding of processes of achievement. A summary analysis of the main empirical sections follow: South Asian educational achievement processes in the educational life-cycle, the perennial dichotomy of the school versus the home in the achievements of South Asians and an evaluation of teacher perspectives – those who hold power and act as gatekeepers to the successes and failures of South Asians in education. Taxonomical and theoretical developments emanating from this research are also presented as well as suggestions for further research in this area.

The educational life-cycle

Although this study was concerned with the processes of South Asians in education between the ages of 14–19, it was found that early schooling experiences were nevertheless generally regarded *positively* by most South Asian pupils and students and considered an *enjoyable* experience by the majority of *all* respondents (see Chapter 4). By the fact of later immigration, some of the South Asian Muslims, who came to Britain as young children, found that a negative early start impacted them later on. A few of the Bangladeshi and Pakistani respondents, here, reported that it was difficult to adjust at first. A positive start in education is missing for certain South Asian groups and it affects their later development. For others, positive interaction with other pupils and the teachers in schools was widely acknowledged. It can be seen therefore the extent to which South Asian experiences in education can begin to diverge based on immigration history and incorporation into what is often the 'bottom' of the education system.

In the transition from primary to secondary education, differences were found between South Asians based on social class and the effectiveness of schools. In the transition to selective schooling in particular, the social class background of parents was the most important factor closely followed by adequate preparation for the common entrance examinations. South Asian parents from lower social class positions differed in their attitudes towards selective schooling compared with their middle-class peers. Some of the poorer South Asian parents were encouraged by the idea of selective schooling but felt that they did not possess the financial means to support their children through it. The alternative view was that these schools were intended for other, more affluent, South Asians – a class-conscious perspective. Teachers in the selective schools also indicated that there were high numbers of South Asians sitting entrance tests but inadequate preparation tended to affect *all* candidates as well as South Asians. The issue here relates to a lack of economic, cultural and social capital on the part of certain South Asian groups. Where South Asian groups are in a position to take educational advantage they do so. They are maximising returns on investment in education and have very high aspirations for their children. Working class and poorer South Asians do not always posses the 'capital' and although aspirations remain high there are no means to facilitate the particular forms of educational progress being considered. Selective education remains for the very few.

The question of setting in schools and its effects upon pupils and students was explored in some detail as it is an important way in which the educational experiences of ethnic minority and South Asian pupils differ. In reality, teachers place different pupils in different ability sets based on perceived ability. It has been shown the extent to which this has impacted on individuals who believed they had been placed in sets lower than their abilities would suggest. Moreover, it was found that children were set in various ways, particularly for the national curriculum core subjects and more subtly for others. The way in which pupils are set has considerable ramifications for later educational opportunities. Subtle judgements, on occasions biased against ethnic minorities and South Asians, can make every difference to an individual's subsequent educational development opportunities. In terms of choosing

GCSE and 'A' Level subjects, pupils from all the schools provided the view that they had little choice over GCSE subjects as there appeared to be limited flexibility in the way in which subjects could be chosen. Some South Asian pupils, in particular a number of the Muslims (Bangladeshis, Pakistanis and East African Asians), in both selective and comprehensive schools, took additional modern language or religious studies GCSE subjects, both inside and outside of schools (see Chapter 5). Pupils and students felt they were affected positively and directly by parent stimuli during this process.

It was found that middle-class parents were generally inclined to permit their children and the teachers in the selective schools to decide on GCSE subjects, however. It was South Asian parents with children in comprehensive schools that were more likely to take greater involvement in the subject selections made. It was normally found that the schools were important in this GCSE selection process, but, where possible, parents took the impetus to exert an authourity and in some cases directly influencing their children's choices. Teachers also agreed with the notion that South Asian parents tended to be positively involved in the selection of GCSE subjects. In the survey of teachers, however, it was found that some parents were thought to be somewhat narrow in the choice of their children's GCSEs and 'A' Levels. Overall, South Asian pupils from selective schools picked subjects because of the school's academic ethos – its institutional *habitus*. In the comprehensive schools, vocational courses were taken alongside GCSE subjects. Parents stated that they had endeavoured to ensure that the educational paths taken by their children were as uncomplicated as possible by providing as much as they could. Although it is understood that South Asian parents are strongly motivated for their children to perform well, significant differences emerged, however, with the extent of educational knowledge that parents had. Nonetheless, all parents were strongly motivated for their children, irrespective of their children's gender or religion, with few exceptions. The notion that young South Asian Muslim Bangladeshi and Pakistani women were restricted after compulsory leaving age did emerge significant through pupils, students and teachers. Some of the teachers and some college students, in particular, did highlight instances of being restricted from education. Rather, all young South Asian women are encouraged by parents, with the added pressure to perform than to be removed but there remain genuine instances of some experiencing difficulty and a strong perception on the part of teachers of its existence. As the pupils and students progress above GCSE level (16+), differences are found between the experiences of pupils from selective and comprehensive schools. Reasons for performance disparity in examination results, necessarily, are directly attributable to the effect of schools. In the selective schools, pupils chose to carry on to the sixth-form almost without question. Pupils from selective schools invariably wish to enter elite universities for higher education. There also appears a high preference from pupils in the selective schools to study medicine at university – although not considered very positively by senior teachers and headteachers. Empirical research in this area confirms that medicine is not a particularly good career for ethnic minorities. Both selective and comprehensive school pupils and many of the college students wished to proceed through further education and enter higher education even before contemplating the idea of entering the labour market (see Chapter 6).

Invariably, all the South Asian pupils and students reported that they wished to attend university at some stage. Teachers felt that the South Asian pupils and students were self-assured in selecting their educational paths and were often aiming for the elite universities, given the selective status of some of the schools. Motivation arising out of the wish to be removed from economic and social exclusion led many South Asians to aim high. There were disparities, however, between institutions and social class levels. Less likely were students to attend universities or colleges of higher education further away from home simply because of the cost incurred to the individual. Consequently, universities nearer home were attractive to *all* would-be South Asian degree students. Teachers were aware of the ambitions of South Asian parents and their children who were particularly keen to read science- or medicine-related subjects.

It was the Indians emanating from higher socio-economic positions that were able to take greater advantage of a selective education system, thereby improving their positions. Conversely, Bangladeshis and Pakistanis living in inner-city areas, enter local schools where resources are limited and the infrastructures of schools do not permit the same degree of access to educational and ultimately occupational opportunity.

Responsibilities: parents or teachers?

It has been shown that aspects of culture, religion, socialisation and language act interdependently to construct the educational life-cycle of the young South Asian as a multifaceted experience. Both parents and their children are convinced in their enthusiasm for educational achievement but in the analysis of the question of whether it is parents or teachers that are responsible for the education of South Asians differences are found between groups in their attitudes towards relationships with the school, on the one hand, and, on the other, experiences within the home. Students were more critical of their white teachers and it appeared that most of the negative experiences were mentioned by the South Asian Muslims. Many were concerned by the lack of expectation on the part of teachers and their inability to recognise their potential or needs. These students were critical of their teachers because of their reflexive outlook and increased maturity (as opposed to pupils interviewed in schools who were still experiencing secondary schooling). South Asian parents presented few, if any, direct criticisms of teachers. When the question of teacher ethnicity was raised, however, middle-class South Asian parents wished for effective teachers *per se*, irrespective of ethnicity. Less affluent South Asian parents were in favour of same-ethnicity teachers, especially in their ability to potentially facilitate 'Asian' problems to which white teachers may otherwise be less sympathetic. Pupils and students responded to this question in a similar way. Same-ethnicity teachers were considered useful in situations where certain cases arise, which could be both domestic and school-specific, and not easily recognised or ameliorated by other teachers (see Chapter 7). Middle-class parents stated that they would look first at their own children when it came to actual achievements with South Asian parents from the lower social classes certain that the school would be at fault and not their children. Interestingly, more socially mobile parents negatively regarded other South Asian parents that were not in the fortunate position of raising their standards in the same way. These parents were more likely to directly associate members of their own ethnic minority community with their children's underachievement. They felt that many of these other parents were ill-informed of the ways in which to achieve in education. A genuine shift in class-consciousness emerged in these South Asian parents.

Turning to the home lives of South Asian children and their parents, additional differences were recognised. All South Asian pupils and students alluded to the notion that, given the nature of the religion as well as some of the cultural practices of parents and communities, being a Muslim in advanced Western economies presented complications (see Chapter 7). Young South Asian Muslim women were not only beginning to identify strongly with their religion, in comparison with men, but they also sought to discover a 'proper' Islam rather than the apparently outmoded religio-cultural practices of parents. This identity formation and development led to certain demands made by Muslim pupils and students in *all* the schools and colleges in this study to form active societies and provide, for example, prayer facilities and organisational influence. Religion is important in the school and college lives of South Asian Muslims, inside of school hours and outside too. Muslims were far more likely to have attended after-school supplementary schools. It may explain part of the reason why religion in schools and colleges is in such high demand. It was also ascertained that there were distinct differences between parents on the levels of their religious adherence. The small number of Muslim mothers interviewed reported being the most religious within the home. In general, South Asian Muslim parents are convinced of the values and scriptures of Islam and wished to ensure that the greatest possible depth of knowledge, understanding and application was extended to their children, even if they were less knowledgeable themselves. On the whole, young South Asian Muslim women found ways of working with parents to make them better understand the advantages and opportunities that are generated through education. This is reflected in the significant recent improvements in educational performance by this group although it is far from perfect. Conversely, more socially integrated Hindu parents are sure that their children remain religious but not at all impacting their education at home or at school. Sikh parents ranged in their attitudes towards religion in relation to the social class levels they occupied. More affluent Sikh parents kept their religious and cultural identities intact in the main but their children felt less bound.

Parental motivations are highest among South Asian groups that seek social mobility through the education of their children, nevertheless, underperformance is still apparent and has become the norm for certain South Asian Muslim groups. For South Asian Muslims in Birmingham, their reaction to education is an adaptation to the limited opportunities faced. It leads to disparities between parental and school expectations, fuelling disillusionment, which consequently discourages teachers, parents and pupils. It is the marginalised occupational positions that South Asian immigrants originally found themselves in that are subsequently reproduced for their children in the inner-city areas they continue to live. Certain South Asians receive a limited education because of the unequal structure of contemporary society and the way in which the education system reinforces them. The privileged sustain themselves not only through their own education but also through the *mis*-education of others.

Teachers and their views evaluated

It was relatively clear that many teachers provided encouraging rejoinders to questions in relation to South Asians and their education. The reason was that many of the schools were able to apply 'progressive policies' in order to ameliorate the disadvantaged positions of certain disadvantaged groups, namely the South Asians. Teachers in inner-city comprehensive schools that were more critical of South Asian pupils invariably originated from schools performing significantly lower than citywide and national averages.

In schools, there were issues in the comprehensive schools in relation to the expression of masculinity on the part of some young South Asian men. It is a reaction to their disenfranchised social and economic positions impacting them negatively in education. They regard their futures as limited and thus develop an attitude which does not value the education they receive. These young South Asian Muslim men were thought to display an amalgamation of expressed masculinity combined with certain patriarchal religio-cultural norms and values. For the young South Asian women, teachers argued that they tended to group together and that it was not automatically inside of the classrooms. Outside-of-school socialisation patterns impacted on inside-of-school socialisation patterns and vice versa. For teachers the perception of Islam became associated with gender. In both cases, it is not Islam itself which leads to such assumptions, rather the way in which Islam is practised by some South Asian Muslim groups in Britain and, to an extent, how worldwide events are perceived. British South Asian Islam is organised and facilitated along the cultural practices and structures observed in the sending regions before migration and teachers' perception of Islam is affected by negative media portrayals of wider global events. In a sense, young South Asian Muslims are disadvantaged in education because of the lower social class positions they have inherited as well as the way in which a view of the religion of Islam has been distorted by the popular media and its impact upon people's general awareness of the religion and East–West relations in contemporary episodes of geopolitical history.

Many teachers in the comprehensive schools believed that the use of English was inadequate for many South Asian Muslims, consequently affecting their performance in the classroom. Language use was also found to be an important factor in how South Asian Muslims socialised. Inner-city schoolchildren were thought to lack the ability to express themselves fluently. There is a socio-pathological line to this argument which suggests that the South Asian groups are at fault and it is one used by many of the inner-city senior teachers and headteachers (Abbas, 2003a). In relation to the ethnicity of the teacher, the roles that ethnic minority teachers play in the inner-city comprehensive schools are thought to be important for a number of reasons but in the selective schools it is believed that the overall ability of the teacher matters more than their ethnicity (this view was shared equally by pupils, parents and teachers). Senior teachers and headteachers in selective schools, in particular, are of the view that ethnic minority applications for teaching posts were not forthcoming to their schools. Anecdotal evidence shows the effects of South Asians not opting for education or teacher-training degrees considerably limiting their availability as teachers in the graduate teacher market. When they do emerge, it has been known that they may prefer to teach in inner-city schools in order to empower children from similar backgrounds to themselves or to avoid racism in mainly white schools. Nevertheless, in the current climate, teachers are required to *perform* and it was argued that 'racist' teachers would not be found in inner-city schools because of the demands placed upon them by ethnic minority pupils and their educational needs. The curriculum was still considered to be outmoded and laden with imperial and colonial sentiment, history, literature and worldview. And so it is necessary to make changes to the curriculum to reflect the more recent history of post-war Britain as well as celebrate the successes of otherwise unrecognised ethnic minority historians, poets, artists, explorers, agitators and so on.

Teachers were becoming more aware of the situations of South Asians and are therefore more able to provide the necessary educational resources and environment for pupils. Given the competitive nature of school league table systems, where in the past unwitting racism may well have prevailed, teachers are now far more conscious of addressing such issues – both because of race relations legislation as well as central government drivers.

Taxonomy of South Asians in education

The central hypothesis in this research questioned the process of educational achievements and whether the additional factors of religion and culture are able to explain the way in which the educational achievements of South Asians differ as well as how they bring about the out comes being considered. In reality, disadvantage in educational opportunity is further characterised by social and religio-cultural elements within the behavioural characteristics of certain South Asian groups, given that social class and the effect of schools are recognised as principally important factors. Conversely, it is the advantaged status of certain Indian (essentially Hindu, Sikh and East African Asian) groups in society which permits them to take full benefit of existing educational opportunity structures. As well as occupying higher social positions in mainstream society, they are also able to send their children to schools that are selective and fee-paying through the realisation of economic, cultural and social capital. They have adopted additional strategies within the home, helping Indian parents to ensure greater educational success for their children. These South Asian groups have been positively integrated into society and have been able to increase their social and economic positions through education. These are the few.

Since the earliest phases of post-war immigration, settlement, racialisation and ethnicisation of ethnic minorities, the education system has undergone many changes. There has been a steady rise of national attainments in GCSEs and 'A' Levels. It has resulted in a dramatic move in the population of students through the education system, especially through higher education. In the midst of this immense sea change, inequalities have invariably persisted and intensified. Furthermore, based on the immigration of other South Asians over time and the way in which communities have been socially stratified, wider divisions have emerged in the educational achievements of South Asians. The gulf between high and low achievers began to widen during Thatcher in the 1980s and under Major and Blair in 1990s. It continues to widen under Blair today. In an attempt to further embrace the *laissez-faire* approach to education, central government policy has increasingly sought to provide parents with a choice of school for their children. The choice, however, is seen as a limitation for working-class and ethnic minority parents. The education system has essentially become a function of capitalism and increasingly so in recent periods of British educational history. Education in England is not a fair system but is riddled with inequality. The attitudes of certain disadvantaged South Asian parents towards schools and teachers are informed by an experience of failure and their own negative experiences of education. It is recognised that South Asian groups who tend to be located in poorer inner-city areas are less likely to be seen as desirable commodities by teachers, with increasing segregation as white parents choose to remove their children from certain ethnic minority-concentrated schools. Social class positions are important because educational knowledge in the current market place results in some ethnic minorities remaining uninformed because of their economic and social marginalisation. Some Bangladeshi and Pakistani parents, as a result, are distinctly disadvantaged. Market forces have had the effect of polarising certain groups and alienating them from potential educational advantage while permitting others to excel. These are the many.

It is important to develop a taxonomic framework as the analysis and findings have indicated a series of important and new insights. The study has evaluated the economic and social predicaments facing South Asians in Birmingham and religio-cultural manifestations have been highlighted in an attempt to evaluate more fully the nature of South Asians in educational settings. Given the broad social class and ethnic differences found between South Asian groups, this research was designed to determine the nature of divergence in educational achievement processes for successful and unsuccessful groups. The research attempted to delineate processes, recognising foremost the heterogeneity of South Asians and their schools. A research project of this size and complexity, incorporating the wider variables of ethnicity, class, gender, religion and culture in a study of differentiated South Asian groups in education.

Table 9.1 highlights the nature of difference in the different types of educational institutions that exist. They characterise the 'dominant ethical taxonomy' of factors in the educational performance of South Asian groups in different educational settings. South Asian children

Table 9.1 Taxonomy of South Asians in education

Characteristics	Comprehensive schools	Selective schools
Ethnicity	Bangladeshis and Pakistanis (Muslims)	Indians (Hindus and Sikhs), East African Asians
Social class	Working class, 'under-employed', unemployed (proletariat, lumpenproletariat)	Middle class, 'upper' working class (bourgeoisie, petit bourgeoisie)
Gender roles – male	Expressed masculinity	Contained masculinity
Gender roles – female	Some subjugation and dependence	Free-willed and independent
Parental occupation	Manual, semi-skilled, technical	Professional, management
Language in school	Bilingual (mother tongue teaching assistance)	Monolingual (English the dominant language)
'Choice' of higher education	Local and 'new' universities	National and 'traditional' universities
School policy	Antiracist-multicultural	Multicultural

socialised into the dominant culture have a big advantage over children not socialised into this culture, as schools reproduce a general set of dominant cultural values and ideas. In cultural terms, each type of educational experience permits the individual to speak a 'certain language', but some are more successful than others in being understood. The ability to 'speak the language' of the educational system and teachers produces a huge advantage. Thus, children who have been socialised into dominant cultural values appear to the teacher to be 'more gifted'.

In this respect, Bourdieu argues one of the major roles played by the school is *social elimination*, which involves the progressive removal of pupils from access to higher knowledge and social rewards (Bourdieu also calls this differentiation – the need to 'make pupils different' in ways that are recognised as valid by a dominant culture.) Elimination itself is achieved in two main ways. First, through an examination system designed to gradually fail or exclude pupils. Working-class pupils are far more likely to underperform in examinations because their cultural capital is less significant. Second, through self-elimination, as working-class South Asian children quickly come to realise that they do not 'speak the same language' as the education system. It offers them little that is culturally useful and they leave the education system at the earliest possible opportunity. Such children learn that their chances of educational success (as measured in terms of qualifications) are small and they realistically assess the possible future avenues open to them (which normally means lower-paid employment instead of further and higher education). South Asians in comprehensive schools do not possess the economic, cultural and social strengths of their middle-class peers in selective schools and, as such, their educational opportunities are limited by the extent to which they can generate the kind of 'capitals' needed through working with parents and making efforts to better learn in schools, all in an attempt to 'learn the language', 'get on' and 'get ahead' as well as they can.

In reality, the determination to achieve in education is eminently affected by the will of parents. It is also apparent, however, that variable knowledge on the part of parents exists on the way in which achievement is best attained. Middle-class South Asian parents acquire 'hot knowledge' to become more informed of educational opportunities through social networks and contacts rather than from the information provided by the schools themselves, particularly in relation to the choice of secondary schooling. It is also determined by the strength and ethos of the school itself – its institutional *habitus*. Schools reflecting the dominant social and cultural values of society are reproduced in the pupils. Parent education levels are significant as they are closely associated with the educational successes of children, particularly in relation to access into higher education. It proposes that social class is not the only factor and the education of parents is also important. It also suggests opportunities for ethnic minorities and South Asians to make a genuine difference as they are not so rigidly structured in class terms as Marxian theory and analysis would point.

It is Bangladeshis and Pakistanis, nevertheless, who enter local primary and comprehensive schools that tend to be located in the inner cities of Birmingham. These schools have a propensity to be under-resourced, with teaching of limited quality and generally lower overall examination results. Other South Asians that are more fortunate live in the outer cities or in suburban areas, have greater economic capital at their disposal and attend schools that are more effective (or selective schools in inner-city areas). Although parents are just as highly motivated they also tend to be more informed. The experience of young South Asian Muslim women, however, remains interesting. Recent research continues to find the group to be more successful in education compared with their male peers, largely through the active involvement of parents and the realisation of how important education is for women too. Parents are increasingly being open-minded and supportive although there is more to do to get parents to realise, understand and appreciate. The negative perceptions of some teachers towards young Muslim women, however, expressed the greatest concern in relation to the stereotyping of religions and genders.

It was the aim of this research to discover the ways in which the educational achievements of South Asians vary. To this end, a qualitative study of South Asians has addressed issues of social class, religion and culture in relation to South Asian educational achievement processes. It is established, given a large city such as Birmingham with its tapestry of post-war immigration and industrial decline, that there are many South Asian groups entering an array of differing schools and colleges. Some of these educational institutions have absorbed ethnic minority pupils since early periods and as a result have found ways to ameliorate the situations of disadvantaged South Asian groups while at the same time providing every opportunity for South Asians that are equipped with the necessary cultural capital to proceed in education. The resolve and purpose of South Asian children and their parents have not relented in this period and the wish to achieve in education still remains strong for economic and social reasons, for all South Asians. Social class combined with cultural and social capital, teacher attitudes towards certain ethnic minority groups and the effects of schools are the most decisive factors in the educational (under)achievements of South Asians.

Suggestions for further research

A distinctively qualitative methodological approach has been to engender grounded theory in the development of answers to empirical, conceptual and analytical questions on how South Asians perform in education. The study focused on the specific ethnic category of South Asians (and the three significant groups within them) and used differing forms of schooling within the city of Birmingham, UK, to determine the findings in this area.

At the micro level, new research could look into peer group socialisation, gender roles and the impact of religion and culture on education more closely. At the macro level, further research may wish to integrate the changing nature of the British education system and the increased movement towards organisational efficiency with questions of ethnic minority educational performance. Further studies need to take into consideration the current economic and social positions of various ethnic minorities in Britain. Certainly, it is apparent that in certain parts of the city, schools are applying constructive antiracist-multicultural education policies to improve the experiences of ethnic minorities in education. Further research here might examine how teachers and schools utilise these encouraging developments so that they may be applied elsewhere or considered more as part of evidence-based policy-relevant findings in this area.

Appendix A: Methodology

At the outset, important questions were asked on how this study would need to be carried out, what precise questions would be asked and in which way. Answers were led by current research in this area which suggested limitations to quantitative data on ethnic minority comparisons and the usefulness of group-orientated qualitative research in the study of education. A qualitative methodological approach was taken and the various experiences of it are elaborated upon below.

A particular facet of the research design for the current study was the omission of a white control group. It was felt less significant as a great deal of comparative, albeit more quantitative, research exists in the field (Maughan and Rutter, 1986; Kysel, 1988; Nuttall *et al.*, 1989; Smith and Tomlinson, 1989; Drew, 1995). In-depth interviews and sample surveys were the chosen methods – a combination of detailed first-hand accounts accompanied with descriptive statistics from the attitudinal and experiential surveys. During the time of the author's study, a number of ethnographic research emerged in this field, including studies of specific differences between South Asians as well as experiences at the level of different South Asians (Basit, 1997a; Haw, 1998; Ahmad, 2001 – on young Muslim women; Debnath, 1998; Haque, 1999 – on young Bangladeshis; Bhatti, 1999 – on all South Asians). Methodologically, the current research used a distinctive qualitative framework based on a range of selective and comprehensive schools and further education colleges. By involving a relatively large sample of actors (137 long interviews – with pupils, parents and teachers; 176 survey responses [109 college students, 67 teachers]), detailed open-ended statements were used to engender 'grounded theory' through qualitative empiricism (Glaser, 1968). Certain elements of the presentation of data also involved the use of case-study examples (Yin, 1994). A final imperative was the extent to which the study could provide valuable insights into the *processes* of education for specific groups. It is argued policymakers can use sociology of education research to directly improve professionalism in schools (McIntyre, 1997; Wrigley, 1997; Hargreaves, 1999; Mortimore, 1999).

The fieldwork for the research was carried out between February 1996 and March 1999. There were five separate data gathering exercises: interviews with South Asian school pupils, a postal survey of college students, interviews with South Asian parents, interviews with teachers and a teachers' attitudinal survey. It is with great care that respondents were interviewed and surveyed using recognised social science research methods. Every aspect of the data gathering process was rigorously scrutinised and piloted before execution (Wilson, 1998). Additional periods were required when after each interview or survey stage, time was needed to transcribe, collate, code, deconstruct, interpret, analyse and compartmentalise the data. To assist in the analysis qualitative and quantitative computer software packages were used, namely Atlas Ti and SPSS (Statistical Package for Social Scientists).

Interviews

Secondary school pupils: selective and comprehensive

To determine most effectively how different South Asians perform in relation to their social class, ethnicity and gender it was felt important to allow for a wide variation in the sample of schools to be used for the interviews. The educational institutions, however, were ultimately 'selected on an opportunity sampling basis', with the aim of discovering processes in vastly differing educational settings, the foundation of study resting on the comparability of South Asian groups in polarised settings. The schools used in the study (sampled schools) were finally selected at the end of 1995. Originally, eight were thought most suitable but only six were ultimately selected (one girl's selective fee-paying school, a boy's selective school, a girl's selective school and three inner-city comprehensive schools [one county, one voluntary-aided, one foundation]).

In the process of determining interviews with school pupils, 'contact teachers' from each of the sampled schools were originally asked to select a random sample of South Asian pupils from their current GCSE and 'A' Level students. Given different ratios of South Asian pupils in each of the schools, teachers were asked to select up to 30 pupils of mixed ability and social class backgrounds. From the comprehensive schools, the contact teachers were asked to divide their sample equally by gender. The schools and the contact teachers drew up a list of potential respondents and a letter of introduction was sent to the parents of each child. The schools wrote to parents, with a reply-slip at the base of the letter, accompanying the author's letter.

Interviews with pupils began in February of 1996 and ended in July of 1996. During the semi-structured interviews, pupils were asked questions relating to secondary school entry, GCSE choice at 13+, examination success at GCSE, 'A' Levels and potential higher education entry. They were also asked to discuss the role of parents, teachers, siblings, friends, relations, wider community structures and religious and cultural influences potentially thought to impact on their education. Aspects of religion and culture, social class and the effects of schools were considered in particular. All the pupils were individually interviewed using a tape recorder for approximately one hour each. Two young women refused to be tape-recorded. All the interviews were conducted on school premises during the respondent's free time and in English. Interviews took place in a designated room often with contact teachers nearby. A small number of interviews were conducted during lunch breaks mainly because of imminent examinations or tests.

Table A.1 below lists the sampled schools and highlights their essential characteristics. It is seen that St Aiden's and New Heath schools are located in the same inner-city ward of Small Heath. Longlake School is a large comprehensive school situated in the adjacent inner-city ward of Moseley. Rosebud School and Psi Grove schools, although selective, are located in the inner-city wards of Handsworth and Aston. Omega High School for Girls is an independent school with a national reputation for high academic success and is located in the affluent area of Edgbaston. All the schools contained a sixth-form. The funding status of schools is currently under review by central government but the definitions stated below were relevant at the time of the study.

Table A.1   Sampled schools, pupils, status and location

School	Ward	Entry status	Sex status	Age-range	Male (%)	Female (%)	Total (%)
Omega High	Edgbaston	Selective and fee-paying	Girls	11–18	–	6 (100)	6 (100)
Rosebud	Handsworth	Selective	Girls	11–18	–	24 (46)	24 (100)
Psi Grove	Aston	Selective	Boys	11–18	12 (100)	–	12 (100)
Longlake	Moseley	Comprehensive	Mixed	11–18	7 (64)	4 (36)	11 (100)
St Aiden's	Small Heath	Comprehensive	Mixed	11–18	7 (58)	5 (42)	12 (100)
New Heath	Small Heath	Comprehensive	Mixed	11–18	11 (46)	13 (54)	24 (100)
Total	–	–	–	–	37 (42)	52 (58)	89 (100)

Source: Adapted from Department of Education and Skills, 2003 (www.dfes.gov.uk. Accessed 17 December 2003).

Forty-seven per cent of the total pupils in the sample were derived from the three selective schools (one fee-paying and two grammar) [42/89]. Although not entirely reflective of the situation of all South Asians in education, in aiming to discover the ways in which differences are found between South Asians, a high proportion of selective schools and sampled pupils invariably adds to greater empirical and theoretical development. Table A.1 also shows there were more younger women than men.

Eighty-nine pupils were interviewed. Table A.2 shows the religion, ethnicity and gender composition of the pupil sample. It is important to note the high number of Pakistanis. In part, it reflects local population concentration ratios (BEIC, 1993). Nevertheless, the fact that two of the schools are girls' schools and there is only one boys' school is important to consider. Given the general population levels of Bangladeshis and Pakistanis in Birmingham the high presence of Muslims in the sample reflects the local demography (Owen, 1992; Owen and Johnson, 1996; Phillips, 1998). It needs to be stated that this study was not a quantitative exercise, however, and the variations in the samples reflect a wider need to develop greater theoretical understanding.

Table A.2   Ethnicity, gender and religion of study school pupils

Sex	Muslim (%)	Sikh (%)	Hindu (%)	Total (%)
Male	24 (41)[a]	6 (43)	7 (43)	37 (42)
Female	35 (59)[b]	8 (57)	9 (57)	52 (48)
Total	59 (100)	14 (100)	16 (100)	89 (100)

[a] [16 Pakistanis, 6 Bangladeshis, 2 East African Asians], [b] [25 Pakistanis, 7 Bangladeshis, 3 East African Asians].

The age-range of respondents is shown in Table A.3. The average age for school pupils was 16 years and two months. The study schools were originally informed that a random selection of South Asian pupils was needed to reflect the broad range of the South Asian intake within the school. The types of pupils available were naturally differentiated across the six study schools and widely in cases but the process of determining them was the same for each of the schools. Teachers were expected to help determine a suitable range of pupils for the purposes of interviewing that would help the motivations of this research in the best of ways, and they largely did. At Omega High, however, pupils were asked to take part during a school assembly and, as such, only six volunteered.

It is without doubt that there are inconsistencies between sample sizes and that some South Asians are concentrated in some schools more than others. Moreover, the fact that three of the schools are selective and single-sex with one that is also fee-paying is not necessarily reflective of the situations of all schools in Birmingham and indeed of South Asians within them. Moreover, this particular sampling approach resulted in more young women than men and more Pakistanis than any other group. A significant advantage of this particular make-up of the sample, of course, is that it helps to contextualise theoretical and conceptual development and this is the most important factor to consider.

A potential problem with the type of qualitative data gathered is that it essentially deals with a range of South Asians receiving their education at different stages of the educational life-cycle and in vastly differing types of institutions. Pupils were interviewed at length on the nature of their schooling, invariably up to the point at which they were in the educational process. For sure, not only were responses geared by the age of the pupil and his or her relative experience but also by the nature of the pupils themselves (i.e. class and personality). Pupils from selective schools were far more likely to be apt in responding than their inner-city peers (at the time of interviewing, it was possible to make field-notes on general matters. The use of such are incorporated intrinsically into the analysis. Particular points of observation, such as dress code, posture and confidence levels remain distinct features of that field-note memory. Another significant aspect of this was seen in terms of the number of many Muslim woman respondents that wore the *Hijab* (whether full or just the headscarf) during interviews. As such, the sampling of these 89 school pupils was not intended as a statistical study but rather the articulation of the way in which educational experiences are revealed through individual

Table A.3   Age of school pupil sample

Age	14–15 (%)	15–16 (%)	16–17 (%)	17–18 (%)	18–19 (%)	Total (%)
Longlake	–	3 (9)	4 (17)	2 (10)	2 (100)	11 (13)
Psi grove	–	6 (17)	–	6 (30)	–	12 (13)
St Aiden's	–	12 (34)	–	–	–	12 (13)
Rosebud	8 (89)	4 (11)	9 (40)	3 (15)	–	24 (27)
New Heath	–	9 (26)	8 (35)	7 (35)	–	24 (27)
Omega High	1 (11)	1 (3)	2 (9)	2 (10)	–	6 (7)
Total	9 (100)	35 (100)	23 (100)	20 (100)	2 (100)	89 (100)

life histories in their particular educational contexts and with a significant sample of young South Asian men and women so as to permit something meaningful to be said about South Asian differences in education. As a cautionary note, however, although an impartial method was adopted for the purposes of accurately determining an unbiased sample it is apparent teachers may have exercised their own discretion and considered some pupils more suited for interview than others, particularly if the school's image, performance levels and antiracist-multicultural education policies were thought to be scrutinised.

South Asian parents

South Asian parents were interviewed to explore the various ways in which they exercised an influence over their children's education and how they related to their children's teachers and schools – directly and indirectly. In March 1997, once the pupil interviews had been completed and analysed the six schools were re-contacted to arrange interviews with parents. A letter to parents was written and, again, the schools wrote an additional letter to parents with a reply-slip at its base. Pupils were asked to take letters home to parents and return reply-slips directly to the school. Of the 169 letters sent to parents, unfortunately, only fifteen responded positively, of which eleven were successfully interviewed. It was felt this number was too small a sample to provide sufficient information and it was decided to find relevant parents through 'snowball sampling'. These parents were selected by 'purposively sampling' South Asian parents known to be of varying ethnicity, social class and gender (McNeill, 1990). Ultimately, 25 parents were interviewed using a semi-structured list of questions on the diverse educational experiences of differing South Asian groups. Interviews were conducted in various South Asian languages and dialects; namely Mirpuri, Punjabi, Urdu and Hindi (some Bangladeshi fathers were also able to speak in Urdu/ Hindi). All the interviews were tape-recorded. The duration of interviews ranged from one hour to as long as two or three. Occupational positions of parents ranged from entrepreneurs and medical doctors to factory workers, taxi drivers, the 'under-unemployed' and the unemployed. They also varied in age, South Asian ethnicity and gender. The last of the interviews was carried out in March 1998. Table A.4 profiles the South Asian parents in the overall sample.

It is recognised that South Asians live in varying levels of prosperity and, as such, the extent to which 'a traditional English education' has been eulogised reveals itself in distinct forms by parents. English universities are regarded highly, a perspective based largely on a colonial education system and other remnants left by the British in South Asia. It has been stated that 'an Indian parent from an urban area, with a higher education even though working in an unskilled job, may expect his son to do well in school; while a rural, semi-literate parent might regard the fact that his children attend school as a major achievement' (Tomlinson, 1984, p. 34). Therefore, it was important to interview differing South Asian parents to draw out their perceptions of and attitudes towards their children in education. The sample of parents, although relatively small, does provide variations by ethnicity and social class, reflecting the types of schools and students sampled in this study. From the start of the process until the last of the parent interviews, an entire 12 months had passed. Such was the length of time it took to overcome difficulties and to ensure that a representative sample of South Asian parents was ultimately ascertained.

Table A.4   Profile of South Asian parent sample

No.	Parent	Religion	Occupation	Ethnic origin	Location
1	Mother	Hinduism	Homemaker	India	Edgbaston
2	Father	Hinduism	Scientist	India (via Kenya)	Harborne
3	Father	Islam	Restaurateur	Bangladesh	Aston
4[a,c]	Father	Islam	Post-office manager	Bangladesh	Great Barr
5	Father	Islam	Restaurateur	Bangladesh	Handsworth
6[c]	Father	Islam	Unemployed	Bangladesh	Small Heath
7[c]	Father	Islam	Unemployed	Bangladesh	Small Heath
8	Father	Islam	Paediatrician	India (via Tanzania)	Harborne
9	Father	Islam	Ambulance driver	Pakistan	Saltley
10[c]	Father	Islam	Taxi driver	Pakistan	Saltley
11	Father	Islam	Print worker	Pakistan	Saltley
12	Father	Islam	Entrepreneur	Pakistan	Moseley
13	Father	Islam	Civil servant	Pakistan	Small Heath
14[c]	Father	Islam	Unemployed	Pakistan	Small Heath
15	Father	Islam	Restaurateur	Pakistan	Sparkbrook
16[c]	Father	Islam	Retired factory worker	Pakistan	Sparkhill
17[c]	Father	Sikhism	Entrepreneur	India	Handsworth
18	Father	Sikhism	Entrepreneur	India	Handsworth Wood
19	Father	Sikhism	Entrepreneur	India	Harborne
20[c]	Grandfather	Hinduism	Retired teacher	India (via Kenya)	South Yardley
21[c]	Mother	Hinduism	Civil servant	India	Harborne
22[b]	Mother	Islam	Part-time employee	Anglo-Pakistan	Small Heath
23[c]	Mother	Sikhism	Entrepreneur	India	Hamstead
24	Mother	Sikhism	Pharmacist	India	Harborne
25[c]	Mother	Sikhism	Receptionist	India	Sandwell

[a] English wife.
[b] Pakistani husband.
[c] Parents of pupils from sampled schools.

A note on interviews with parents and pupils

Both sets of interviewing were time-consuming and particularly in relation to parents quite difficult to arrange. Although many of the interviews were often more like pleasant conversations, others were more difficult because of having to prompt younger respondents who were sometimes shy, nervous or wished to provide merely single-worded answers. Keeping question consistency with parents of vastly different social class backgrounds, religions and dialects was imperative. Inherent within the experiences of many South Asian parents is how they have adopted/adapted to the ways of the host society in order to maximise their economic opportunities. Some had succeeded while others were merely beginning. Some parents were highly educated with children in selective schools who were more concerned with the Oxford college they would favour. Others were keen to ensure their children were performing but felt powerless to engage with them at a religio-cultural, inter-generational or at an educational level – and were often entirely submissive to the comprehensive school or college their children were attending. Nevertheless, each interview with both pupils and parents was a rewarding, fulfilling experience, enriching the researcher and the research in terms of providing specific primary data for this particular study.

Teachers

It has been argued teacher opinions and values are important to evaluate, especially given the vastly divergent academic and vocational routes taken by South Asian school pupils and college students in the last decade (Abbas, 2002c). The interviewing of teachers began in November of 1998 and ended in March of 1999. Respondents were interviewed during school hours using a semi-structured list of questions. There were some difficulties experienced in interviewing teachers. St Aiden's School could not continue its involvement with the study and, in effect, had to pull out. In addition, certain contact teachers from the colleges moved out of employment. To counterbalance the limited numbers teachers from other schools with similar characteristics were purposively sampled. Interviews were carried out primarily with school headteachers, deputy headteachers, principals and senior teachers from the sampled schools and colleges. Altogether, 23 teachers were interviewed, eight of which were sampled from other schools.

Teachers ranged in status and years of employment experience. The teachers interviewed made detailed statements on the nature of South Asian educational achievements. Teachers expanded upon questions relating to parents, religion and the culture of pupils. There were, however, potential hazards by interviewing teachers in this way. Given the subject matters of 'race', ethnicity and achievement in education, teachers were likely to be extra-sensitised to researcher objectives. As such, teachers may have informed the researcher only part of all the information felt important, especially if the researcher is seen to take away sensitive information, never to return. It remains important, nevertheless, to work out whether teachers were not telling just the truth but also whether they were party to any untruths. Table A.5 profiles the teacher sample.

It was felt by the researcher that all the contact teachers, nevertheless, were committed to this research from very early on and after almost four years of cooperation, for teachers to have made inaccurate claims or value judgements towards the end of the research is felt to be limited. Indeed, many of the statements were frank revelations and opinions and they were very much based on the development of trust. All the interviewed teachers provided forthright responses to probing questions in an open manner. Teachers expressed a genuine desire to actively engage with the research and to help improve their knowledge of South Asian pupils in education. The full range of responses from teachers, often in very senior positions, provided informative insights into thoughts, processes,

Table A.5 Profile of teacher sample

No.	School/College	School status	Sex	Ethnicity*	Position
1	Inner-City School (A)	Comprehensive	Male	White	Senior teacher
2	Inner-City School (A)	Comprehensive	Female	White	Headteacher
3	Inner-City School (A)	Comprehensive	Female	White	Teacher/16–18 coordinator
4	Inner-City School (B)	Comprehensive	Male	African-Caribbean	Senior teacher
5	Inner-City School (B)	Comprehensive	Male	White	Senior teacher
6	Cherrywood College	16–19	Male	Pakistani	Lecturer
7	Inner-City School (C)	Comprehensive	Male	African-Caribbean	Headteacher
8	Inner-City School (C)	Comprehensive	Male	Sikh-Indian	Teacher
9	Inner-City School (D)	Comprehensive	Male	White	Headteacher
10	Cherrywood College	16–19	Male	Pakistani	Assistant principal
11	Longlake	Comprehensive	Male	White	Deputy Headteacher
12	New Heath	Comprehensive	Male	White	Deputy Headteacher
13	Omega High	Selective and fee-paying	Female	White	Headteacher
14	Psi Grove	Selective	Male	Sikh-Indian	Head of physics
15	Psi Grove	Selective	Male	White	Deputy Headteacher
16	Rosebud	Selective	Female	White	Head of sixth-form
17	Rosebud	Selective	Female	White-European	Headteacher
18	Rosebud	Selective	Female	White	Teacher
19	Rosebud	Selective	Female	White	Teacher
20	St Margaret's	16–19	Male	White	Senior lecturer
21	St Margaret's	16–19	Male	White	Vice principal
22	St Margaret's	16–19	Female	White	Head of department
23	St Margaret's	16–19	Female	White	Senior lecturer

Note: Inner-city comprehensive schools *A, B, C* and *D* were used to supplement sampled school and college teacher interviews.
* White refers to English unless otherwise stated.

understanding and behaviours in both elite schools and inner-city comprehensive schools. The maintenance of a committed relationship with the schools and the teachers allowed for greater research objectivity in the long run.

Surveys

Colleges and South Asian students

After completing the pupil interviews a survey of college students was carried out. The aim of this sub-project was to discover the attitudes of older South Asians on their retrospective experiences of school. It was found that the older pupils in the interviews in the schools were far more reflective and engaging with the subjects of discussion. It was interesting to see students, who were only slightly older, 'looking back' on their very recent experiences. Furthermore, it was given that many students who are at further education colleges were formerly pupils in comprehensive schools. This permitted a balanced perspective in relation to the view of the 14–19 education process *per se*. Random samples of South Asian students from two further education colleges (Cherrywood and James Watt) and one sixth-form college (St Margaret's) were acquired and subsequently used to survey students. The college students were asked almost identical questions but, here, respondents selected their responses from a finite set of attitudinal statements, although space was provided for students to write down their experiences. This resulted in very valuable data (Abbas, 2002a).

Using the student databases of the three colleges, each of the respective contact teachers were asked to draw up a sample of 150 South Asian students equal in terms of age, gender, course level, perceived ability and the three South Asian groups (i.e. Bangladeshis, Indians and Pakistanis). A combined list of 403 randomly sampled South Asian college students were assembled from the three colleges. Students were sent a postal questionnaire with a first-class reply-paid envelope. All but Cherrywood College sent a covering letter by the contact teacher. The entire survey provided a response rate of 27 per cent (James Watt College, 34 per cent; Cherrywood College, 19 per cent; St Margaret's College, 47 per cent). In more detail, from James Watt College, 146 students were sampled resulting in 37 responses and from Cherrywood College, 154 students sampled provided 21 responses. The St Margaret's College sample consisted of the entire South Asian second- and third-year student body. Here, there were seven Bangladeshis [five boys, two girls], 50 Indians [23 boys, 27 girls] and 54 Pakistanis [31 boys, 23 girls]. A combined set of 111 students was sampled, of which 51 responded to the survey. In total, 109 college students responded positively to the questionnaires, sent to the three colleges and received during July 1996 to December 1996.

Respondents were provided a multiple choice attitude-scale questionnaire which also asked experiential questions. The questions revolved around themes similar to those asked of pupils. Respondents were asked to reflect upon their specific experiences of school, relationships with teachers, the effects of religion and the home, the roles their parents played as well as to write down anything they had to say in addition. Nevertheless, the predicament with a research experiment of this type was with the wording of questions and the responses from which individuals were expected to select. Responses individuals decided upon not only had to be based on the validity to students but also in the wording of questions and statements (Oppenheim, 1992). Table A.6 shows the ethnicity and gender of the college student respondents. Over a quarter of the respondents were young Pakistani women. One respondent did not state their ethnicity or gender.

In terms of religious identification, of the 106 valid responses received (one value missing, one atheist and one not giving an identity), 65 per cent categorised themselves as Muslim, 25 per cent Hindu and eight per cent Sikh. Table A.7 shows where the college students stated they were born.

Of the 16 Bangladeshis in the sample, six were born in Bangladesh. Of the 53 Pakistanis, 15 were born abroad, either in Pakistan or outside of Britain. Ninety-two per cent of Indian students were British-born. As such, it is possible to suggest there is still some migration (family re-unification) to Britain by some Bangladeshi and Pakistani groups compared with the more firmly established positions of Indians.

Aspects of the personal data revealed the Bangladeshis and Pakistanis were more likely to have unemployed fathers. Pakistani fathers and mothers were far more likely to have retired from work. Bangladeshi fathers were least likely to be in full-time employment. Muslim (Bangladeshi and Pakistani) mothers were most likely to be homemakers. There was a high rate of Indian mothers found to be in full-time employment.

Table A.6   College student's ethnicity and gender

Sex	Bangladeshi (%)	Indian (%)	Pakistani (%)	Total (%)
Female	7 (53)	24 (44)	28 (62)	59 (55)
Male	9 (47)	15 (56)	25 (38)	49 (45)
Total	16 (100)	39 (100)	53 (100)	108 (100)

Table A.7   College student's place of birth

Place of Birth	Bangladeshi (%)	Indian (%)	Pakistani (%)	Total (%)
Birmingham	9 (56)	26 (70)	35 (66)	70 (66)
UK, not Birmingham	1 (6)	8 (22)	3 (6)	12 (11)
Pakistan	–	–	11 (21)	11 (10)
Bangladesh	6 (38)	–	–	6 (6)
Kenya[a]	–	2 (5)	2 (4)	4 (4)
Abroad[a]	–	–	1 (2)	1 (1)
India	–	1 (3)	–	1 (1)
Kashmir[a]	–	–	1 (2)	1 (1)
Total	16 (100)	37 (100)	53 (100)	106 (100)

[a] Categories are self-ascribed.

Schools and teachers

After all the interviews with teachers had been completed, an attitude-scale questionnaire was handed out to teachers from four of the sampled schools. The aim was to maintain an element of critical distance as well as to buttress the range of would-be teacher respondents given also the relatively small but selective sample of interviews. Five of the sampled schools, save for St Aiden's School, and only St Margaret's of the three colleges were provided questionnaires. Attempts made to further encourage the other contact teachers to assist were to no avail. The closeness of examinations at that time of year and perhaps an element of research fatigue may well have led to teachers assuming no further contact with the researcher until the dissemination of the research. Only four of the sampled schools had replied by the end of July 1999. By that stage it was felt no further primary data was needed. A letter was written to all the remaining contact teachers and they were informed they would be made aware once the research was complete.

In sum, 67 successfully completed responses were obtained from teachers in four of the six sampled schools. Table A.8 shows the ethnicity and gender of the teachers responding to the survey.

The range of teachers surveyed was diverse. Thiry-eight per cent [24/64] of teachers had been employed for less than four years and 23 per cent [15/64] between five and nine years. Only eight per cent [5/64] of the teachers had been employed for more than 20 years. Fifty-eight per cent of the total sample was women. It is clear that there was an overwhelming preponderance of teachers from selective schools in the survey [64 per cent]. It is reflective of the sampled school pupils, of which 47 per cent were from selective schools. The majority of the teachers sampled from Rosebud, Psi Grove and Omega High schools were white women. The New Heath Schoolteacher sample was the most ethnically diverse.

Table A.8 Teacher's school, ethnicity and gender

Ethnicity	Sex	Rosebud (%)	Psi Grove (%)	New Heath (%)	Omega High (%)	Total (%)
White	Male	1 (11)	14 (82)	6 (25)	2(12)	23 (34)
	Female	8 (89)	2 (12)	10 (42)	14(82)	34 (51)
White-other	Male	–	–	2 (8)	–	2 (3)
	Female	–	1(6)	1 (4)	1(6)	3 (5)
Pakistani	Male	–	–	2 (8)	–	2 (3)
	Female	–	–	1 (4)	–	1 (2)
Indian	Male	–	–	1 (4)	–	1 (2)
British-Indian [a]	Female	–	–	1 (4)	–	1 (2)
Total		9 (100)	17 (100)	24 (100)	17 (100)	67 (100)

[a] Category is self-ascribed. White refers to English unless otherwise stated.

Politics and social research method

During the in-depth interviews it was important that respondents felt comfortable in answering questions and confidently imparted to the researcher their beliefs, opinions and values towards all aspects of education (Denscombe, 1984). The proficiency has to be developed and harnessed early on in the data gathering process (McCracken, 1988; Bell, 1993; May, 1993). To improve the quality of the data, the researcher has to 'actively listen', keeping the interview 'focused ... infilling and explicating' where data is lacking and identifying clues from respondents. The interview 'is not just a device for gathering information. It is a process of constructing reality to which both parties contribute and by which both are affected. Interviewers put something of themselves into an interview ...' (Open University, 1994, p. 60). The interview is an educative process – for both the interviewed and the interviewer. It permits the ability to come together around a set of important considerations and for them to be fully discussed and elaborated upon. Nevertheless, it is the specific considerations of power, ideology and shared ethnicity that are important in the rationalisation and assessment of interview dynamics in specific relation to the current study. There are implications for the researcher, the researched and the overall findings that are likely to be generated. These are discussed below.

It is important to elaborate upon the gender and the ethnicity of the researcher. A South Asian Muslim man studying the educational experiences of young South Asian women potentially constitutes a dilemma for social science research. To eliminate the potential for disparity, extra care was taken during the data gathering process to remain aware of the power dynamics inherent in the interchange of information, to remain sensitive of exploring religio-cultural issues when respondents felt it too difficult to discuss, to avoid discussing sensitive issues and to not use the process itself as an act of politicising, problematising or sensationalising the research question. As such, by concentrating on a phenomenological methodological approach, to ensure that the voices of young women are used to disclose their own stories impartially, respondents have been able to present accounts of their life histories incorporating a range of perspectives and aspirations that help to inform impartial research on the nature of experience for different young South Asian women in education. The function of the researcher has to be transparent; therefore, aspects of ethnicity, gender, linguistic ability, cultural awareness and education class were ubiquitous considerations in the interaction between the researcher and the researched.

To effectively produce sound social science research the personification of the 'ideal researcher' was generated; not simply during the data gathering process but also as part of the interactions and confrontations embroiled within. For example, in attempting to negotiate passage into educational institutions various appearances had to be kept with gatekeepers to ultimately gain access to potential respondents. When interviewing pupils, the researcher had to demonstrate he was young enough to engage with respondents but mature enough to remain detached. Similarly, with parents, the researcher had to be considered a professional with genuine social science interests ensuring that all the ethical standards of research were being adhered to. In addition, great care was required so as not to be drawn into politically or religiously charged conversation. Each experience, nevertheless, was achieved through the management of impressions (Goffman, 1990) as well as through the utilisation of appropriate social science methods.

Given the sensitivity of attitudes towards ethnic minorities in education, an additional area raised is empowerment through knowledge. The antiracist education perspective encourages the researcher to actively challenge common-held beliefs about 'race'. Antiracist educationists, 'seek not only to highlight forms of inequality and injustice, but view the research act itself as constituting a deliberate challenge to the *status quo* ... [adding] to emancipatory knowledge' (Troyna and Carrington, 1989, p. 206, *original emphasis*). With this type of research, however, caution must be taken not to move the focus of interest towards race relations *per se* and away from racism in education such that the education system itself becomes the focus of attention. Nevertheless, it is important to challenge stereotypes which give rise to racism in educational settings and in research terms to accurately determine aspects of 'biography, culture and history ...' as '... the education system is part of a wider system of constraints which, often unwittingly, serves to maintain black people in a position of structural subordination' (Mac an Ghaill, 1989a, p. 271–84). As an example of 'empowerment research', Mac an Ghaill's (1989b) study focused on providing a voice for the disadvantaged and disaffected in education. The process of talking to respondents in detail about their experiences was something Mac an Ghaill argued respondents found helpful – as it provided information and knowledge on what they could expect as well as helping them to rationalise their structurally subordinated positions. A criticism levelled against Mac an Ghaill's work was that giving a voice to marginalised groups does not mean that they have been empowered – for that real change is required not just development of an individual's knowledge. He responds by saying his research showed what it is to be empowered irrespective of change to material conditions (Devine and Heath, 1999).

The view that researchers can challenge the negative outcomes of ethnic minorities in educational settings is critiqued by 'methodological purists' (a label constructed by the late Barry Troyna; see Troyna, 1993a), who regard the approach 'a fundamental error of "critical" research to assume that it is possible to pursue both knowledge and practical goals simultaneously' (Hammersley, 1998, p. 32). Taking a politicised perspective in the conduct of research, therefore, should be regarded as a move away from acceptable forms of social science research methodology, although the idea that it is something often done in the name of research is not unknown (Hammersley, 2000, 2001). Nonetheless, an important aspect to consider is that racism takes many different forms in the educational life-cycles of certain ethnic minority individuals and groups. Carrington and Troyna (1998) argue that questions of racism as well as educational disadvantage are fundamental to any study of ethnic minorities in education no matter how they are politicised in the sphere and domain of academic discourse.

Furthermore, it is possible that the interaction between the researcher and the researched itself may give rise to the perception and experience of ethnicity, especially if there are questions relating to identity (Song and Parker, 1995; see also Basit, 1997a; Haw, 1998; Bhatti, 1999). It is argued, nevertheless, that a researcher with shared ethnic characteristics is less likely to pathologise or stereotype and more likely to remain 'ethnically correct' (Brar, 1992, p. 195). Still, one of the most important roles of the researcher is they remain 'curious' in the field and indeed courageous in the face of all manners of resistance or obstacles placed before them. There is a need for 'confidence in their ability to impart scientific value to whatever they find out . . . insights of value and curiosity must be informed' (Beyer, 1992, p. 66). In educational settings in particular, 'such work requires the building of relationships of mutual trust and respect between the researcher and the pupils' (Gillborn and Drew, 1992, p. 554).

Shared ethnic characteristics with the researched together with sensitivity to questions revolving around ethnic identity provide greater opportunity for the processes of educational achievements to be better understood. Although there are factors in relation to the politics of the research and the shared ethnicity of the researcher that can affect how interviews are carried out and the type of information gleaned, there is still a range of important 'checks' that can be made to ensure that bias and partisanship are significantly reduced. Oppenheim (1992) states that there may be a problem with the sample in the first instance; it may well be biased. Poor rapport between the respondent and the interviewee is also an issue. Questions that are altered subtly might lose their original objectivity – which is related to poor prompting, biased probing and re-arranging the order. Some of these questions might be leading, 'putting words into respondent's mouths'. The following need to be addressed at the outset: attitudes, opinions, expectations of the interviewer; the tendency for the interviewer to see the respondent in their own image; the tendency for the interviewers to see answers supporting preconceived notions; misperceptions on the part of the interviewer of what is being said; and, misunderstanding on the part of the respondents of what is being asked (Cohen *et al.*, 2000).

A real and genuine consideration therefore is that of power. It is the case that it is the interviewee who is under scrutiny; power is held in the hands of the interviewer. Matters are compounded when the researched are often marginalised, disaffected, powerless and potentially vulnerable. There are further aspects to consider when there is shared ethnicity between the researcher and the researched as well as the fact that the researcher is in a position to more positively engage with the subject matter by remaining aware of the pitfalls when the 'politics of the research' and the act of empowering the disadvantaged becomes the end-goal. Indeed, qualitative researchers in this area of study have a role to ensure that they are accurately identifying the cause of or the explanation for the problem however much it may be deemed politically sensitive. At the same time, it is important for the researcher to appropriately exploit the factors of shared ethnicity so as to maximise the depth, detail and insight of the information, without the interaction of researcher and researched itself affecting the findings.

In the field of research that is the sociology of education in relation to ethnic minorities in the British context, two broad schools of thought place the onus of achievement in either (a) the structures of the education system with certain ethnic minorities necessarily at the bottom of the hierarchy (Weis, 1985; Ogbu, 1997) or (b) in the particular social and cultural norms of certain groups which inhibit their progression beyond a certain point (that is, based on religio-cultural, patriarchal and inter-generational factors). What is important is that ethnicity is not provided with explanatory status on its own – there are wider factors to take into consideration and often achievement tends to be more about how well parents are educated, how good the schools and their teachers are, what kind of religio-cultural norms and values impact some groups more than others, and the degree to which groups possess the kinds of wider social and cultural capital necessary to succeed in education that the majority or those who hold power *per se* are often more in a position to operationalise.

For other social scientists engaging in research, questions of a sensitive nature, where shared ethnicity between the researcher and the researched is a feature and a qualitative methodological approach is taken, the issues of power, ideology and shared ethnicity remain. Inevitably, the specifics will vary from study to study but the approach taken on each occasion will require similar sets of thinking from the researcher. In the end, the wish to produce sound social knowledge ought to be the aim of all researchers but is tempered by the need to ensure that correct methods have been used in the appropriate way, given research questions involving complex issues of a political or ideological nature.

Appendix B: Evaluating Performance

It is important to evaluate the way in which the schools and colleges and the South Asian pupils and students in this study performed in relation to each other as well as in relation to citywide and national results. The information used here is available from Birmingham LEA and from data provided publicly by the Department of Education and Skills (BCC, 2002; DfES, 2003).

Educational achievements in Birmingham

The relative proportions of ethnic minorities in Birmingham schools in 1997 can be seen below in Table B.1. As local population numbers have shown, Pakistanis are the largest ethnic minority group in the city and, as such, they are the largest group in number within the schools (approximately one in six of all pupils). The Bangladeshi figure however is considerably smaller in comparison to the other South Asian groups (approximately one in 33 of all pupils). The Indians are the same in number as African-Caribbean groups (approximately one in 10 of all pupils).

Based on the following statistics made available from Birmingham LEA, Table B.2 clearly shows that average 5+ A–C GCSE passes for South Asians have increased over the period 1995 to 2002. Young Pakistani men were the lowest performing of all the South Asian groups in this period. Young African-Caribbean men achieved the least in comparison to all other groups. In sharp contrast to the young African-Caribbean men, African-Caribbean women achieved nearly twice as well as the men did. Young Indian men and women performed best of all groups, followed by the whites, Bangladeshis, Pakistanis and African-Caribbeans.

It is apparent from Table B.2 that the greatest improvement in performance has been made by the young South Asian women – with Indian young women exhibiting the greatest overall net improvement during this period. The relative ability of young Bangladeshi and Pakistani women performing well needs to be

Table B.1 Children in Birmingham comprehensive schools [1997]

Ethnicity	Primary (%)	Secondary (%)	Population 1991 Census (%)
White	61	57	79
Pakistani	16	16	7
African-Caribbean	7	8	6
Indian	6	9	5
Bangladeshi	3	3	1

Source: Adapted from Osler and Hill (1999, p. 39).

Table B.2 Pupils achieving 5+ A–C GCSE grades [1998–2002]

Ethnic group	1998 (%)	1990 (%)	2000 (%)	2001 (%)	2002 (%)	Improvement 1998–2002 (%)
African-Caribbean boys	13	20	19	17	25	+12
African-Caribbean girls	28	30	31	34	39	+11
Bangladeshi boys	28	31	30	27	43	+15
Bangladeshi girls	36	40	42	50	52	+16
Indian boys	40	43	49	49	57	+17
Indian girls	50	55	61	65	69	+19
Pakistani boys	21	26	27	31	33	+12
Pakistani girls	31	32	41	42	44	+13
White boys	34	33	36	39	41	+7
White girls	44	45	45	50	52	+8
All boys	30	32	34	35	39	+9
All girls	42	44	47	48	51	+9
Total	36	38	41	41	45	+9

Source: BCC, 2002.

set in the context of the ambitions of this group as well as the changing attitudes towards and experiences of South Asian young Muslim women in education. As such, these educational achievements of South Asians in Birmingham provide a picture which shows that Indians are the highest performers and Pakistanis the least. Caution, however, is needed in the interpretation of these results as total numbers in each sub-category of ethnic minority group distort finer group variations. Also, the idea that performance is rising so fast needs to be set in the context of a considerably slower start and a much lower starting point.

Note

Since the time of the study the performances of all students at 5+ A–C GCSE and 'A' Level have been increasing and during this period the performances of schools and colleges have risen or fallen in relation to their continued development in some cases or systematic underachievement in others.

Notes

Chapter 1

1. The term South Asian refers to people who originate from Bangladesh, India or Pakistan. The term East African Asian includes people who arrived from Uganda, Kenya and Tanzania before entering Britain but are broadly of Indian origin.The term white refers to people of largely Anglo-Saxon descent. It is occasionally interchanged with ethnic majority, White-British or White-English.

2. It is argued that 'race' has no biological foundation as it is based on a socially deterministic attempt to reify hierarchical relationships between those that hold power and those that are subservient to it (Miles, 1982; Bulmer, 1986). The development of racial categories based on phenotypical and skin colour characteristics emerged to legitimise the imperialisation and colonialisation of distant lands for the greater accumulation of capital through exploitation (Greene, 1970; Marx, 1978; Runnymede Trust, 1984; Banton, 1987). Ethnicity is defined as the set of defining factors distinguishing one individual or group from another – whether defined by the viewer or the viewed (Fenton, 2003). The essential determinants and features of racism are still prevalent in society and the negative features of 'race' and racism need to be considered *a priori* in any sociological study of 'race' and education (Carter and Green, 1996; see also Back and Solomos, 2000, for a first-rate reading on theories of 'race' and racism). More pertinently, it is argued that 'race' is a function of British Empire itself and although it no longer exists in anywhere near the shape it once did the air of confidence and overriding superiority that the British people had remains part of the national psyche. In the words of Duffy (2002, p. 138), 'we are still dogged by the myth of our empire and its aftermath. Centuries of regarding ourselves, however impoverished economically and culturally as at least "better than the heathen" adds to our feelings of superiority over all foreigners which, when it is seen to be manifestly untrue as in European league tables for education, child poverty or sports, turns to aggression and arrogance born of shame and frustration'.

3. It is important to note that the idea of *educational (under)achievement* needs conceptual clarity, particularly in relation to assessing differential levels of scholastic performance (Plewis, 1988, 1991). Educational sociologists define underachievement in relation to groups or individuals that perform at levels below an overall mean (Burgess, 1986).

4. At the time of writing, detailed information from the 2001 Census has not been made available. Nevertheless, it is important to state that the 1991 Census found Birmingham contained seven per cent of all ethnic minorities in Britain. Furthermore, 57 per cent of Birmingham's ethnic minority population was found to be located in seven of the city's 39 wards (Handsworth, Soho, Sparkbrook, Sparkhill, Small Heath, Sandwell and Aston). It was further ascertained that almost half of the city's African-Caribbean groups lived in six wards (Handsworth, Soho, Aston, Ladywood, Sandwell and Sparkbrook). Over

70 per cent of South Asians were found to be living in eight wards (Aston, Handsworth, Sandwell, Small Heath, Soho, Sparkbrook, Sparkhill and Washwood Heath). In particular, Indians were found concentrated in the Handsworth area, with Pakistanis in Small Heath, Sparkbrook and Sparkhill. Bangladeshis were found mainly in Aston and Sparkbrook. The Chinese were found to be dispersed in Birmingham as they are elsewhere in Britain.

In addition, the 1991 Census showed that in Britain, 55 per cent all ethnic minorities were British-born. In Birmingham, over half of Indians and Pakistanis were British-born in contrast to 60 per cent of Birmingham's Bangladeshis who were born overseas. Ten per cent of Birmingham's Indians were born in East Africa. Forty-four per cent of the South Asian population was below the age of 17, including 36 per cent of Indians, 49 per cent of Pakistanis and 55 per cent of Bangladeshis compared with 21 per cent of whites. Young South Asians accounted for a significant part of each South Asian strong as well as of the total population of the city (BEIC, 1993).

5. The religion question was asked for the first time in the 2001 Census. Although a voluntary question, 92 per cent of individuals provided a response nationally. Muslims accounted for 14.3 per cent of the city's population (140,000), with Pakistanis numbering under over 105,000 (74 per cent of Muslims in Birmingham). Although it is the seventh highest Muslim population as a proportion of a British city it is twice as large as the single highest concentration of Muslims (outside of London). In April 2001, nine per cent of *all* British Muslims [16 m] and 16 per cent of Britain's entire Pakistani population of 658,000 were found to be located in the city of Birmingham (ONS, 2003).

It is difficult estimate the proportion of Pakistanis in Britain who are actually from the Azad Kashmir district. Based on personal observation, a significant majority in the West Midlands, the North and South of England is Azad Kashmiri although the category itself is not recognised in official statistics. The term 'Mirpuri' is also used instead of Pakistanis or Azad Kashmiri. The term 'Azad Kashmiri' has not quite yet become accepted parlance in academic or practitioner discourse. It is important to state, however, that some people would not consider Azad Kashmir to be part of Pakistan at all but would neither wish to be identified as Pakistanis.

6. School exclusions, or more specifically *school suspensions* or *school expulsions*, was something that New Labour inherited when it came into power in 1997. School exclusions were considered a specific problem because they lead to unemployment, poverty and even criminality. Vulliamy (2001) argues that the process of inclusion and exclusion are inextricably linked. The intensified focus on 'standards, league tables, targets and blame' is at odds with the idea of 'social inclusion'. Rather, it is important to realise that problems are often a function of particular 'socio-cultural arrangements in both schools and wider society'.

A recent analysis of Birmingham school 'exclusion' rates found that the accepted pattern of young African-Caribbean men being excluded from school was being reproduced for Pakistanis. In inner-city Birmingham LEA maintained schools it was found that of the South Asians, Muslims were most likely to be excluded compared with the Sikhs and Hindus. Using 1994–1995 and 1995–1996 Birmingham LEA data, it was noted that there was, 'an increase in the permanent exclusions of Asian pupils – which may be directed particularly against Muslim rather than Sikh or Hindu pupils' (Mehra, 1999, p. 470).

7. Institutional racism is best defined as, 'the production of racial inequality in a wide range of institutions by the normal processes of their operation, the irrelevance of the intentions of the personnel involved, the historical developments of racial exclusion and oppression and the interrelationships of institutions, resulting in the cumulative nature of the inequalities' (Williams, 1985, p. 327). More recently, the Macpherson Report (1999, section 5, paragraph 34) stated that it is, 'the collective failure of an organisation to provide an appropriate and professional service to people because of their colour, culture, or ethnic origin. It can be seen or detected in processes, attitudes and behaviour which amount to discrimination through unwitting prejudice, ignorance, thoughtlessness and racist stereotyping which disadvantage minority ethnic people'.

Chapter 2

1. It is important to state the three broad sociological schools that exist in relation to the theorisation of 'race' and ethnicity. First, the notion of *class ideological distortion* is central in understanding how ethnicity is subservient to capitalism – so much so that stratification by ethnicity serves capitalism. Second, *negatively privileged status groups* is a neo-Weberian conceptualisation that helps to rationalise the positions occupied by different groups. From the Marxian point of view, economic factors are often considered more crucial but it is also possible to pursue the neo-Weberian strategy of complexity in stratification. Economic, cultural and social capital can be seen to be a function of class – a distinctly Marxian notion – and ethnicity which can be explored using a neo-Weberian perspective. Third, there is the 'New Ethnicities' project, where ethnicity is seen to be autonomous and distinct from the capitalist mode of production. It also adds further insight into the experiences of ethnic minorities in 'host societies', moving from the dull and crude dichotomies of 'black' or 'white' towards a more complex picture. Here, issues of assimilation, integration, cultural pluralism and multiculturalism become the topics of debate. The latter provides a relevant policy perspective.
2. Willis (1977) draws heavily (if not almost entirely) on the concept of cultural capital when he uses the idea of working-class cultural histories, experiences, customs and traditions to explain *why working-class kids get working-class jobs*. Similarly, it is argued that teachers and pupils interact in the classroom in ways that draw implicitly on concepts of cultural capital (teacher-perceptions of family background being particularly important, for example). A range of writers including Bernstein (1971), with his concept of restricted and elaborated language codes and Jackson (1968), with his development of ideas relating to the 'hidden curriculum' could also be included in these particular examples of early and relevant research in this field.
3. Bonding is considered in its most literal form: marriage. The most common form of marriage is between first cousins; sons and daughters of siblings, especially brothers (patrilineal parallel cousins). Consanguineous marriages refer to marriage between people of the 'same blood' (second cousins or closer relatives, that is, first cousins once removed, first cousins, double first cousins,

uncles and nieces, and aunts and nephews). A recognised issue is the extent to which Pakistanis are overly involved in consanguineous marriages (Shaw, 2001). It is apparent that some of the health risks associated with such marriages are negated once social class factors are taken into account (Ahmad, 1996), but what is important, however, are the social and cultural consequences of the current practice.

Chapter 3

1. It must be noted, however, that both the Taylor (1973) and Gupta (1977) studies involved respondents who had experienced most of their education overseas and were in the process of merely completing their compulsory education in England.

Chapter 4

1. It is important to elaborate upon the way in which bilingual pupils perceive their first and second languages. Based on research conducted in Birmingham, it was found that Punjabi-speaking Sikh parents put pressure on their children to develop an accurate use of the language. However, children were not always able to develop their language use in accordance with their parents' wishes and developed a preference for English. The move was reinforced by the mainstream use of English within schools. It was found that when 'pupils feel negatively about their literacy they are likely to compromise their academic achievement'. As such, 'a first step would be to recognise and disseminate the good practise which is going on ... where learner's home language is recognised and used not only in the classroom but in the curriculum as a vehicle for learning, and where there is development of multiliteracies in the classroom' (Martin and Stuart-Smith, 1998, p. 253).
2. The Bohra (Shia) Muslims maintain a particular form of cultural identity. They can be recognised by distinct community characteristics; namely, belonging to the commercial classes and retaining strong religious organisations. Much of this is derived from historical antecedents with location in the Gujarat region of India. Sojourning in East Africa before immigration to Britain, these Muslims are distinctive in their ways and operate in sophisticated micro-societies (Agrawal, 1978).
3. For data related to parent sample, see Table A.4 (p. 152).
4. For data related to teacher sample, see Table A.5 (p. 154).

Chapter 7

1. Recent large-scale research from North America (Portes and MacLeod, 1996, 1999) and the Netherlands (Wolbers and Driessen, 1996) has identified language within the home to be crucial in the educational achievements of ethnic minorities in these countries. In Britain, a recent study of Bangladeshi

mothers and their children in local primary schools found that they experienced difficulties in being able to talk to teachers. The difficulty was not because of a narrow vision of their children's education or the teachers themselves but because parents did not feel confident in their use of the English language (Blackledge, 1999). It seems, for ethnic minorities in education, the question of language use is significant and one that is also found in other advanced economies.

2. In a recent ethnographic study of young South Asian Muslim women and their education it was found that they developed a sense of British and Islamic identity based on the degree of 'freedom' and 'control' provided to them by their parents. These young Muslim women recognised their Islamic heritage but they can also positively integrate into mainstream society. Negotiation resulted in women remaining in education but forsaking male relationships (Basit, 1997a,b).

3. In a study of ethnic minority schoolchildren from comprehensive schools in Wales it was found that young South Asian Muslim men and women were least acculturated into society. It was argued that the reasons for this related to the vast gulf experienced between the home and school. The home lives of respondents were driven by the needs of the collective rather than the individual. This was further compounded when differences emerged between genders in attitudes towards education. Young men were, in the main, given considerably more importance than women by South Asian parents within the home, whereas the schools promoted more equal gender roles. Muslims saw that it was important to retain family norms and values. Ghuman (1997) argues that Muslims from South Asia possess a religiosity which carries with it elements of a culture that is subsequently maintained in the host society. In contrast, the Hindu religion, in existence for much longer, is considered to be more tolerant of surviving alongside new religions and also offers greater equality towards women, as seen in the worshipping of female deities (see also Ghuman, 2002).

4. Both British Bangladeshis and Pakistanis are experiencing the rapid development of an Islamic and national identity among the younger generations (Beckerlegge, 1989; Eade, 1989, 1990; Peach, 1990; Gardner and Shuker, 1994).

5. The Salman Rushdie Affair, The Gulf War (1990–1991), Bosnia-Herzegovina (1993–1998), the Oklahoma Bombing (1996) and more recently the Taliban (1995–2001), Algeria (1993–), Grozny (1999), Kosova (1999), The 'War on Terror' in Afghanistan (2001–2002), the Iraq War (2003) and a number of other global events since the terrorist attack on the World Trade Centre and The Pentagon in 2001 have placed Muslims everywhere at the centre of media and news controversy (Asad, 1990; Modood, 1990, 1998; Ahmed, 1992; Kundnani, 2000; Abbas, 2001). At the beginning of the twenty-first century, British Muslims are found to be under greater scrutiny, especially in the light of ever-turbulent changes in Eastern Europe, the Middle East and South East Asia (Ahmed, 1995; Peach and Glebe, 1995; Halliday, 1996; Runnymede Trust, 1997; Ali, 2002). Among these more recent events, Palestine (1948–) and Kashmir (1947–) continue to trouble the minds of Muslims in Britain and in the rest of the world. Muslims in Britain are increasingly identifying themselves with a wider Islamic identity and one that transcends national, linguistic and regional affiliation.

6. Combining questions of religious and ethnic identity is a complex scenario. It involves not only an analysis of ethnic and religious ties but it also incorporates notions of religious observation. A recent study found that young Pakistanis identified themselves more with an Islamic rather than a British, English or Pakistani identity. Not only do individuals make a distinction between a religious and an ethnic identity but these ethnic identities are 'clear cut'. Religion is without doubt a defining characteristic of any ethnic group but it cannot, 'be assumed that religious identity is necessarily subsumed by ethnic identity' (Jacobson, 1997, p. 238; see also Modood, 1994; Samad, 1998; Sardar, 2003).

Chapter 8

1. Recent research on young South Asian women and the relationships they formed in school and away at university has shown the extent of socialisation differences between groups. Of those in education, white women had different family-oriented values and activities and formed sexual relationships in a different way. They developed sexual relationships with men often at an early age. South Asian women did not because of cultural taboos, cultural norms and parental control. Muslim women were discouraged from entering into relationships with men. Any relationships formed tended to be hidden from parents as it would cause embarrassment in the community. Indeed, South Asian women were expected to remain chaste until marriage. Many of the South Asian women in the study expected an arranged marriage. This scenario tended to apply less for Hindu women compared with their Sikh or Muslim peers. Of the young South Asian women that had left home either to attend university or to be in work, a number of them had altered their relationship patterns. These young South Asian women were influenced by new peer groups which looked upon sexual relations outside of marriage more openly. Although, here, these South Asian women were moving away from the situations of arranged marriages they, nevertheless, did not wish to disrespect the wishes of the family in the long run (Hennick *et al.*, 1999).

Bibliography

Abbas, T. (2001) 'Media capital and the representation of South Asian Muslims in the British press: an ideological analysis', *Journal of Muslim Minority Affairs* 21(2): 245–57.
—— (2002a) 'A retrospective study of South Asian further education college students and their experiences of secondary school', *Cambridge Journal of Education* 32(1): 73–90.
—— (2002b) 'The home and the school in the educational achievements of South Asians', *Race Ethnicity and Education* 5(3): 292–316.
—— (2002c) 'Teacher perceptions of South Asians in Birmingham schools and colleges', *Oxford Review of Education* 28(4): 447–71.
—— (2003a) 'The impact of religio-cultural norms and values on the education of young South Asian women', *British Journal of Sociology of Education* 24(4): 411–28.
—— (2003b) 'Structural and cultural racism in the educational underachievement of British South Asian Muslims', in K. Jacobson and P. Kumar (eds) *South Asians in Diaspora: histories and religious traditions*. Leiden: Brill.
Abraham, J. (1989) 'Testing Hargreaves' and Lascey's differentiation-polarisation theory in a setted comprehensive', *British Journal of Sociology* 40(1): 46–81.
Adonis, A. and S. Pollard (1997) *A Class Act: the myth of Britain's classless society*. London: Hamish Hamilton.
Afshar, H. (1989) 'Education: hopes, expectations and achievements of Muslim women in West Yorkshire', *Gender and Education* 1(3): 261–72.
Agrawal, B. (1978) 'The Bohras: identity maintenance', *Eastern Anthropologist* 32(4): 597–601.
Ahmad, F. (2001) 'Modern traditions? British Muslim women and academic achievement', *Gender and Education* 13(2): 137–52.
Ahmad, W. (1996) 'Consanguinity and related demons: science and racism in the debate on consanguinity and birth outcome', in C. Samson and N. South (eds) *The Social Construction of Social Policy: methodologies, racism, citizenship and the environment*. London: Macmillan.
Ahmed, A. (1992) *Postmodernism and Islam*. London: Routledge.
—— (1995) ' "Ethnic cleansing": a metaphor of our time?', *Ethnic and Racial Studies* 18(1): 1–25.
Aitkin, M. and N. Longford (1986) 'Statistics modelling issues in school effectiveness studies', *Journal of Royal Statistical Society A* 149(1): 1–43.
Ali, T. (2002) *A Clash of Fundamentalisms: crusades, jihads and modernity*. London: Verso.
Anwar, M. (1979) *The Myth of Return: Pakistanis in Britain*. London: Heinemann.
Asad, T. (1990) 'Multiculturalism and British identity in the wake of the Rushdie Affair', *Politics and Society* 18(4): 455–80.
Back, L. and J. Solomos (1992) 'Black politics and social change in Birmingham, UK: an analysis of recent trends', *Ethnic and Racial Studies* 15(2): 327–51.
—— (eds) (2000) *Theories of Race and Racism*. London: Routledge.

Back, L., M. Keith, A. Khan, K. Shukra and J. Solomos (2002) 'The return to assimilation: race, multiculturalism and New Labour', *Sociological Research Online* 7(2), <http://www.socresonline.org.uk/7/2/back.html>.

Ball, S. (1981) *Beachside Comprehensive*. Cambridge: Cambridge University Press.

—— and C. Vincent (1998) ' "I heard it through the grapevine": "hot" knowledge and school choice', *British Journal of Sociology of Education* 19(3): 377–400.

——, M. Maguire and S. McRae (1998) ' "Race", space and the further education market place', *Race Ethnicity and Education* 1(2): 171–89.

——, D. Reay and M. David (2002a) ' "Ethnic choosing": minority ethnic students, social class and higher education choice', *Race Ethnicity and Education* 5(4): 333–57.

——, J. Davies, M. David and D. Reay (2002b) ' "Classification" and "Judgement": social class and the "cognitive structures" of choice of Higher Education', *British Journal of Sociology of Education* 23(1): 51–69.

Ballard, R. (ed.) (1994) *Desh Pardesh: the South Asian presence in Britain*. London: Hurst.

—— and S. Vellins (1985) 'South Asian entrants to British universities: a comparative note', *New Community* 12(2): 260–5.

Banton, M. (1987) *Racial Theories*. Cambridge: Cambridge University Press.

Basit, T. (1997a) *Eastern Values, Western Milieu: identities and aspirations of adolescent British Muslim girls*. Aldershot: Ashgate.

—— (1997b) ' "I want more freedom, but not too much": British Muslim girls and the dynamism of family values', *Gender and Education* 9(4): 425–39.

Bates, R., R. Figueiredo and B. Weingast (1998) 'The politics of interpretation: rationality, culture, and transition', *Politics and Society* 26: 221–35.

Beckerlegge, G. (1989) *Nation Formation and Religious Education: the concerns of Muslims in Britain and Bangladesh*. Centre for the Study of Islam and Muslim–Christian Relations, Muslims in Europe, no. 44. University of Birmingham.

Bell, J. (1993) *Doing Your Research Project*, Second Edition. Buckinghamshire: Open University Press.

Bernstein, B. (1971) *Class, Codes and Control, Vol. 1*. London: Paladin.

Berrington, A. (1996) 'Marriage patterns and inter-ethnic relations', in D. Coleman and J. Salt (eds) *Ethnicity in the 1991 Census, volume I: demographic characteristics of the ethnic minority population*. London: HMSO.

Berube, M. (2000) *Eminent Educators: studies in intellectual influence*. London: Greenwood Press.

Beyer, J. (1992) 'Researchers are not cats – they can survive and succeed by being curious', in P. Frost and R. Stablein (eds) *Doing Exemplary Research*. California: Sage.

Bhachu, P. (1985) 'Parental education strategies: the case of the Punjabi Sikhs in Britain', *New Community* 12(1): 9–21.

—— (1991) 'The East African Sikh diaspora: the British case', in S. Vertovec (ed.) *Aspects of the South Asian Diaspora*. Delhi: Oxford University Press.

Bhatti, G. (1999) *Asian Children at Home and at School: an ethnographic study*. London: Routledge.

Birmingham City Council (BCC) (2002) *Examination and Assessment Results 2002*. Birmingham, UK: Birmingham City Council.

Birmingham Economic Information Centre (BEIC) (1993) *1991 Census topic reports: ethnic groups in Birmingham*, Birmingham City Council Economic Information Centre, Birmingham, UK.

Blackledge, A. (1999) 'Language, literacy and social justice: the experiences of Bangladeshi women in Birmingham, UK', *Journal of Multilingual and Multicultural Development* 20(3): 79–93.

Blair, M. and M. Cole (2002) 'Racism and education: the imperial legacy', in M. Cole (ed.) *Education, Equality and Human Rights: issues of gender, 'race', sexuality, special needs and social class*. London: Routledge-Falmer.

Bourdieu, P. (1986) 'The forms of capital', in J. Richardson (ed.) *Handbook of Theory of Research for the Sociology of Education*. London: Greenwood Press.

—— (1990) *In Other Words: essays towards a reflexive sociology*. Cambridge: Polity Press.

—— and J. C. Passeron (1998) *Reproduction in Education, Society and Culture*, Reprinted. London: Sage.

Brah, A. and R. Minhus (1985) 'Structural racism or cultural differences: schooling for Asian girls', in G. Weiner (ed.) *Just a Bunch of Girls*. Milton Keynes: Open University Press.

Brah, A. and S. Shaw (1992) *Working Choices: South Asian young Muslim women and the labour market*. London: Department of Employment Research Paper No. 91.

Brar, H. (1992) 'Unasked questions, impossible answers. The ethical problems of researching race and education', in M. Leicester and M. Taylor (eds) *Ethics, Ethnicities and Education*. London: Kogan Page.

Brittan, E. (1976) 'Multiracial education. Teacher opinion on aspects of school life. Part 2. Pupils and teachers', *Educational Research* 18(3): 182–92.

Brown, M. (2000) 'Religion and economic activity in the South Asian population', *Ethnic and Racial Studies* 23(6): 1035–61.

Bulmer, M. (1986) 'Race and ethnicity', in R. Burgess (ed.) op. cit.

Burgess, R. (1986) (ed.) *Key Variables in Social Investigation*. London: Routledge.

Burnhill, P., C. Garner and A. Mcpherson (1990) 'Parental education, social class and entry into higher education 1976–1986', *Journal of Royal Statistical Society A* 153: 233–48.

Carrington, B. and B. Troyna (eds) (1998) *Researching Racism in Education: politics, theory, and practice*. Buckingham: Open University Press.

Carter, B. and M. Green (1996) 'Naming difference: race-thinking, common sense and sociology', in C. Samson and N. South (eds) *The Construction of Social Policy: methodologies, racism, citizenship and environment*. Basingstoke: Macmillan.

Castles, S. and G. Kosack (1973) *Immigrant Workers and the Class Structure in Western Europe*. London: Institute of Race Relations and Oxford University Press.

Cheng, Y. and A. Heath (1993) 'Ethnic origins and class destinations', *Oxford Review of Education* 19(2): 151–65.

Coe, R. and C. Fitz-Gibbon (1998) 'School effectiveness research: criticisms and recommendations', *Oxford Review of Education* 24(4): 421–38.

Cohen, L., L. Manion and R. Morrisson (2000) *Research Methods in Education*, Fifth Edition. London: Routledge-Falmer.

Cole, M. (1998a) 'Racism, reconstructed multiculturalism and antiracist education', *Cambridge Journal of Education* 28(1): 37–48.

—— (1998b) 'Re-establishing antiracist education: a response to Short and Carrington', *Cambridge Journal of Education* 28(2): 235–8.

Coleman, J. (1988) 'Social capital in the creation of human capital', *American Journal of Sociology* 95: ss. 95–120.

Coles, M. (1997) 'Race equality and school improvement: some aspects of the Birmingham experience', *Multicultural Teaching* 15(2): 12–20.

Commission for Racial Equality (CRE) (1988) *Medical School Admissions: report of a formal investigation into St. George's Hospital Medical School.* London: CRE.

—— (1992) *Set to Fail? Setting and banding in secondary schools.* London: CRE.

—— (1996) *Roots of the Future.* London: CRE.

Connolly, P. (1992) 'Playing it by the rules: the politics of research in "race" and education', *British Education Research Journal* 18(2): 133–48.

—— (1994) 'Shades of discrimination: university entry data 1990–1992', in S. Haselgrove (ed.) *The Student Experience*, pp. 20–34. Milton Keynes: Open University Press.

Cote, S. and T. Healy (2001) *The Well-Being of Nations: the role of social and human capital.* Paris: Organisation for Economic Co-operation and Development.

Craft, M. and A. Craft (1983) 'The participation of ethnic minority pupils in further and higher education', *Educational Research* 25(1): 10–19.

Crook, D., S. Power and G. Whitty (1999) *The Grammar School Question: a review of research on comprehensive and selective education.* London: University of London Institute of Education.

Crozier, G. (1999) 'Is it a case of "we know when we're not wanted"? The parents' perspective on parent–teacher roles and relationships', *Educational Research* 41(3): 315–28.

Dale, A., N. Shaheen, V. Kalra and E. Fieldhouse (2002) 'Routes into education and employment for young Pakistani and Bangladeshi women in the UK', *Ethnic and Racial Studies* 25(6): 942–68.

David, M. (1991) 'Comparisons of "Educational Reform" in Britain and the USA: a new era?', *International Studies in Sociology of Education* 1: 87–109.

Dayha, B. (1974) 'The nature of Pakistani ethnicity in industrial cities', in A. Cohen (ed.) *Urban Ethnicity.* London: Tavistock.

—— (1988) 'South Asians as Economic Migrants', *Ethnic and Racial Studies* 11(4): 439–56.

Deakin, N. (1970) *Colour, Citizenship and British Society.* London: Panther.

Debnath, E. (1998) 'Youth, gender and community change: a case study of young Bangladeshis in Tower Hamlets', Unpublished PhD Thesis. University of Cambridge School of Education.

Demack, S., D. Drew and M. Grimsley (2000) 'Minding the gap: ethnic, gender and social class differences in attainment at 16, 1988–1995', *Race Ethnicity and Education* 3(2): 117–43.

Denscombe, M. (1984) 'Interviews, accounts and ethnographic research in teachers', in M. Hammersley (ed.) *The Ethnography of Schooling: methodological issues*, Second Edition. Driffield: Nafferton.

Department of Education and Employment (DfEE) (1998) *Teachers – meeting the challenge for change*, Green Paper. London: HMSO.

Department of Education and Science (DES) (1977) *Education in Schools: a consultative document*, Green Paper. London: HMSO.

Department of Education and Skills (DfES) (2003) *Research & Statistics Gateway*, http://www.dfes.gov.uk/rsgateway/. Accessed 17 December 2003.

Desai, R. (1963) *Indian Immigrants in Britain.* London: Oxford University Press and the Institute of Race Relations.

Devine, F. and S. Heath (1999) *Sociological Research Methods in Context*. Basingstoke: Macmillan.

Drew, D. (1995) *'Race', Education and Work: the statistics of inequality*. Aldershot: Avebury.

—— and B. Fosam (1994) 'Gender and ethnic differences in education and the youth labour market', *Radical Statistics* 58: 16–32.

——, J. Gray and D. Sporton (1997) 'Ethnic differences in educational participation of 16–19 year olds', in V. Karn (ed.) *Ethnicity in the 1991 Census. Volume 4. Employment, education and housing among ethnic minority populations of Britain*. London: Stationary Office.

Duffy, M. (2002) *England: the making of myth from Stonehenge to Albert Square*. London: Fourth Estate.

Eade, J. (1989) *The Politics of Community: The Bangladeshi community in East London*. Aldershot: Avebury.

—— (1990) 'Nationalism and the quest for authenticity: the Bangladeshis in Tower Hamlets', *New Community* 16(4): 493–503.

Edwards, T. and S. Tomlinson (2002) *Selection isn't Working: diversity, standards and inequality in secondary education*. London: Catalyst Forum.

Eggleston, J. (1986) *Education for some: the educational & vocational experiences of 15–18 year-old members of minority ethnic group: a report on a research project for the Department of Education & Science*. Stoke-on-Trent: Trentham.

Esmail, A., P. Nelson and S. Everington (1996) 'Research note: ethnic differences in applications to United Kingdom Medical Schools between 1990–1992', *New Community* 22(3): 495–506.

Feinstein, L. and J. Symons (1999) 'Attainment in Secondary School', *Oxford Economic Review* 51: 300–21.

Fenton, S. (2003) *Ethnicity*. Cambridge: Polity.

Figueroa, P. (1995) 'Multicultural education in the United Kingdom: historical development and current status', in J. Banks (ed.) and C. Banks (Assoc. ed.) *Handbook of Research on Multicultural Education*. New York: Macmillan.

Fine, M. (1991) *Framing dropouts: notes on the politics of an urban high school*. New York: New York State University Press.

Floud, J. and A. Halsey (1958) 'The sociology of education', *Sociology* 7(3): 165–93.

Foster, P. (1990) 'Cases not proven: an evaluation of two studies of teacher racism', *British Educational Research Journal* 16(4): 335–48.

—— (1992) 'Equal treatment and cultural difference in multi-ethnic schools: a critique of the teacher ethnocentrism theory', *International Studies in Sociology of Education* 2(1): 89–103.

—— (1993) ' "Methodological pluralism" or "a defence against hype"? Critical readership in research in "race" and education', *New Community* 19(3): 547–52.

Gardner, K. (1992) 'International migration and rural context in Sylhet', *New Community* 18(4): 579–90.

—— and A. Shuker (1994) ' "I'm Bengali, I'm Asian, and I'm living here', in R. Ballard (ed.) op. cit.

Ghuman, P. (1980) 'Punjabi parents and English education', *Educational Research* 22(2): 121–30.

—— (1995) *Asian Teachers in British Schools: a study of two generations*. Clevedon: Multilingual Matters.

—— (1997) 'Assimilation or integration? A study of Asian adolescents', *Educational Research* 39(1): 23–35.

—— (2002) 'South-Asian adolescents in British Schools: a review', *Educational Studies* 28(1): 47–59.

Gibson, A. and P. Bhachu (1988) 'Ethnicity and school performance: a comparative study of South Asian pupils in Britain and America', *Ethnic and Racial Studies* 24(3): 239–62.

Gibson, A. and S. Asthana (1998) 'Schools, pupils and examination results: contextualising school performance', *British Education Research Journal* 24(3): 269–82.

Gillborn, D. (1990) *'Race', Ethnicity and Education: teaching and learning in multiethnic schools.* London: Unwin Hyman.

—— (1998) 'Racism and the politics of qualitative research: learning from controversy and critique', in B. Carrington and B. Troyna (eds) op. cit.

—— and D. Drew (1992) ' "Race", class and school effects', *New Community* 18(4): 551–65.

—— and D. Drew (1993) 'The politics of research: some observations on "methodological purity" ', *New Community* 19(2): 354–60.

—— and D. Gipps (1996) *Recent Research on the Achievements of Ethnic Minority Pupils.* London: HMSO.

—— and H. Mirza (2000) *Educational Inequality: mapping race, class and gender.* London: OfSTED.

—— and D. Youdell (2002) 'The new IQism: intelligence, "ability" and the rationing of education', in J. Demaine (ed.) *Sociology of Education Today*, Second Edition. Basingstoke: Palgrave.

Gilroy, P. (1990) 'The end of anti-racism', *New Community* 17(1): 71–83.

Glaser, B. (1968) *The Discovery of Grounded Theory: strategies for qualitative research.* London: Widenfeld and Nicolson.

Glennerster, H. (1972) 'Education and inequality', in P. Townsend and N. Bosanquet (eds) *Labour and Inequality.* London: Fabian Society.

Goffman, E. (1990) *The Presentation of Self in Everyday Life.* Reprinted. London: Penguin.

Goldstein, H. and G. Woodhouse (2000) 'School effectiveness research and education policy', *Oxford Review of Education* 26(3/4): 353–63.

Goldthorpe, J. (1996) 'Class analysis and the reorientation of class theory: the case of persistent differentials in educational attainment', *British Journal of Sociology* 47(3): 481–512.

Granovetter, M. (1973) 'The strength of weak ties', *American Journal of Sociology* 78: 1360–80.

Gray, J., D. Jesson and B. Jones (1986) 'The search for a fairer way of comparing schools' examination results', *Research Papers in Education* 1(2): 91–120.

Gray, J., D. Jesson and N. Sime (1990) 'Estimating differences in examination performances of secondary schools in six LEAs: a multilevel approach to school effectiveness', *Oxford Review of Education* 16(2): 137–59.

Greene, F. (1970) *The Enemy: notes on imperialism and revolution.* London: Jonathan Cape.

Grosvenor, I. (1997) *Assimilating Identities: racism and educational policy in post 1945 Britain.* London: Lawrence and Wishart.

Gupta, Y. (1977) 'The educational and vocational aspirations of Asian immigrant and English school leavers', *British Journal of Sociology* 28(2): 185–98.

Halliday, F. (1996) *Islam and the Myth of Confrontation: religion and politics in the Middle East*. London: IB Taurus.

Halsey, A., A. Heath and J. Ridge (1980) *Origins and Destinations: family, class and education in modern Britain*. Oxford: Clarendon Press.

Hammersley, M. (1998) 'Partisanship and credibility: the case of antiracist education research', B. Carrington and B. Troyna (eds) op. cit.

—— (ed.) (2000) *Taking Sides in Social Research: Essays on partisanship and bias*. London: Routledge.

—— (2001) 'Whose side was Becker on? Questioning political and epistemological radicalism', *Qualitative Research* 1(1): 91–110.

Hanifen, L. (1916) 'The rural school community center', *Annals of the American Academy of Political and Social Science* 67: 130–8.

Haque, Z. (1999) 'Exploring the validity and possible cause of the apparently poor performance of Bangladeshi students in British secondary schools', Unpublished PhD Thesis. University of Cambridge School of Education.

—— (2000) 'The ethnic minority "underachieving" group? Investigating claims of "underachievement" amongst Bangladeshi pupils in British secondary schools', *Race Ethnicity and Education* 3(2): 145–68.

—— and J. Bell (2001) 'Evaluating the performances of minority ethnic pupils in secondary schools', *Oxford Review of Education* 27(3): 357–68.

Hargreaves, D. (1967) *Social Relations in a Secondary School*. London: Routledge and Kegan Paul.

—— (1999) 'Revitalising educational research: lessons from the past and proposals for the future', *Cambridge Journal of Education* 29(2): 239–49.

Haw, K. (1998) *Educating Muslim Girls: shifting discourses*. Buckingham: Open University Press.

Heath, A. and P. Clifford (1990) 'Class inequalities in education in the twentieth century', *Journal of Royal Statistical Society A* 153(1): 1–16.

—— and D. McMahon (1997) 'Education and occupational attainments: the impact of ethnic origins', in A. Halsey, H. Lauder, P. Brown and A. S. Wells (eds) *Education – culture, economy and society*. Oxford: Oxford University Press.

Hennick, M., I. Diamond and P. Cooper (1999) 'Young Asian women and relationships: traditional and transitional', *Ethnic and Racial Studies* 22(5): 867–91.

Hof, L. and J. Dronkers (1994) 'Differences in educational attainment of children from various groups of recent immigrants in the Netherlands: class, family or migrant culture?', *Migration: a European journal of intercultural migration and ethnic relations* 26: 5–48.

Holdsworth, C. and A. Dale (1997) 'Ethnic differences in women's employment', *Work, Employment and Society* 11(3): 435–57.

Hurrell, P. (1995) 'Do teachers discriminate? Reactions to pupil behaviour in four comprehensive schools', *Sociology* 29(1): 59–72.

Jackson, P. (1968) *Life in Classrooms*. New York: Holt Rinehart and Winston.

Jacobson, J. (1997) 'Religion and ethnicity: dual and alternative sources of identity among young British Pakistanis', *Ethnic and Racial Studies* 20(2): 238–56.

Jenkins, R. (1992) *Pierre Bourdieu*. London: Routledge.

Joly, D. (1989) *Ethnic Minorities and Education in Britain: interaction between the Muslim community and Birmingham Schools*. CSIC Research Papers: Muslims in Europe, no. 41, University of Birmingham Centre for the Study of Islam and Muslim–Christian Relations.

Joshi, S. and B. Carter (1984) 'The role of Labour in the creation of a racist Britain', *Race and Class* 25(3): 53–70.

Kalekin-Fishman, D., G. Verma and P. Pitkänen (2002) 'Conclusions', in P. Pitkänen, D. Kalekin-Fishman and G. Verma (eds) *Education and Immigration: settlement policies and current challenges.* London: Routledge Farmer.

Kelly, A. (1988) 'Ethnic differences in science choice, attitudes and achievements in Britain', *British Educational Research Journal* 14(2): 113–27.

Khan, V. (ed.) (1979) *Minority Families in Britain: support and stress.* London: Macmillan.

Kidd, J. and M. Wardman (1999) 'Post-16 course choice: a challenge for guidance', *British Journal of Guidance and Counselling* 27(2): 259–74.

Kundnani, A. (2000) ' "Stumbling on": race, class and England', *Race & Class*, 41(4): 1–18.

—— (2001) 'From Oldham to Bradford: the violence of the violated', *Race and Class* 43: 105–10.

Kysel, F. (1988) 'Ethnic background and examination results', *Educational Research* 30(2): 83–90.

Lightbody, P., S. Nicholson, G. Siann and D. Walsh (1997) 'A respectable job: factors which influence young Asians' choice of career', *British Journal of Guidance and Counselling* 25(1): 67–79.

Little, A. (1975) 'Performance of children from ethnic minority backgrounds in primary schools', *Oxford Review of Education* 1(2): 117–35.

—— (1981) 'Education and race relations in the United Kingdom', in J. Megarry, S. Nisbet and E. Hoyle (eds) *World Yearbook of Education.* London: Kogan Page.

—— (1986) 'Educational inequalities: race and class', in R. Rodgers (ed.) *Education and Social Class.* London: Falmer.

Lynch, J., C. Modgil and S. Modgil (eds) (1992) *Education for Cultural Diversity.* London: Famler.

Mac an Ghaill, M. (1988) *Young, Gifted and Black: student–teacher relations in the schooling of black youth.* Milton Keynes: Open University Press.

—— (1989a) 'Coming-of-age in 1980s England: re-conceptualising black students' schooling experience', *British Journal of Sociology of Education* 17(2): 163–86.

—— (1989b) 'Beyond the white norm: the use of qualitative methods in the study of black youth's schooling in England', *Qualitative Studies in Education* 2(3): 273–87.

—— (1996) 'Sociology of education, state schooling and social class: beyond critiques of the New Right hegemony', *British Journal of Sociology of Education* 17(2): 163–76.

—— (1999) *Contemporary Racisms and Ethnicities.* Buckingham: Open University Press.

Macpherson Report (1999) *The Stephen Lawrence Inquiry.* Report of an Inquiry by Sir William Macpherson of Cluny. London: Stationary Office.

Martin, D. and J. Stuart-Smith (1998) 'Exploring bilingual children's perceptions of being bilingual and biliterate: implications for educational provision', *British Journal of Sociology of Education* 19(2): 237–54.

Marx, K. (1978) 'On imperialism in India', in R. Tucker (ed.) *The Marx-Engels Reader.* Second Edition. London: Norton.

Mattausch, J. (1988) 'From subjects to citizens: "East African Asians" ', *Journal of Ethnic and Migration Studies* 24(1): 121–41.

Maughan, B. and M. Rutter (1986) 'Black pupils' progress in secondary schools: II. Examination attainments', *British Journal of Developmental Psychology* 4: 19–29.

May, T. (1993) *Social Research: issues, methods and process*. Milton Keynes: Open University Press.

McCracken, G. (1988) *The Long Interview*. California: Sage.

McIntyre, D. (1997) 'The profession of educational research', *British Educational Research Journal* 23(2): 127–40.

McNeill, P. (1990) *Research Methods*, Second Edition. London: Routledge.

Mehra, H. (1999) 'The permanent exclusion of Asian pupils in secondary schools in central Birmingham', *Multicultural Teaching* 17(1): 42–8.

Miles, R. (1982) *Racism and Migrant Labour*. London: Routledge and Kegan Paul.

—— (1989) 'Nationality, citizenship, and migration to Britain, 1945–1951', *Journal of Law and Society* 16(4): 426–42.

Modood, T. (1990) 'British Muslims and the Rushdie Affair', *Political Quarterly* 1(62): 143–60.

—— (1993) 'The number of ethnic minority students in British higher education', *Oxford Review of Education* 19(2): 167–81.

—— (1994) 'Political Blackness and British Asians', *Sociology* 28(4): 859–76.

—— (1998) 'Anti-essentialism, multiculturalism and the "recognition" of religious groups', *Journal of Political Philosophy* 28(4): 859–76.

—— and M. Shiner (1994) *Ethnic Minorities and Higher Education: why are there differential rates of entry?* London: Policy Studies Institute.

——, R. Berthoud, J. Lakey, J. Nazroo, P. Smith, S. Virdee and S. Beishon (1997) *Ethnic Minorities in Britain: diversity and disadvantage*. London: Policy Studies Institute.

Mortimore, P. (1999) 'Does education research matter?', *British Education Research Journal* 26(1): 5–24.

Nuttall, D. and A. Varlaam (1990) *Differences in Examination Performance*. London: Inner London Education Authority Research and Statistics.

——, H. Goldstein, R. Prosser and J. Rasbash (1989) 'Differential school effectiveness', *International Journal of Educational Research* 13: 769–76.

Office for National Statistics (ONS) (2003) *Census 2001*. http://www.statistics. gov.uk/census2001.

OfSTED (1996) *The Teaching of Reading in 45 Inner London Primary Schools*. London: HMSO.

—— (1997) *The Annual Report of Her Majesty's Chief Inspector of Schools: standards and quality in education 1996/97*. London: HMSO.

—— (1999a) *Raising the Attainment of Minority Ethnic Pupils*. London: HMSO.

—— (1999b) *Primary Education: A review of primary schools in England, 1994–1998*. London: HMSO.

Ogbu, J. (1997) 'Racial stratification and education in the United States: why inequality persists', in A. Halsey, H. Lauder, P. Brown and A. S. Wells (eds) *Education – culture, economy and society*. Oxford: Oxford University Press.

Open University (1994) *Educational Research Methods*. Milton Keynes: Open University Press.

Oppenheim, A. (1992) *Questionnaire Design, Interviewing and Attitude Measurement*. London: Pinter.

Osler, A. and J. Hill (1999) 'Exclusion for school and racial equality: an examination of government proposals in the light of recent research evidence', *Cambridge Journal of Education* 29(1): 33–62.

—— and Z. Hussain (1995) 'Parental choice and schooling: some factors influencing Muslim mothers' decisions about the education of their daughters', *Cambridge Journal of Education* 25(3): 327–47.

Owen, D. (1992) 'Ethnic minorities in Great Britain: settlement patterns'. 1991 Census Statistical Paper No. 1. University of Warwick Centre for Research in Ethnic Relations, University of Warwick.

—— and M. Johnson (1996) 'Ethnic minorities in the Midlands', in P. Ratcliffe (ed.) *Ethnicity in the 1991 Census vol. 3: Social Geography and Ethnicity in Britain: geographical spread, spatial concentration and internal migration.* London: HMSO.

Parekh, B. (1989) 'The hermeneutics of the Swann Report', in G. Verma (ed.) *Education for all: a landmark in pluralism.* London: Falmer.

Parker-Jenkins, M. (1995) *Children of Islam: a teacher's guide to meeting the needs of Muslim pupils.* Stoke-on-Trent: Trentham.

Peach, C. (1990) 'Estimating the growth of the Bangladeshi population', *New Community* 16(4): 481–91.

—— and G. Glebe (1995) 'Muslim minorities in Western Europe', *Ethnic and Racial Studies* 18(1): 26–45.

Penn, R. and H. Scattergood (1992) 'Ethnicity and career aspirations in contemporary Britain', *New Community* 19(1): 75–98.

Phillips, D. (1998) 'Black minority ethnic concentration, segregation and dispersal in Britain', *Urban Studies* 35(10): 1681–702.

Pilkington, A. (1999) 'Racism in schools and ethnic differentials in educational achievement: a brief comment on a recent debate', *British Journal of Sociology of Education* 20(3): 411–17.

Plewis, I. (1988) 'Assessing and understanding the educational progress of children from different ethnic groups', *Journal of the Royal Statistical Society A* 151(2): 316–26.

—— (1991) 'Underachievement: a case of conceptual confusion', *British Educational Research Journal* 17(4): 377–85.

Portes, A. and J. Sensenbrenner (1993) 'Embeddedness and immigration: notes on the social determinants of social action', *American Journal of Sociology* 98: 1320–50.

—— and P. Landolt (1996) 'The Downside to Social Capital', *The American Prospect* 26 (May–June): 18–21.

—— and D. MacLeod (1996) 'Educational progress of children of immigrants: the roles of class, ethnicity and school context', *Sociology of Education* 69: 255–75.

—— and D. MacLeod (1999) 'Educating the second generation: determinants of academic achievement among children of immigrants in the United States', *Journal of Ethnic and Migration Studies* 25(3): 375–96.

Power, S. (2000) 'Missing: a sociology of educating the middle class', in J. Demaine (ed.) *Sociology of Education Today.* London: Macmillan.

Prais, S. (2001) 'Grammar schools' achievements and the DfEE's measures of value-added: an attempt at clarification', *Oxford Review of Education* 27(1): 69–73.

Print, M. and D. Coleman (2003) 'Towards understanding of social capital and citizenship education', *Cambridge Journal of Education* 33: 123–49.

Putnam, R. (1993) *Making Democracy Work: civic traditions in modern Italy.* Princeton: Princeton University Press.

—— (2000) *Bowling Alone: the collapse and revival of American community.* New York: Simon and Schuster.

Ram, M. and T. Jones (1998) *Ethnic Minorities in Business*. Milton Keynes: Small Business Research Trust.

Rampton (1981) *West Indian children in our schools*. London: Department of Education and Science.

Ranger, C. (1988) *Ethnic Minority School Teachers: a survey in eight local education authorities*. London: Commission for Racial Equality.

Rattansi, A. (1992) 'Changing the subject? Racism, culture and education', in J. Donald and A. Rattansi (eds) *'Race', Culture and Difference*. London: Sage.

Reay, D. (1995) 'Using habitus to look at "race" and class in primary school class-rooms', in M. Griffiths and B. Troyna (eds) *Antiracism, Culture and Social Justice in Education*. Stoke-on-Trent: Trentham.

—— (1998) 'Cultural reproduction: mother's involvement in their children's primary schooling', in M. Grenfell and D. James with P. Hodkinson, D. Reay and D. Robbins, *Bourdieu and Education: Acts of practical theory*, pp. 55–71. London: Falmer.

—— (2000) 'A useful extension of Bourdieu's conceptual framework? Emotional capital as a way of understanding mothers' involvement in children's schooling', *Sociological Review* 48(4): 568–85.

—— and S. Ball (1997) ' "Spoilt for choice": the working classes and educational markets', *Oxford Review of Education* 23(1): 89–101.

—— and S. Ball (1998) ' "Making their minds up": family dynamics of school choice', *British Education Research Journal* 24(4): 431–48.

Reeves, F. and M. Chevannes (1981) 'The underachievement of Rampton', *Multiracial Education* 10(1): 35–42.

—— (1988) 'The ideological construction of Black underachievement', in M. Woodhead and A. McGrath (eds) *Family, School and Society*. London: Hodder and Stoughton.

Rex, J. (1987) 'Antiracist and multicultural education', in T. Chivers (ed.) *Race and Culture in Education*. Nelson: National Foundation for Educational Research.

—— and R. Moore (1967) *Race, community and conflict: a study of Sparkbrook*. London: Institute of Race Relations and Oxford University Press.

—— and S. Tomlinson (1979) *Colonial Immigrants in a British City: a class analysis*. London: Routledge and Kegan Paul.

Richardson, R. (1999) 'Unequivocal acceptance – lessons from the Stephen Lawrence Inquiry for Education', *Multiracial Teaching* 17(2): 7–11.

Robinson, F. (1988) *Varieties of South Asian Islam*, Research Papers in Ethnic Relations No. 8. Centre for Research in Ethnic Relations, University of Warwick.

Robinson, V. (1980) 'The achievement of Asian children', *Educational Research* 22(2): 148–50.

—— (1996) 'Boom and Gloom: the success and failure of South Asians in Britain', in C. Clarke, C. Peach and S. Vertovec (eds) *South Asians Overseas: migration and ethnicity*. Cambridge: Cambridge University Press.

Rose, E., N. Deakin, M. Abrams, V. Jackson, M. Peston, A. Vanags, B. Cohen, J. Gaitskell and P. Ward (1969) *Colour and Citizenship: a report on British race relations*. London: Institute of Race Relations and Oxford University Press.

Runnymede Trust (1984) *How Racism came to Britain*. London Institute of Race Relations and the Runnymede Trust.

—— (1997) *Islamophobia: a challenge for us all*. London: Runnymede Trust.

—— (2000) *The Future of Multi-Ethnic Britain*. London: Profile.

Samad, Y. (1998) 'Imagining a British Muslim identification', in S. Vetovec and A. Rogers (eds) *Muslim European Youth: reproducing ethnicity, religion, culture*. Aldershot: Ashgate.

Sammons, P. (1995) 'Gender, ethnic and socio-economic differences in achievement and progress: a longitudinal analysis of student achievement over 9 years', *British Educational Research Journal* 21(4): 465–86.

Sardar, Z. (2003) 'The agony of a 21st-century Muslim', *New Statesmen*, 17 February: 50–2.

Sarup, M. (1991) *Education and the Ideologies of Racism*. Stoke-On-Trent: Trentham.

Shaikh, S. and A. Kelly (1989) 'To mix or not to mix: Pakistani girls in British Schools', *Educational Research* 31(1): 10–19.

Shain, F. and J. Ozga (2001) 'Identity crisis? Problems and issues in the sociology of education', *British Journal of Sociology of Education* 22(1): 109–20.

Shaw, A. (2000) *Kinship and Continuity: Pakistani families in Britain*. Amsterdam: Harwood.

—— (2001) 'Kinship, cultural preference and immigration: consanguineous marriage among British Pakistanis', *Journal of the Royal Anthropological Institute* 7: 315–34.

Shiner, M. and T. Modood (2002) 'Help or hindrance? Higher education and the route to ethnic equality', *British Journal of Sociology of Education* 23(2): 209–32.

Short, G. and B. Carrington (1996) 'Anti-racist education, multiculturalism and new racism', *Educational Review* 48(1): 65–77.

—— (1998) 'Reconstructing multicultural education: a response to Mike Cole', *Cambridge Journal of Education* 28(2): 231–4.

Siann, G., A. Knox, E. Thornley and R. Evans (1990) 'Parents, careers and culture: the view of ethnic-minority and ethnic-majority girls', *British Journal of Guidance and Counselling* 18(2): 156–69.

Singh, R. (1990) 'Ethnic minority experience in higher education', *Higher Education Quarterly* 44(4): 344–59.

Sivanandan, A. (1982) 'From resistance to rebellion: Asian and Afro-Caribbean struggles in Britain', *Race and Class* 23(2/3): 111–52.

Smith, D. and S. Tomlinson (1989) *The School Effect: a study of multi-racial comprehensives*. London: Policy Studies Institute.

Song, M. and D. Parker (1995) 'Commonality, difference and the dynamics of disclosure in in-depth interviewing', *Sociology* 29(2): 241–56.

Stopes-Roe, M. and R. Cochrane (1987) 'The process of assimilation in Asians in Britain: a study of Hindu, Muslim and Sikh immigrants and their young adult children', *International Journal of Comparative Sociology* 28(1/2): 43–56.

—— (1990) *Citizens of this Country: the Asian-British*. Clevedon: Multilingual Matters.

Strand, S. (1999) 'Ethnic group, sex and economic disadvantage: association with pupils' educational progress from baseline to end of Key Stage 1', *British Educational Research Journal* 25(2): 179–202.

Swann Report (1985) *Education for all*. London: Department of Education and Science.

Tanna, K. (1990) 'Excellence, equality and educational reform: the myth of South Asian achievement levels', *New Community* 16(3): 349–68.

Taylor, J. (1973) 'Newcastle upon Tyne: Asian pupils do better than whites', *British Journal of Sociology* 29(4): 431–47.

—— (1976) *The Half-Way Generation: a study of Asian youths in Newcastle upon Tyne*. Windsor: National Federation for Educational Research.

Taylor, M. and S. Hegerty (1985) *Best of Both Worlds . . . ? A review of research into the education of pupils of South Asian origin*. Windsor: National Federation for Educational Research.

Taylor, P. (1993) 'Minority ethnic groups and gender access in higher education', *New Community* 19(3): 425–40.

Thomas, G., P. Vass and R. McClelland (1997) 'Parents in a marketplace: some responses to information, diversity and power', *Educational Research* 39(2): 85–194.

Tomlinson, S. (1984) *Home and School in Multicultural Britain*. London: Batsford.

—— (1987) 'Curriculum option choices in multi-ethnic schools', in B. Troyna (ed.) *Racial Inequality in Education*. London: Tavistock.

—— (1992) 'Achievement, assessment and the school effect', in J. Lynch *et al.* (eds) op. cit.

—— (2001) *Education in a Post-Welfare Society*. Buckingham: Open University Press.

Troyna, B. (1978) 'Race and streaming: a case study', *Educational Review* 30(1): 59–65.

—— (1984) 'Fact or artefact: the "educational underachievement" of black pupils', *British Journal of Sociology of Education* 5(2): 153–66.

—— (1985) 'The "great divide": politics and practices in multicultural education', *British Journal of Sociology of Education* 6(2): 209–24.

—— (1992) 'Can you see the join? An historical analysis of "multicultural" and antiracisst education policies', in D. Gill, B. Mayor and M. Blair (eds) *'Race', Education and Society: structures and strategies*. London, Sage.

—— (1993a) 'Underachiever or misunderstood? A reply to Roger Gomm', *British Education Research Journal* 19(2): 167–84.

—— (ed.) (1993b) *Racism and Education: research perspectives*. Milton Keynes: Open University Press.

—— and B. Carrington (1989) ' "Whose side are we on?" Ethical dilemmas in research on "race" and education', in R. Burgess (ed.) *The Ethics of Educational Research*. London: Falmer.

—— and J. Williams (1986) *Racism, education and the state*. London: Croom Helm.

Vellins, S. (1982) 'South Asian students in British universities. A statistical note', *New Community* 10(2): 206–12.

Vincent, C. (1995) 'School, community and ethnic minority parents', in S. Tomlinson and M. Craft (eds) *Ethnic Relations and Schooling: policy and practice in the 1990s*. London: Athlone.

Vulliamy, G. (2001) 'Review essay: a sociology of school exclusions', *British Journal of Sociology of Education* 22(1): 177–84.

Ward, R. (1983) 'Race relations in Britain' in A. Stewart (ed.) *Contemporary Britain*. London: Routledge and Kegan Paul in association with the British Journal of Sociology.

Weis, L. (1985) 'Seeing education relationally: the bottom and the top', *International Journal of Sociology and Social Policy* 5(4): 61–73.

White, A. (2002) *Minority ethnic groups in the UK*. London: Office for National Statistics.

Williams, J. (1985) 'Redefining institutional racism', *Ethnic and Racial Studies* 8: 323–46.

Willis, P. (1977) *Learning to labour: how working class kids get working class jobs.* New York: Columbia University Press.

Wilson, J. (1998) 'Preconditions for educational research', *Educational Research* 40(2): 161–7.

Wolbers, M. and G. Driessen (1996) 'Social class or ethnic background? Determinants of secondary school careers of ethnic minority pupils', *Netherlands Journal of Social Sciences* 32(2): 109–26.

Woodrow, D. (1996) 'Cultural inclinations towards studying mathematics and sciences', *New Community* 22(1): 23–38.

Woolcock, M. (2001) 'The place of social capital in understanding social and economic outcomes', *Canadian Journal of Policy Research* 2: 11–17.

Wright, C. (1986) 'School processes – an ethnographic study', in J. Eggleston op. cit.

—— (1987) 'Black students – white teachers', in B. Troyna (ed.) *Racial Inequality in Education.* London: Tavistock.

—— (1990) 'Comments in reply to the article by P. Foster, "Cases not proven: an evaluation of two studies of teacher racism"', *British Educational Research Journal* 16(4): 351–5.

Wrigley, T. (1997) 'Raising achievement for Asian pupils', *Multiracial Teaching* 16(1): 21–30.

Yin, R. (1994) *Case Study Research: design and methods*, Second Edition. London: Thousand Oaks.

Index